SOUTHERN PRESBYTERIAN PULPIT

Some Other Solid Ground Titles

SOUTHERN PRESBYTERIAN PULPIT

A Collection of Sermons from the Nineteenth Century

by

Ministers of the
Southern Presbyterian Church

Solid Ground Christian Books
Birmingham, Alabama USA

Solid Ground Christian Books
PO Box 660132
Vestavia Hills AL 35266
205-443-0311
sgcb@charter.net
www.solid-ground-books.com

SOUTHERN PRESBYTERIAN PULPIT
A Collection of Sermons from the Nineteenth Century

by Ministers of the Southern Presbyterian Church

Originally published by The Presbyterian Committee on Publication,
Richmond, Virginia, 1896

Cover design by Borgo Design
Contact them at borgogirl@bellsouth.net

COVER IMAGE: The identity of the men on the cover is as foll
Upper Left – John L. Girardeau
Upper Right – Moses D. Hoge
Lower Left – Robert L. Dabney
Lower Right – Benjamin M. Palmer

ISBN- 978-159925-2001

PREFACE.

Two motives have prompted the issue of this volume. There has been a distinct demand for a book of practical sermons, suitable for reading in the public worship of God when conducted by ruling elders of the church. It would seem easy, from the many sermons published, to supply this demand, and yet the selection is often very difficult. We are sure that, under such circumstances, our people will be glad to hear from one of our own ministers.

But, in addition to this motive, it has seemed very desirable to put in permanent form some examples of the work of our Southern Presbyterian pulpit, which is, we are confident, second to none in eloquence, doctrinal purity, persuasiveness, and practical power.

It will add much to the value of this collection that the readers will have before them an excellent likeness of the author of the discourse to which their attention may be directed.

August, 1896.

CONTENTS.

CONTENTS.

CONTENTS.

The Transforming Power of the Gospel.

BY REV. B. M. PALMER, D. D.

Pastor of the First Presbyterian Church, New Orleans, La.

" Therefore, if any man be in Christ, he is a new creature : old things are passed away; behold, all things are become new."— 2 Cor. v. 17.

A NOTED scoffer was once arrested in his noisy invective against Christianity by two simple questions, to which a direct and candid answer was challenged: What would be the effect upon the world if all men were sincere Christians? and, on the other hand, what would be the effect upon the world if all men were consistent infidels? In the silence which followed these questions was manifested the skeptic's defeat. For you observe that he could not return a truthful answer to one or the other without abandoning his own case. The argument is a valid one, founded upon the moral effect of the two systems as compared one with the other. If Christianity is found to be a system whose principles, heartily adopted, will relieve the world of most of the evils by which it is oppressed and convert this earth into a paradise, then, surely, it is the last of all systems that men ought to decry. If, on the other hand, infidelity, overturning Christianity, destroys the foundations on which all virtue and morality are based, then it is the last of all systems that ought to be upheld. The text sets forth this transforming power of the gospel over the characters and lives of men.

9

I need scarcely pause to expound the beautiful, though simple, expression, "if any man be in Christ Jesus"; for you remember there are two correlative expressions—to be in Christ, is one; for Christ to be in us, is the other; and these two expressions are employed in the New Testament to cover, upon the right hand and upon the left hand, the whole gospel. To be in Christ is to be united to him by a living faith; so that we are clothed with his righteousness and, as is beautifully expressed in another Scripture, "We are accepted in the beloved." Christ is in us when the Holy Spirit forms the image of Christ in our hearts. We are made new creatures in him; and then the Spirit carries forward the work of sanctification, until at length we are translated to the world of glory.

If any man be in Christ, then, he is entirely transformed; "old things are passed away: behold, all things are become new." But let us precisely understand the nature of the claim; it is by no means affirmed that all who profess Christianity experience, in like degree, this transforming change. Alas, my hearers, many who profess to be the children of God are in "the gall of bitterness and in the bonds of iniquity." The number is larger still of those converted by the Spirit of God, who are, nevertheless, imperfectly developed Christians. And in none of those who are the purest and best is this development completed till death. Not till then is the likeness to Christ made perfect by the last touches of the divine artist, and we are delivered forever from the presence and being of sin, as before we were, in a measure, delivered from its power and dominion. But, in all stages of the work, the nature and the reality of this transforming change may distinctly be traced.

What is it, then, which gives to the gospel its transforming power? How comes it to pass that whenever it takes hold upon the sinner it makes him a new creature—old things passing away and all things becoming new? I have three special answers to return to this question, all which are so important that I must break each into distinct specifications.

I. The gospel has this transforming power over the characters and lives of men BECAUSE IT UNDERTAKES TO DEAL WITH SIN IN ITS ESSENCE AND ROOT, AND NOT WITH SIN IN ITS EXTERNAL FORMS OR OUTWARD MANIFESTATIONS. In this particular you perceive that the gospel is separated, by a long interval, from all the systems of moral reform which are devised by men. We have associations for the suppression of intemperance and of gambling. We have voluntary organizations, by precept and example to build up specific virtues in the world. All these associations, however praiseworthy, are, from the very statement of the case, merely palliative, whilst the gospel claims to be distinctly remedial. These schemes of reform strike at particular evils; they lop off the diseased branches of the tree. The gospel undertakes to go behind all these down to the sin, which lies at the root of every vice. It undertakes to effect a radical cure—not to remove the diseased limb of the tree, but to engraft upon the trunk, and to send down into its roots the virtue of a new life. The gospel transforms the character of man and makes him a new creature in Christ for the simple reason that it deals with sin in its interior nature rather than in its external form. This will be made plain if we view the gospel under four different aspects.

1. *It is the only system which undertakes to provide a perfect pardon and to readjust man's relations to the violated law.* In every government, human or divine, the first

thing to be considered is our relation to the law.   Immediately upon transgression, the law seizes the offender's person, brings him before the tribunal of justice, convicts him under the evidence, fixes upon him the sentence of condemnation, and holds him in prison, awaiting the execution of the penalty.   Of necessity, therefore, in seeking relief, his first concern will be to settle with the law and to cancel its indictment.   It does not make a particle of difference, at the first, how the man feels as to his transgression; whether he glories in it, or is sorry for it; whether, if released from punishment, he will lead a life of obedience or repeat his trespass to the end. The first and absorbing question is how to escape the infliction of the penalty which he has incurred.   How shall he come forth from the shadow of his prison and walk in the free air of heaven with an erect form, and look without a blush in the faces of other men.

Now, this is just what the gospel undertakes to do for the sinner.   It provides a perfect pardon, and secures it upon principles of strict justice and law.   The imperfection of human government is in nothing more manifest than in the fact that it never can exercise mercy except at the expense of justice.   The criminal can never escape the penalty without inflicting a certain amount of injury upon the country and the law.   If he escape by any defect in the evidence he is turned loose again to prey upon society as before.   If executive clemency sets aside the deliberate judgment of the court, a shock is given to the stability of government by the collision between its two departments, which ought to be mutually supporting.   But in the gospel, the justice and integrity of God are as completely vindicated as in the punishment of the transgressor.   Whilst the sinner escapes the penalty, the law of God is more firmly established than before.

Such a pardon, in which every claim of law is satisfied, goes to the root of the sinner's case, so far as his guilt is concerned, for the reason that it is a pardon which can be sealed upon the conscience and give it perfect peace.

2. The gospel provides that *the sinner shall, by repentance, put away the sin from himself.*   Not only does God cast his iniquities into the sea and remember them against him no more, but his grace enables the sinner to concur in a solemn act of repudiation on his part also, whereby he is doubly separated from the sins which he bewails.   It is thus expressed by the Apostle Paul: "That I may win Christ and be found in him, not having mine own righteousness which is of the law, but that which is through the faith of Christ, the righteousness which is of God by faith."   The first element in repentance is, of course, a true knowledge of sin—its very nature being opened to the spiritual eye so as to be seen in its hidden deformity.   The second element is a thorough hatred of that sin, the vileness of which is so clearly perceived, and then bitter grief for its commission.   After this comes the honest endeavor to turn away from it.   Thus repentance, like a sharp sword, cleaves between a man and his sins—causes them to be cast behind his back with a most thorough repudiation— and leads him to strive with a vigorous purpose after new obedience.   What a wonderful system! which not only blots out the sin from the divine record, but gives power to the transgressor himself to put the offence away, as disowned and rejected forever!   In striking thus directly at the dominion of sin, no less than its guilt, the remedial character of the gospel is disclosed.

3. *In the new birth is communicated a superior and divine life to the soul "dead in trespasses and sins."*   The spirit-

ual life, which man possessed before the fall, consisted in the holiness of nature in which he was created. In the loss of his original rectitude, man became spiritually dead. Hence, in the definition of original sin, as given in our standards, this "want of original righteousness" is placed between "the guilt of Adam's first sin" and "the corruption of our whole nature," as being the nexus by which the two are bound together. The legal process may be briefly stated thus: Adam being constituted in the covenant the representative and head of his posterity, his act, whether of obedience or of sin, would, by virtue of this headship, become putatively their act. The legal effect of this imputation of Adam's sin would be to separate man from God, with the consequent loss of that holiness in which he was created—and upon the loss of this original righteousness the entire corruption of nature must ensue. When, therefore, Christ, the second Adam, takes the sinner's place under the law, and satisfies its claim, the righteousness of the substitute is reckoned to the sinner as his own—precisely as before in the imputation of the first Adam's transgression. The guilt being now removed, and the sinner being legally restored to the divine favor, the spiritual life, which had been forfeited under the curse, must be restored. This is done by the Holy Spirit in the new birth, whereby the sinner is quickened into spiritual life through the principle of holiness once more implanted in the soul.

In the power of this new and divine life the sinner puts forth the act of faith which appropriates Christ's righteousness, and takes into actual possession what had previously been legally reckoned as the ground of reconciliation with God. By the same power he exercises also the repentance above described, by which he becomes, on his part, separated practically, as before legally, from the sins he deplores.   In the impartation of this new life is begun the process by which the sin is eventually destroyed, whose guilt has already been pardoned, and its dominion already broken.   But this introduces to the topic of the section that follows.

4. As stated above, the salvation of the sinner is not completed without *the entire elimination of sin from the nature itself*, in the sanctification and glorification of the believer.   Language and thought alike fail in depicting this blessed consummation.   It almost staggers belief that man shall not only be delivered from the dominion of sin, but eventually from its very presence and being. We accept it only upon the divine testimony, and because it is the logical outcome of the scheme of grace itself.   If, in regeneration, a divine life is communicated to the sinner, its characteristic energy must, by its own expulsive force, drive out the sin which obstructs its growth.   The power of sin is daily weakened, and there comes a moment, it may be in the instant of death, when the last stain is washed away in the Saviour's atoning blood, and the being of sin is forever destroyed in the soul.   Transformed into the image of his divine Redeemer and Head, the believer ascends to heaven with a nature as holy as that in which he first came from his Creator's hand.   The peer now of spotless angels who never sinned, he teaches them the song of redeeming grace, to which they can only respond in the mighty chorus, "Blessing and honor and glory and power be unto him that sitteth upon the throne, and unto the Lamb forever and ever."

Is not the gospel, then, a glorious remedy for sin, going down to its root to destroy it there in the very seat of its life?   It seals upon the conscience a perfect pardon,

which takes away all guilt; it cuts out the cancer from
the man himself through the surgery of an honest repentance; it breathes a divine life into the soul that was
separated from God, and completes its beneficence by
the extirpation of sin itself and the transfiguration of the
saint in glory.   Here is no palliation of an inveterate
disease, but its radical cure in a fourfold deliverance from
the *punishment*, the *dominion*, the *pollution*, and the *being*
of sin.   Well may the apostle say, "If any man be in
Christ, he is a new creature: old things are passed away;
behold, all things are become new."

II. The gospel is thus transforming in its influence
BECAUSE THE POWER IS DIVINE BY WHICH IT WORKS.
It is a law of nature that, wherever there is motion there
is power behind it as the cause.   Now, when you ask
for the power by which this transformation is wrought
in the character of the sinner, the answer ascribes the
change to the power of God alone.   There are one or
two specifications under this head also:

1. *It is the concurrent power of each person of the Godhead in their official distinction.*   God, in the Scriptures,
is revealed as Father, Son and Holy Ghost.   These are
plainly distinguished from each other, so that the Father
is never confounded with the Son, nor the Son with the
Spirit.   Offices are assigned to each, which are so dis-
tinctive that they can neither be transposed nor consoli-
dated.   Affections are attributed to them which belong
only to persons, such as anger and grief.   The distinction, therefore, is not of attributes belonging to, nor of
relations and offices discharged by, one and the same
individual, but it is a distinction of persons in the adorable Trinity, who are yet revealed, however incomprehensible the mystery, as the one only living and true
God.

It follows, from this unity of being, that the trinity of persons must concur in every action of the Deity, whether it be in creation, providence, or grace. We accordingly find in the Scriptures all the divine works referred now to one and now to another of these three persons respectively. The distinct agency of each is, however, not clearly drawn until we come to the scheme of redemption. As to the works of creation and providence, the distinction is sufficiently intimated as the exercise of power *from* the Father, *by* the Son, and *through* the Spirit; *from* the Father, in the way of original and supreme authority; *by* the Son, in the way of immediate efficiency; *through* the Spirit, in the way of a completing and applying agency.

If this distinction should appear to you vague and uncertain, it becomes amazingly clear and full in the scheme of grace. In this the Father, as the first in the order of thought, is the immediate representative of the Godhead (holds in his hands the reins of universal empire), administers the law and fastens its penalty upon the transgressor. It is the office of the Father, in the covenant of redemption, to accept the Son as the sinner's substitute under the law; to give the commission under which this Son shall act as the Mediator; to accept the sacrifice by which man's sin is expiated; to justify all those to whom this perfect righteousness is imputed; and to crown this Redeemer and all his seed with everlasting glory. The Son, in the distinction of his personality as the Son, undertakes the sinner's cause; endures the penalty of sin in his stead; renders the obedience in which he had failed; ascends to heaven to plead the merit of his sacrifice; sues out the sinner's right to pardon and life, and sends forth the Holy Spirit under his royal commission to work this complete salvation

2

into the experience of men. Whilst the Holy Ghost, the third of this trinity in unity, reserves to himself the final office in this scheme of grace, in applying the redemption purchased by Christ and making the believer meet for glory and immortality beyond the grave.

Here, then, is not only divine power, but that power concurrently wielded by each person of the Godhead in each of the three parts of the scheme of grace. How can it fail to produce the effect which is stated in the text? If the power of the Father decreeing this salvation, and the power of the Son executing it, and the power of the Holy Spirit applying it—if it all bears directly upon the sinner's case, he must be changed into the image of his Creator, from glory unto glory. The immediateness of this applied power from each of the persons of the Godhead gives additional security to the result, leaving no opportunity for the intrusion of any disturbing agency which shall arrest the completion of that which grace has begun.

2. *It is power springing out of spontaneous love; not intermittent, but constant.* There are those of scientific taste who amuse themselves with the effort to discover perpetual motion, just as the alchemists of old sought for the water of life, or labored to transmute the baser metals into gold. Assuming that for all movement there must be a force, and endeavoring by a combination of natural forces to compensate for the loss of energy experienced in producing motion, they hope to arrive at movement which shall never cease. But the secret of all force is found at last in the divine will; and God's will is always effective, because God always lives. Interpose as many secondary causes as you please, you are compelled, by the law of thought which seeks for the efficiency of every cause, to ascend to the eternal purpose

and thought of the infinite Jehovah.   Multiply the links
as you may, you must have at last the ring-bolt which
suspends the chain from the arm of him who is himself
uncaused.

But we would be overwhelmed by this conception of
infinite power if it were not the free movement of infinite
love as well.   "Herein is love; not that we loved God,
but that he loved us, and sent his Son to be the propitiation for our sins."   It is power, indeed; but power
springing from a nature of love, always under the direction of infinite wisdom and benevolence.   It will, therefore, be a constant force, carrying the provisions of the
gospel to their last result.   When power and love combine the believer may well utter the triumphant challenge, "Who shall separate us from the love of Christ?
Nay, in all things we are more than conquerors through
him that loved us."

3. *It is the power pledged in the stipulations and promises
of the divine covenant.*   The pledge, you perceive, is twofold, in the stipulations between the parties to the covenant, and in the promises made to those who receive its
benefits.   But who are the parties?   Only the persons
of the adorable Godhead.   Far back in the silence of
past eternity, before sun, moon, or stars shone in the
firmament, or any creature had been fashioned—in the
far-off ages when only God was, the Eternal Three devised the scheme by which man should be released from
the thraldom and guilt of sin.   The distribution of offices,
which must be severally discharged, involved certain
stipulations between those who assumed the various
parts.   The Father gave to the Son those whom he
should redeem; the Son came under obligation to rescue
these from eternal death : the Holy Ghost gave his
pledge to apply this redemption to all those for whom it

was wrought.   Can this solemn compact fail without a rupture in the Godhead?

The salvation thus secured under these mutual stipulations is made over to the sinner under "exceeding great and precious promises" which are "yea and amen in Christ Jesus."   With what tender emphasis our faith is here assured.   Wherever the sinner is found on the face of the earth, the gospel comes with its repeated "Verily, verily, I say unto you."   Yes, sinner, yes, it constantly proclaims, Whosoever believeth shall be saved.   Then comes the blessed "Amen"; the benediction which follows the affirmation and seals the promise under its own exultation.   "So be it," sounds the triple voice in the pavilion of the Godhead!   "So be it," says the law in the person of the Father; "So be it," cries divine mercy in the person of the Son; "So be it," cries infinite grace in the person of the Holy Ghost. The grand "Amen" rings through the upper temple in the song of angels, while the glad echo goes up from a redeemed earth to give a new tone to the music of heaven.

Surely, he who trusts in the Lord Jesus plants his feet upon a rock—upon the Rock of Ages, the eternal rock; the rock of God's own rectitude, his infinite justice and unchangeable truth.   With such guarantees, the gospel can never fail to accomplish its last result in the transfiguration of the believer.

III.   The gospel is thus transforming in its power BECAUSE IT BRINGS THE WHOLE AGENCY OF MAN INTO CO-OPERATION WITH THAT OF GOD.   God is unchangeable in his works as well as in his being.   Having made man holy and put him under law, he will never contravene the principles of this economy, but will hold him to his responsibility in the scheme of salvation as dis· tinctly as in the fall.   No man ever trusted in the Saviour without a consciousness of his concurrence in the acceptance of the ''great salvation.'' The pardon is never sealed upon us until we embrace him who offers it. Not only in the first exercise of faith and repentance is this human concurrence brought into view, but through the long conflict with indwelling sin, and in the assured hope with which the Christian mounts from the bed of death to sit at the right hand of the King in his glory. It is in the free play of all his faculties, as they are emancipated from the bondage of sin, the transforming energy of divine grace finds its manifestation.

Arresting all discussion at this point, I press upon your attention one or two practical inferences. The first is, *the grave responsibility which is herein laid upon Goa's children.* So far as the Scriptures inform us, redeemed sinners are the only representatives of God's most majestic work, and of the most important and holy principles which he has undertaken to reveal to the creature. What a responsibility! We undertake to say to the universe that there is pardon, consistent with holiness, justice and truth, for the sinner that will accept it. Is our testimony challenged, and do we say the Bible affirms it? Let the Bible speak for itself. God is his own witness when he puts these immortal truths on record in this book. But when we are asked about this pardon we must draw the answer from our own experience, because the pardon purchased with blood has been sealed upon our conscience, and has given us peace and ''joy in the Holy Ghost.'' Upon this personal knowledge our testimony must be based. We say the power of this gospel is seen in making the Christian purer and holier, until at last he is made perfect in Christ's image. How do we know it? The Scriptures affirm it. But where is our testimony corroborating the truth of God's holy word unless we experience this deliverence from the power and dominion of sin?

What an august testimony to bear before the world! Angels bend from their high places in order to hear it; and the world in which we live holds us under their jeers and taunts if we do not act consistently with these high professions. For this reason, God converts men in all conditions of life. The King upon his throne is made a witness and the beggar on the street, that in all these walks of life men may testify to the riches and efficacy of divine grace.

My brethren, this should be with us the main business and purpose of life. The first question which should come to every professing Christian is, whether this or that consists with his character as a child of God. We have no right to put our testimony under suspicion by being anywhere where a Christian ought not to be—by doing anything which a Christian ought not to do. Is the responsibility fearful? Let us remember that it is also a blessed responsibility. The joy of life is found in its weighty trusts. It is worth little if we cannot testify to some truth, and throw out some principle which shall help our fellow-men on their ascending path from earth to heaven. Just because these responsibilities are so immense, they ought to be taken by us as a crown of glory. And we shall be upon the edge of the millenium when the church herself shall fully recognize the binding nature of her own vow of consecration; when she shall consent to draw the line exactly as the world draws it, sharp and clear betwixt themselves and us.

The second inference is, that *the only hope of a perishing world is in the gospel of the grace of God*. The reformation from external vices may bring relief to society from many ills which oppress it, but they work no radical cure, even of these. The waters can be healed only in the fountain from which they flow. And let the unconverted man see how all practical difficulties are removed out of the way of his salvation. He says, with a strange orthodoxy availing himself of a truth which he detests, that he has no power to believe or repent and turn away from sin. Grant it; but here is the power, in God if not in man; and all that power is offered without reserve to those who will simply yield to its exercise. The sinner is conscious of power to resist God's truth. We ask that he shall cease this resistance, and not grieve the Holy Spirit by smothering his convictions of sin. It is true, there is no power in the unrenewed man to turn from sin to holiness; but there is power in God, and the only hope for a world of sinners is, that they will become "willing in the day of his power," and appear before his throne at last as the drops of the morning dew.

THE CHANGING WORLD AND THE UNCHANGING GOD.

BY REV. MOSES D. HOGE, D. D.,

Pastor of the Second Presbyterian Church, Richmond, Va.

"And, Thou, Lord, in the beginning hast laid the foundation of the earth; and the heavens are the works of thine hands. They shall perish, but thou remainest : and they all shall wax old as doth a garment; and as a vesture shalt thou fold them up, and they shall be changed; but thou art the same, and thy years shall not fail."—HEB. i. 10, 11, 12.

HERE we have disclosed to us in most impressive terms the contrast between the mutability of all created things and the unchanging God

The earth, with its apparently firm foundations and the seemingly steadfast heavens, are declared to be alike unsubstantial. As they represent what is supposed to be most durable, there is something startling in the quiet assertion, "they shall be changed," "they shall perish."

But if the pillared firmament can be shaken, if the great globe itself is to dissolve as an exhalation and vanish like a vision of the night, then the inference is irresistible that all that mortal men can construct by manual skill or mental force; that all the pageants of time and sense, that all the creations of genius and all the pomp and pride of human glory, are still more evanescent.

Nothing terrestrial bears the stamp of indestructibility. The things that are seen are temporal, and not only so, but instability is their characteristic even during their brief survival.

It is so evident that this law of change is divinely decreed that we are impelled to inquire for what ends God fills human life with so much perturbation.   This is my theme to-day—the ethics of change, the moral uses of vicissitude ; and I hope to show that the very fluctuations of our present state of being, that what we call the accidents that befall men; that the crosses and disappointments which are so common, as well as the blessings that fill the heart with gratitude and joy— that these are so many instrumentalities by which God shapes and moulds human character, and by which he teaches men how so to use this present life as to be prepared for life eternal.   The Scriptures assert that a life of continuous prosperity and success breeds false security, leads men to presume on the future and to forget God.   ''Because they have no changes, therefore they fear not God.''   They take what we call providence as the natural course of human events, and, gliding along on a smooth sea with prosperous gales, there is nothing to remind such that there is one who rides upon the clouds and directs the storm, and then at his will makes all calm again.

So far as the *fact* is concerned that change characterizes human affairs, there is nothing that is more readily, and nothing that is more generally, admitted.   In a great variety of ways the Scriptures announce this truth and try to impress it upon the memories and hearts of men.   Sometimes they state the fact in plain, didactic language, and sometimes they use the most graphic and glowing figures, that by imagery and metaphor they may deepen the impression that the world is a world of perturbation, and that God intends us to live in the midst of vicissitude.   I find this stated in one short line which inspiration has put upon record: "The fashion of this world passeth away."   "The *pageant* of this world passeth away" like the plays performed on the dramatic stage, where the scenery is perpetually shifting, where actors come and go, where there are representations of imaginary situations and delineations of imaginary characters and events, the one rapidly following the other, until the curtain drops and the play is over.   "All the world's a stage," and the actors are the men and women whose smiles of joy and tears of woe make up the comedy or the tragedy of the fleeting show.   And so time moves on until it runs its appointed round, and the great curtain drops on the drama of completed human history.

We have the same truth announced under a different figure, where inspiration tells us that, "Here we have no continuing city."   Many of the works of men possess great permanence.   The great capitals of Old World empires, with their stately temples, with their strong, triumphal arches, with their massive walls fortified by tower and bastion, with their gigantic granite amphitheatres—these were structures that seem to have been destined to defy the hand even of that greatest of all destroyers, time.   And yet these cities became the prey of successive conquerors.   Again and again they were captured and pillaged and desolated, and the banners of successive victors waved in triumph over the towers that were deemed impregnable.   At last decay and disintegration followed the ruthless work of the invader, and a mightier force laid those cities low, until the time has come when the very sites they once occupied is a matter of dispute.

Antiquarians engage in long controversies as to the very places where these imperial cities stood, some of them that bore the boastful name of "Eternal." How will it be with the cities of the present generation? I shall not remind you of Macaulay's prediction of a man sitting in the midst of a vast solitude on a broken arch of London bridge and sketching the ruins of the cathedral of the world's metropolis. I have no predictions to make with regard to the doom of the mighty cities that now dominate the nations, and into which all the resources of power and influence seem to be concentrating; cities by and by to rule the continents, and ultimately to rule the world.

We see no signs of decay and dissolution in the sovereign cities of the earth in the present time; and yet there is a sense in which the old text is just as true of London and Paris and Berlin and New York and San Francisco as it was true of those cities of which I have just made mention, that "Here we have no continuing city." The city may remain, but you and I must go.

How few of the inhabitants of any city live in houses which they themselves built. The great majority of people occupy houses through which the representatives of successive generations have passed; and with regard to those who built and who own the dwellings in which they live, they are but the temporary tenants. Presently their children will sit at the head of the table and manage all the affairs of the household, and sometimes talk very tenderly and very kindly about what father and mother did in their day. We are only the transient inhabitants of the places we call home, and therefore it is true of us that "Here we have no continuing city." The very habitations endeared to us, it may be, by many hallowed associations, will fall first into the hands of our children and afterwards they will pass into the hands of utter strangers, and it may be that the very tradition

will be lost as to who once lived there and as to who was
the founder of the house.

But it is not worth while, in the illustration of my
theme, that I should ask you to indulge in retrospects.
It is enough to invite you to give me the testimony of
your present observation. What is it? It is this: that
you see the inhabitants of any city with which you are
familiar very rapidly changing. There is not a month
that I do not meet with some one who visits this church
who worshipped here, it may be, ten or twenty years
ago. I hear the same old, sad story. They all say that
it revives many pleasant memories to be within these
walls again, but as they look over the congregation it is
a new and strange one to them. It was only here and
there that they recognized a face that they had ever seen
before. There may be one man in this house, but not
more than one, who heard the first sermon that I preached
here. We constantly see changes in the people around
us, whether we live in the town or the country. Last
week you settled an account with a man, but you will
never settle another account with him, and the reason is
that he has gone to his last account. The other day you
met with a man and you shook hands with him. You
did not dream that that friendly pressure was the last.
The other day a neighbor of yours moved into another
residence. Well, since then you know he has moved
again, and now he has found another home. It is the
place we call the long home. A few Sundays ago one
sat beside you in the church, and heard just what you
heard. He listened to the same discourse to which you
listened. He united in singing the same hymns of
praise. He heard the sounds that mercy utters from the
cross, but now no voice of invitation, no melody of Zion
awakens one emotion. Nothing stirs the heart that lies

so chill and still in the coffin, and no music penetrates that dull, cold ear of death. "Here we have no continuing city."

This is a fact that ought to do more than make us pensive; it ought to remind us that the same changes we see in our friends they see in us. You meet a friend that you have not seen for several years, and, you do not tell him so, on the contrary, you avoid giving him any intimation of what you observe, but you are very much startled to see what a change time has made in him; to see how white his hair has become, and how decrepit his form is, and how uncertain his movements are. Well, he looks at you, and just what is passing through your mind is passing through his. So we are all moving along on the same stream, and we are all moving along with exactly the same rapidity. You think people grow old a great deal faster than you do, but we are all borne upon the bosom of the same flood and with a common celerity. None of us have it in our power to look up as Joshua did and say: "Sun, stand thou still" until I complete this grand enterprise to which my heart is linked, and to which my life is consecrated. Alas! we cannot lengthen out the short allotted span, no matter how intense may be the desire to live, no matter how impassioned may be the longing to complete the chosen task. Nothing can turn back by one degree the dark shadow that moves with dread certainty over life's dial. We have no continuing city.

Again the figure changes, and the Bible reminds us that "life is a day," not like a long, lingering, summer day; rather like a crisp, winter day, bright but brief. You watch the delicate flush of dawn, and it almost brings tears into the eyes to see the tender grace and sweetness of the early summer morning. By and by

the landscape grows brighter and the heavens more
brilliant, and the sun goes up to its zenith; but it does
not stand there in the mid-heaven, for presently it begins
to decline, and by and by it goes down with a sombre,
mellow glory, not so bright and not so cheery as the
morning ray, but with a pensive glory it goes down to
its western bed, and then the evening comes.   So infancy is that tender break of day; that sweet, bright
dawn; but how quickly infancy merges into youth, and
how soon youth matures into middle age.   Then, when
middle age comes, how swift the decline and how soon
the shadows of evening and the cold dews begin to settle
around us.   Then comes the night, "in which no man
can work."

Again the figure changes, and we are told that life is
like the "troubled sea."   If there is anything whatever
that is an impressive emblem of life, it is the sea with
its unrest; the sea with its perpetual moan; the sea that
is always changing its face—bright and blue when the
heaven is clear above, black and ominous when clouds
darken the sky; sometimes sleeping in a deceitful calm,
and then, at the wind's voice, waking into fury; the sea
with its tides ebbing and flowing through its mighty
heart, and with resounding surge washing the shores of
all continents.   Oh! what an emblem this is of human
life!   Life, with its surprises and fluctuations, with its
uncertainties and perpetual perturbations.

I do not know of anything that is seen, or that has
been created, that does not bear the impress of change
and decay.   This is true of all the works of men to
which I have made reference; but there are some works
of men that are far more permanent than great cities,
than triumphal arches, than colossal columns.   It is a
great mistake to think that these things represent what

is most enduring in the world.   There is the kingdom
of mind—the kingdom of mind that outlasts matter—
the triumphs of mind, and the structures that genius
rears which are far more enduring than those that the
architect can ever erect.   See how the intellects of men
have been held spell-bound in unquestioning obedience
to the great philosophies that in turn have subjugated
thought and given direction to the ethical beliefs of mankind; the philosophies of Plato, of Aristotle, of Epicurus,
and the successive philosophies which have displaced
them in modern times—the one chasing the other like
shadows over a plain.   Sir Walter said one day, as he
looked at a painting and shook his head: ''A painter is
mistaken if he thinks that by a picture he can perpetuate
his fame.''   Said he, ''No man can perpetuate his fame
in that way, because the picture fades and the canvas
upon which it is painted by and by crumbles.   The only
thing that endures is literature.''   My friends, I do not
know of a more sad mistake than that.   With the exception of a few of the classic Greek and Roman writers,
whose pure style, like the pure air of Egypt, keeps bright
and fresh the colors of the interiors of their tombs, there
is nothing more ephemeral than literature.   The very
art of printing, which preserves all other arts, will by
and by make literature an impossibility so far as immortality is concerned, because of the very multiplication of
those products of the human intellect.   Go into the great
libraries of London, or Paris, or St. Petersburg, or in
some of the American cities, and you see nothing more
sad than those vast shelves crowded with the works of
men that once commanded the attention of their generation, but their books lie as unnoticed as mummies in
Egyptian tombs.   There they lie embalmed, without the
possibility of a resurrection.   A great library is a mau-

soleum of dead thought. Therefore, there is no hope of obtaining anything like a permanent renown, even through that long-surviving influence.

When we come to *science*, we think if there is anything that is settled and fixed we will find it there. Not so; there is as much fluctuation in science as there is in general literature. A text-book that was an authority twenty years ago, is only worth the price that the buyer of old paper would give for it; and what are called the exact sciences are so inexact that a book on geology or chemistry that was printed ten years ago is worthless now and everywhere rejected.

But there is one thing far more permanent than the noblest creations of genius, and that is *nature;* but nature itself is not an exception to the law of change. Look at the mountain, look at the sea, and you say, "There is something over which time has no influence." Wait a bit. A man comes, we will say, from the Old World. He emigrates in his boyhood to this country, and after a lapse of fifty years he has a great longing to go back and see his native village. He has a thousand tender memories about it, and thinks if he could only see that village once more he would be willing to leave the world satisfied. He makes the trip and finds the place. Almost at the first glance he says to himself: "I am disenchanted." What an air of desolation and loneliness rests over the place. He walks about and does not recognize a single face as one he ever saw before. He walks about, and people cast careless glances at him as they would at any stranger, but nobody looks at him a second time. He goes to the house where he was born, but it is not tenanted now; it is a ruin. And then he says, "Well, there is one place where I can go and get comfort. I will go to the little spot sacred to the memory of the loved and lost." He goes there, and finds the enclosure broken down. He finds the graves grown over with weeds and briers. He finds the headstone lying some distance from the grave and broken in two; and there is not a place in the world that looks more desolate and lonely. Nobody ever visits that spot now; it is a dolorous solitude. Once affection lingered and wept there, but now all the sighs that are heard there are the sighs of the night wind through the drooping willows, and the only tears are the cold dews that trickle down the broken marbles. "Well," he says, "all this is changed, but nature is not changed." He looks around, and there is the old familiar river, and there are the hills that look just as they did when he last saw them. He says, "Thank God that I find something that is not changed"; and yet, my friends, that is a superficial observation. The whole physical globe is undergoing a perpetual change. The close observer notices how the coasts of some continents are rising, and how the shores of others are depressed. The close observer sees how the ocean now sweeps over vast tracts that once were cultivated, and how others that were once submerged form the homes of busy men. The perpetual mountains crumble, and the everlasting hills bow as they are disintegrated by frost and fire, by the action of the wasting storms and wearing streams. Therefore, we should not be surprised at the statement made in the text: "Thou, Lord, in the beginning hast laid the foundations of the earth, and the heavens are the works of thy hands. They shall perish, but thou remainest; yea, all of them shall wax old as doth a garment; as a vesture shalt thou fold them up and they shall be changed, but thou art the same, and thy years shall not fail."

3

Therefore, when we come to inquire into the moral uses of vicissitude, and what is the grand purpose for which God has placed us in a world of such mutation, we can give briefly, in closing, this answer: it is that we may fix our thoughts and hopes upon something that is both permanent and satisfying.

There are other uses at which we may glance, but this should arrest our supreme regard.

In the fifty-fifth Psalm there is a most pathetic picture. Old King David, wearied with the cares of office, is sitting on the flat roof of his house one evening. He has taken off his crown. It is too heavy, and he has laid it down upon the parapet. He has laid his sceptre at his feet, and sits there and sighs: "Would I were a shepherd lad again. O, that the innocence and sweetness of my early life might come back to replace the pomp and the burdensome cares of empire." Then he looked up and saw a little flock of doves flitting across the sky, their soft plumage glancing in the sun, growing dimmer as they recede, until they reach the western hills, and he said, "O that I had wings like a dove, for then I would fly away and be at rest. O for rest! Rest!"

Vastly mistaken is the man who compares himself to a noble oak, striking its roots deep into the earth, with its great strong branches shooting upwards, upon which the storms of heaven break when they strike it. Man has no such permanence, no such independence. He is more like a vine which has to grow upon a massive wall or upon a strong pillar, otherwise it trails upon the ground and perishes. The worst thing a vine can do is to trail around another vine. Both will fall, and, locked in fatal embrace, will perish. If a vine becomes fruitful, it must be trained to a pillar or a wall. Ah, so it was with that great and yearning heart of David that sought rest. He was taught to say: ''Put not your trust in princes, nor in the son of man in whom is no help; his breath goeth forth, he returneth to his earth; in that very day his thoughts perish.'' ''In that very day man returneth to his earth''; the earth that is *his* because he came out of it and goes back to it; ''earth to earth, ashes to ashes, dust to dust.'' ''In that very day his thoughts,'' no matter how original, how lofty or how profound—it may be thoughts too tender or too delicately personal to be expressed—nevertheless, ''In that very day his thoughts perish.''

Again. If we ask, then, for the ethics, the religious lessons of change, another answer is that God has placed us in the midst of these perturbations to keep our life from becoming stagnant. If there was no change we would all become imbecile. I say if there was no change in the intellectual world, men would, by and by, drivel into impotence. Change is necessary to stir up and quicken and freshen life, just as thunder and storm are necessary to purify the sultry, stifling air. If it were not for these vicissitudes there would be no intellectual and no spiritual development. Change is God's benediction to humanity. No man knows what he can do until he is put in a new situation that calls forth his energies. No man knows the resources that slumber within himself until the exigency comes that wakes them into efficiency. So God puts adversity and prosperity in the world to balance each other and to discipline and develop what is best in man.

Another reason why we are placed in such a world of change is to keep us from presuming on the future. You remember the description that one of the evangelists gives us of the world's fool of the first magnitude—

the greatest fool whose biography has been written—who said, "Soul, thou hast much goods laid up for many years, eat, drink and be merry," as if the soul could be nourished by what grows in the vineyard and the field. The fool uttered a soliloquy, but there were two voices. It was a dialogue; another speaker broke in and said: "This night," not in some future year, but "this night, thy soul shall be required of thee."

Again. Life's changes teach us to avoid the perils of both prosperity and adversity. Do you know the danger of too much success, of a life of uninterrupted prosperity? You say, selfishness and indifference to the interests and happiness of others. It is all that, but another danger of too much prosperity is *discontent*. You thought I was going to say that is the danger of adversity; but one danger of prosperity is discontent. The most discontented men on earth are those who roll in riches and do not know how to make their investments or how to keep their accumulations. The most discontented women on earth are women living in a super-abounding luxury that enervates and surfeits without satisfying. In their discontent they utter more complaints and murmurs in a single day than the poor woman who, stitch by stitch, makes her livelihood in the garret where she toils for her daily crust.

The danger of adversity is doubt—doubt of God's providence, and finally a denial that there is any providence—until at last the person says: "I am no worse than other people, but God seems to think so. He afflicts me, and I do not have anything but trouble. I doubt whether there is any providence at all." And so blank denial of a fundamental truth is the result of too much adversity.

On the otner hand, while prosperity has its dangers,

it opens the way for the cultivation of graces which otherwise would not exist.   If there were no prosperity, where would be room or possibility for humility and for self-denial?   The only man who can deny himself is the prosperous man; the only one who ever really denies himself is the man of abundance.   The poor man is all the while compelled to live a life of self-denial; but the man of abundance can voluntarily choose such a life, and so cultivate a grace that would otherwise be impossible. Where there is no trial there can be no trust.   Where there is no bereavement there can be no resignation. Where there is no disappointment there can be no hope, for how can one hope for what he already possesses? How can the graces of love, joy, peace and holy aspiration grow if they are never exercised?   The vicissitudes of life are the divinely ordained instrumentalities by which God disciplines men and develops their truest and noblest Christian manhood.

Lastly.   Experience and revelation unite in teaching that the soul must have some foundation on which to build and rest secure, which is not subject to mutation; something as enduring as its own immortality, and as satisfying as its capacities for happiness.   But this it cannot find either in the material or intellectual creations of men—not in the noblest or most enduring of them; it cannot find it in human love, however pure and constant; it cannot find it in wealth or fame or power; it cannot find it in nature, whose well-ordered harmonies seem sweet and unvarying as the song of the morning stars.

Where, then, is the foundation on which the deathless soul may erect its immortal hopes and find its eternal rest and peace and blessedness?   The answer comes, all else must change and pass away, "BUT THOU RE-

MAINEST.'' God is the soul's infinite necessity, the soul's eternal satisfaction. He alone is immutable. He cannot be changed by anything that is without, for there is nothing external to himself which he did not create. Creatures possess no powers which he did not confer on them, and he never formed anything that was capable of harming himself. Therefore, he can be changed by nothing from without. Nor from anything within. Being self-existent, he is dependent upon none for his life. Being perfectly happy, he can never wish to be anything but what he is. Being omnipotent, he has power to be what he wishes to be; and being eternal, he can be what he wishes to be forever. A being infinitely blessed can desire no change, for were there any height of happiness or glory above him he would not be infinite.

Through the measureless eternity he will sit upon his throne in the unimpaired greatness of his supremacy. So perfect is he that the flight of unnumbered ages will not behold the kindling of another beam in his immeasurable glory, nor will the flight of unnumbered ages behold amid these glories one ray, now beaming, quenched.

The greatest change ever made in a human life is sometimes caused by a single bereavement, and yet the sorest bereavement may be so sanctified as to become the greatest benediction. There are losses which leave the soul so desolate, so emptied of every earthly joy, that it cries out after God with an intense and impassioned longing never felt before. Were there no God to help, its desolation would deepen into despair.

One way, then, by which the soul learns to know God is through its own great necessities which he alone can satisfy. Were we never in trouble we never could know what a loving Father he is. Did we shed no bitter tears we never could know how soft the hand that wipes them away. If bereavement never caused our hearts to bleed, we could never know how gentle the hand is that binds them up. Our sorrows teach us that he can comfort with more than a mother's tenderness. When we taste the wormwood and the gall, and thus suffer the experience of the bitterness of sin, then we can sing,

> "Sweet the moments, rich in blessing,
> Which before the cross I spend";

or, changing the measure, as we emerge from the darkness, we can prolong the song in strains like these:

> "The opening heavens around me shine
> With beams of sacred bliss,
> When Jesus shows his heart is mine,
> And whispers, I am his."

Then the soul's wish for wings like a dove's is satisfied. It fluttered a moment against the window, and then a friendly hand reached forth and took it into the gospel ark, there safely to abide and sweetly to rest with the life hid with Christ in God, preparatory to the time when a nobler rest shall be enjoyed in the place where the discipline of vicissitude will be needed and known no more, and where the only change will be from one degree of glory to another as the soul advances in endless conformity to the divine image of purity and blessedness in the eternal kingdom of the Father.

"I shall behold thy face in righteousness; I shall be satisfied with thy likeness."

> "O long-expected day, begin."

"ONE JESUS."

BY J. HENRY SMITH, D. D.

Pastor of First Presbyterian Church, Greensboro, N. C.

"Against whom when the accusers stood up, they brought none accusation of such things as I supposed: but had certain questions against him of their own superstition, and of one Jesus, which was dead, whom Paul affirmed to be alive."—ACTS xxv. 18, 19.

THE text occurs in that part of the Acts where St. Luke is recording the statement which the Roman governor, Festus, made of Paul's case to the Jewish prince, Agrippa. Agrippa and Bernice, his sister, had come to Cæsarea, where the Roman governor resided, to salute Festus, the recently appointed successor to Felix. This Agrippa was the son of the Herod whose miserable death is recorded in the twelfth chapter. He was a young man of only sixteen years of age at the time of his father's death, and was living, or going to school, as we would say, in the city of Rome, and enjoying there the friendship and patronage of the emperor Claudius, who was a sort of guardian of the young Jewish prince. In the course of the next ten or fifteen years, by successive grants from the Emperor Claudius and afterwards from Nero, Agrippa had obtained a large portion of his father's kingdom, though not the province of Judea. He was familiar with the Jewish laws from his youth, and had adopted the tenets of the Pharisaic sect. Josephus says, "He was a zealous Jew, at least externally, but not very popular on account of his heathen education and residence in Rome, and his equivocal and somewhat neutral position between Jews and Gentiles.''

At the time of Agrippa's visit to Cesarea, sixteen years had passed away since his father's awful death there, and he was now thirty-two years of age. Festus, the new Roman governor, took advantage of this visit of Agrippa to consult him as one likely to feel more interest, and to be much better informed than himself on the points in question in the case of the man left in bonds by Felix. He recited, therefore, to Agrippa what had taken place, and remarked that nothing of the kind that he had been led to expect had appeared at the trial, that is, they brought no charge of legal or moral wrong as distinguished from mere error of opinion, but, said Festus, they differ with the prisoner on certain questions of Jewish theology or worship, and especially about *one Jesus*, now dead, whom Paul, the prisoner, however, affirms to be alive.

These two words of Festus, ''one Jesus,'' I select as the text, or rather as suggesting the theme of my sermon.

As it regards this Roman official, I infer from the language of Jewish and other historians, that Festus was an upright as well as an active magistrate, and in personal character he was a very much better man than his predecessor, Felix. But we have here to do with his language respecting Jesus Christ. ''One Jesus.'' How strangely now sound these words of Festus as we read or repeat them in the light of this age and in this period of the world and of the Christian church! ''Certain questions of one Jesus.''

Festus, probably, was unable to understand why a difference of opinion about this Jew, Jesus, dead or alive, could be so important and so enlist their feelings. But this much is apparent and indisputable, that though

Festus did not see from his Roman and heathen standpoint why such a question or such a difference of opinion
between Paul and the Jewish elders and priests should
be of such importance, yet both Paul and the Jews did
manifestly so regard it.   Festus saw clearly that the
whole exciting controversy and the main topics of controversy were questions about "one Jesus"—who he
was and what had become of him.   This question, which
both Paul and the Jews considered a question of vast and
vital importance, Festus, just because he was an unen-
lightened heathen, thought very trivial and insignificant.   To him it was passing strange, utterly unaccount-
able, that Paul, an eminent and educated Jew, and a
Roman citizen, too, by birth, should be willing to risk
everything and life itself to maintain his views of Jesus,
and that the Jews of the highest position in church and
state be equally ready and anxious to assassinate him
because of these opinions and his conduct in avowing
and maintaining them.   But the Roman and heathen
magistrate was ignorant and mistaken.   Neither Paul
nor the Jewish officials exaggerated or over-estimated the
importance and far-reaching influence of these questions.
It is utterly impossible to exaggerate their importance.
The question about this Jesus is a great one—important
now as ever—the greatest ever discussed on earth by
mortal man.   And the reason why it is so great a question is that the person about whom the question is raised
is great, and the issue or effect of this question upon
one's eternal destiny is great—great beyond the power
of human thought or language adequately to conceive
or to express.

It is worthy of special note that for ages upon ages
this question has grown in interest and felt importance
as the years have rolled by.   In the present age the un-

believing mind has been looking upon and studying this
very question, and with nothing at all of the careless indifference that characterized these Roman officials.   This
question now agitates the mind of the civilized world
more than any other.

It is strange and interesting, too, to look through the
book of Acts and see how carelessly, if not contemptuously, all these men, Roman officials of high position
and influence, wave away, as beneath their notice, so
trifling a matter as these questions in dispute between
Paul and his fellow-religionists as to this Jesus whenever
the subject is brought before them.   How differently the
matter looked to a spectator in the middle or latter half
of the first century and in the middle or latter half of the
present nineteenth century!   Yes, at that day and, alas,
often still, worldly politicians, statesmen, so-called, high
in office, clothed with great pomp and power, think or
speak and write very lightly of events into which angels
desire to look—events which fill heaven with rapture,
and which will be the theme of grateful and adoring
praises from multitudes which no man can number forever and forever.   Well, just as with the rest, so it was
with Festus.   Says he to Agrippa, "When this man's
accusers stood up, they brought no accusation of such
things as I supposed: but had certain questions against
him about their own Jewish religion and worship, and
about *one Jesus.*"   And now I repeat with all possible
emphasis, is this question as to who and what Jesus is
a small or trivial matter?   Let us consider it as the later
Scriptures and human history illustrate the person and
work and dignity of Jesus Christ.

I say, then, (1), *That merely as a human personage in
this world's history, Jesus is great*—great as a man, great
as a teacher of men, great as a reformer of morals, reli-

gion and civilization. I cannot, of course, enlarge upon this as I would wish, for the three-fold view which I merely indicate would afford rich material for more than an entire discourse.

But let us look at it a while. I deliberately affirm that the life and teachings of Christ divide the morals, the religion, the sentiments and the civilization of the world, and have been doing it ever since his public teaching in Galilee and Judea. Who is Jesus? Thirty years he spent in Nazareth, a poor village not once mentioned in the Old Testament or in Josephus. The New Testament makes no secret of the place which Jesus occupied in the social scale. He was of humble birth and connections, working at the trade of a carpenter, in a private and obscure life. For three years he ministered and taught publicly in Jerusalem, but chiefly in the rural settlements and in several of the obscurer towns and villages of Galilee, and then he suffered death by crucifixion. And yet his thoughts and words have been the inspiration and incentive that has educated and developed men and nations, and produced whatever of real culture and civilization the past ages and the present possess and enjoy, enkindling hopes of still better in the wider spread and heartier reception and influence of his teachings. As a reformer of faith, of morals, of religion, of life, of men, of society and of nations, what name and character has been and is to-day so influential and mighty as the name of Jesus? He left behind him a few spoken words; he never wrote a line. And if all the repetitions, or records of the same events and discourses, in the four Gospels were omitted, the entire and continuous record that would remain would be but a few pages. And while the heroes, statesmen, poets and philosophers of Athens or of Rome, her emperors and soldiers, or this man Festus, his predecessors and successors are dead—yes, doubly dead and gone, so far as present and living power and influence and love and veneration are concerned, Jesus Christ is to-day exalted in the very loftiest niche of admiration and veneration by millions upon millions to whom he is dearer than life. Of all lives ever lived, the most influential confessedly as a man, as a teacher, as a reformer, was the life of this Jesus. Such is the testimony of the centuries. There is absolutely nothing like it in the whole history of the world. The uninspired pages of history attest it.

(2), But further, this Jesus is great because *he is the central subject of the entire Bible*. The Jewish nation, its purpose, its history, its guidance and its Bible, was to prepare the way of "one Jesus." The whole of it—the nation's history and the nation's Bible—like John the Baptist, was the voice of one crying in a wilderness world, "Prepare ye the way of the Lord!" His person, his character, his mission, his life and death, is the theme that explains all. Narrative, history, genealogy, prophecy, sacrifices, ablutions, parables, miracles—all point to and illustrate the name and work of Jesus. The light of truth and mercy and hope, the light of grace and salvation, the light of the Old Testament, the light of the New Testament, the light of all their teachings to guide, to console, to cheer, to sanctify and to save, the light of all hope for man's future here and forever, all comes from this Jesus, well called in prophecy and by himself, "the Light of the world," "the Sun of righteousness." The natural sunlight and color, the variegated and radiant beauty that glows all over the face of the earth, that glitters from the rippling water, that paints the leaves and foliage and flowers of spring-time and summer, that sparkles on the dew drops, that

colors the evening sky with entrancing beauty and
splendor, is not more dependent upon the sun in the
heavens than is the light and beauty and blessedness
of the Bible, its histories, teachings and prophecies dependent upon Jesus. The prime, main object of the
Scriptures is to describe and set forth the Mediator, Jesus
Christ, and his work and kingdom of grace and glory
here and hereafter. "The testimony of Jesus is the
spirit of prophecy;" that is, the grand end and scope of
all revelation is to bear witness concerning "one Jesus."

(3), But further, this Jesus is great *because of his
great, his transcendent work of atonement and redemption*.
By the atonement we mean Christ's satisfying divine
justice by his suffering and death in the place of sinners.
The direct and central design and effect of Christ's death
was to propitiate the principle of justice in the divine
nature. He has satisfied all the demands of law upon
which the favor and fellowship of God were suspended.
This he did by his perfect obedience and sacrifice of himself which he offered up unto God. How clearly is this
stated and reiterated by St. Paul and by all the New
Testament writers. "Being justified freely by his grace,
through the redemption that is in Christ Jesus, whom
God hath set forth to be a propitiation through faith in
his blood, to declare his righteousness for the remission
of sins; that he (God) might be just and the justifier of
him that believeth in Jesus." Contemplate for a while
the priesthood of Christ—himself *as priest* offering himself
as a sacrifice to satisfy divine justice and reconcile us to
God. It is the grandest thought and the most vital and
precious truth of revealed religion! It is, without doubt,
the sublimest event in the annals of time or the records
of eternity. The death of Jesus Christ was peculiar.
It was not a providential event to which he was sub-

jected as you or I are subjected. It was a priestly act
which he achieved. He died as a triumphant agent or
actor; he prevailed against death to live until he himself
said, "It is finished," and then bowed his head in assent and died—died not merely voluntarily, but by positive priestly action giving himself to God. The cross
is itself and justly styled a "chariot of triumph."

Looked at from another point of view, what a spirit of
sublime devotion to God and of self-sacrifice for man
does the cross and death of Jesus display! The position
of Jesus was unparalleled, exceptional and transcen-
dently sublime. Standing before the altar, he confesses
the guilt of his brethren, glorifies the divine justice,
honors and magnifies the law of God (the very law that
dooms them to woe and requires him to suffer), assumes the sinner's place, acknowledges the demands of
truth and righteousness, adores the divine character and
lays down his life—body and soul—as a ransom and
atonement for theirs upon the altar; freely and voluntarily "does and suffers all this, rather than that guilty
and miserable man should perish, or that the divine
government should be insulted with impunity."

Festus never heard, never uttered a name so significant, so rich, so suggestive of goodness and greatness,
as the name of "*one Jesus*." Why, at the time he carelessly repeated this name, and for ages upon ages since,
and in all the ages forever to come,

> ' Floods of everlasting light
>   Freely flash before him;
> Myriads, with supreme delight,
>   Instantly adore him;
> Angelic trumps resound his fame,
>   Lutes of lucid gold proclaim
> All the music of his name;
>   Heaven echoing the theme.

> Sweetest sound in seraph's song,
> Sweetest note on mortal's tongue,
> Sweetest carol ever sung,
>   Jesus,—Jesus,—Jesus!"

(4), But, again, this Jesus is *great in his person and nature as the incarnate Son of God*. For this Jesus was Immanuel, God incarnate, God with us. St. John terms him as he announces him as the subject of his Gospel, "The Word of God"—God's *utterance* to man. God speaks to the world through Jesus over and above what he speaks in nature. I readily admit and maintain that God speaks in nature. In its scenery, processes, productions; in its very silence God speaks to his rational offspring, and speaks intelligently and impressively. God speaks in providence, in its operations, ordinary and extraordinary—in its history and its laws. God speaks in the very nature and constitution of man; in the products of his intellect, his imagination and his tastes, in the achievements of science and art, in the creations of human genius, and in all the utterances of human wisdom and piety, God speaks. But once, only once, in all time, the Godhead tabernacled in flesh.

> "One night while lowly shepherd swains
>   Their fleecy charge attended,
> A light burst o'er Judea's plains
>   Unutterably splendid.
>
> 'Far in the dusky Orient
>   A star, unknown in story,
> Arose to flood the firmament
>   With more than morning glory.
>
> "For heaven drew nearer earth that night—
>   Flung wide its pearly portals—
> Sent forth from all its realms of light
>   Its radiant immortals.

"They hovered in the golden air,
    Their golden censers swinging,
And woke the drowsy shepherds there
    With their seraphic singing."

The word was made flesh, dwelt in our nature, and from within this marvellous veil gave forth its holy and grand announcements. In the person of Jesus God speaks; through his life and in his life as he speaks nowhere else. The first, the lowest, but yet also the last and highest duty of the world is to listen and believe. The command to all ages and to all men is to listen and believe. That command was given of old in Palestine from the open sky beneath which "one Jesus" was standing, and the words are echoing to-day, "This is my beloved Son; hear ye him." And adds St. Peter in the second recorded sermon in the Acts: "Hear him in all things whatsoever he shall say unto you, for every soul that will not hear him shall be destroyed."

(5), But further, this Jesus, of whom the heathen Festus spoke so carelessly, is great *because at that very moment he was and is now "Head over all things for his body the church."* He was at that moment in which Festus uttered the flippant words, "one Jesus," at the right hand of God the Father Almighty, "angels and authorities and powers being made subject unto him"—aye, more, "Far above all principality and power and might and dominion, and every name that is named, not only in this world but also in that which is to come." Every event that was then occurring, or that is now occurring, great or small, until his second coming, did occur, is occurring, and will occur only by, with and under the consent or direction or control of the mediatorial providence of this same Jesus.

3

"Rejoice, the Saviour reigns,
    The God of truth and love ;
When he had purged our stains,
    He took his seat above.
Lift up the heart, lift up the voice ;
Rejoice aloud, ye saints, rejoice.

"His kingdom cannot fail ;
    He rules o'er earth and heaven.
The keys of death and hell
    Are to our Jesus given.
Lift up the heart, lift up the voice ;
Rejoice aloud, ye saints, rejoice."

(6), But further, this Jesus about whom this Roman official spoke so slightingly, if not contemptuously, is great *because he is to be the supreme and final judge and awarder of the everlasting destinies of men and angels.* Festus himself, and every human being is to stand at the judgment seat of one Jesus and receive from his lips his everlasting and irrevocable doom. "The Father judgeth no man, but hath committed all judgment unto the Son, that all men should honor the Son, even as they honor the Father." "He hath appointed a day in which he will judge the world in righteousness by that man whom he hath ordained, whereof he hath given assurance (*i. e.*, indubitable evidence) unto all men by having raised him from the dead." Yes, my hearers, a day of searching and righteous investigation and judgment is coming, when each and all must stand before an omniscient and almighty judge, "one Jesus," who will "render to all according to their works." Oh! how terribly the tables will be turned, as

" On that day, that dreadful day
When man to judgment wakes from clay,"

Festus himself will recognize upon the throne in glorious and judicial majesty, that same Jesus, about whom, thirty years after his resurrection, the Jews and St. Paul, in his presence and before his Roman judgment seat, had disputed. Yes, he had heard them dispute the question (which he thought trivial and superstitious), whether one Jesus was dead or alive; and there he beholds him on the throne, as supreme judge, assigning the destinies of the race.

(7), But further and lastly : this Jesus is great *because such is his connection with the laws and government and throne of God, that every human being in the world (Festus, Agrippa, Bernice, and you and I) must, of necessity, sustain a personal relation to him.* We must be found "*in him*" partaking of his redemption and salvation, or "out of (and apart from) him," and under the bondage and curse of sin, and hopelessly and forever lost. No question is more personal, individual, important and momentous than the question, "What think ye of Christ?"

This matter cannot be avoided or evaded. We must consider and settle it. It is like the question which Pilate, in his confusion, embarrassment and difficulty (how to dispose of Jesus), asked the Jews : "What shall I do with Jesus?" Yes, this awful and mighty question, with all its issues for eternal life or for eternal death, each of us has to settle. How will you decide it? Sooner or later, and often frequently, to every one comes the question which Pilate asked of the Jews, "What, then, shall I do with Jesus who is called the Christ?" If a man cares nothing for the principles of science or art, or takes no interest in politics, he simply lets the subject alone. But this is a matter and a question which you cannot let alone, and which will not let you alone. It will be answered; it must be answered, and it can be answered but in one of two ways.

And no man can settle the matter for you.   Each soul must make its own reply.   Careless, indifferent hearer, do you think to evade replying to this all-important question while, and as long as, you live? I tell you, if you pass your life thus, you have already answered it unconsciously to yourself, it may be, but it has had your reply in the rejection of him.

But when at the judgment you stand before him, the question then will not be, "What shall I do with Jesus?"   The one thought will be "Oh! what will he do with me?"

THE GOSPEL CALL.

BY G. D. ARMSTRONG, D. D.,
Pastor of the First Presbyterian Church, Norfolk, Va.

"The Spirit and the bride say, Come. And let him that heareth say, Come. And let him that is athirst come. And whosoever will, let him take the water of life freely."—REVELATION xxii. 17.

NEAR the commencement of his public ministry, our Lord preached the gospel in the words: "God so loved the world that he gave his only begotten Son, that whosoever believeth in him should not perish but have everlasting life." (John iii. 16.) Many years afterwards, when his atoning sacrifice of himself had been accomplished upon Calvary, and God's acceptance of that sacrifice made known by his resurrection from the dead—when he was about to close his written revelation to his church, intended to be to her ever afterwards "the only infallible rule of faith," he again preached that gospel in the words of the text. I say, he preached, for in both of these passages alike, Jesus Christ is the preacher—John simply records what he heard.

I. ON BOTH OCCASIONS OUR LORD MAKES THE OFFER OF SALVATION, FULL AND FREE, TO THE WHOLE WORLD.

On the first, he traces God's provision of salvation, everlasting life for the perishing, to his love for the world as its fountain head. "There is a deep sense in which God loves the world. All whom he has created he regards with pity and with compassion. Their sins he cannot love; but he loves their souls. 'His tender

53

mercies are over all his works.' (Psalm cxlv. 9.)
Christ is God's gracious gift to the whole world.''—
Ryle. And this gracious gift, our Lord assures us, was
made that ''whosoever believeth in him should not
perish, but have everlasting life.''

The second occasion was very different from the first,
but the offer of salvation made is, if possible, more full
and free than in the first. To understand its language,
we must remember that it was spoken after the church
had entered fully upon the discharge of her commission,
''Go ye into all the world and preach the gospel to every
creature'' (Mark xvi. 15), and her labors had been
crowned with abundant success through the power of
the Spirit working in and with her, he who claimed
for himself the title, ''Jesus . . . the root and offspring
of David, and the bright and morning star'' (Rev. xxii.
16), appeared to the aged John, and in the words of the
text gives expression to his infinite satisfaction in the
work which was being done.

'' *The Spirit and the bride say, Come.*'' ''The Spirit ''
here spoken of is undoubtedly ''the spirit of truth '' who
was to come in Christ's stead and ''abide with the
church forever'' (John xiv. 16), and whose coming and
power was manifested by the wondrous work wrought
in Jerusalem on the first Christian pentecost; and ''the
bride,'' the church herself (see Rev. xxi. 2, 9) through
her apostles, and evangelists, and pastors, and teachers
(Eph. iv. 11), given her for this very ministry.

''*And let him that heareth say, Come.*'' When Stephen,
the first Christian martyr, was stoned, we are told, ''At
that time there was a great persecution against the
church which was at Jerusalem, and they were all scattered abroad throughout the regions of Judea and Sama-
ria, except the apostles, . . . and they that were

scattered abroad went everywhere preaching the word."
(Acts viii. 1-4.) These were not regularly ordained
ministers of the gospel, but, in the language of our day,
"private members of the church," with hearts filled
with the love of Christ and the love of souls, who, driven
by persecution into places where the gospel was unknown, told the story of the cross to all who were willing to listen. And so has it been ever since, especially
in seasons of great revivals of religion; not publicly and
by her regularly ordained ministry alone, but privately,
in the family and in the intercourse of daily life, godly
men and women have been led by the Spirit to "preach
the word," and here Christ gives explicit sanction to
this preaching.

"*And let him that is athirst come.*" These words remind us at once of the call of God by his prophet: "Ho,
every one that thirsteth, come ye to the waters, and he
that hath no money; come ye, buy and eat; yea, come,
buy wine and milk without money and without price."
(Isaiah l. 1.) The man athirst for the water of life is
one who simply feels his need of salvation. There may
be such, even in Christian communities, to whom no
Christian minister has ever especially addressed himself,
and to whom no Christian friend has ever spoken about
the great salvation, who, by the Spirit "who worketh,
when and where and how he pleaseth," has had awakened within him a desire to make all right between God
and his soul. To him, Christ himself here speaks the
word of invitation: "And let him that is athirst come."
And then, that no man can possibly think himself forgotten or excluded from the invitation, he closes the
gospel call in words which remind us at once of the
terms in which he preached it near the commencement
of his public ministry: "*And whosoever will, let him take*

the water of life freely.'' Surely, in no words which human language furnishes could the offer of salvation be made more full and free than in those which our Lord has chosen.

II. THE PUBLICATION OF THIS GOSPEL, FULL AND FREE AS OUR LORD HIMSELF MADE IT, IS, IN THE VERSES IMMEDIATELY SUCCEEDING THE TEXT, ENJOINED UPON THE CHURCH IN TERMS OF AWFUL SOLEMNITY. "I (*i. e.*, I, Jesus) testify unto every man that heareth the words of the prophecy of this book, If any man shall add unto these things, God shall add unto him the plagues that are written in this book; and if any man shall take away from the words of the book of this prophecy, God shall take away his part out of the book of life, and out of the holy city, and from the things which are written in this book." (Rev. xxii. 18, 19.) Whether or not we understand these words, as many expositors do, as God's solemn seal attached to the holy Scriptures, proclaiming the revelation therein made complete and unalterable, there can be no doubt that they cover the case of the gospel call, as contained in the text, in immediate connection with which they were spoken.

In the light shed upon this matter by the subsequent history of the church we can understand, in part, at least, the reason for this solemn warning. Strange and improbable as it might seem at first thought, it is just on this point—the freedom and fulness of the gospel offer of salvation—that the church to which the preaching of the gospel has been committed has shown the strongest disposition to tamper with God's truth—to limit the freedom of the gospel offer, or add to the one condition of salvation, "belief in the only begotten Son of God," which God has prescribed, other conditions of man's devising.

1. Early in the history of the church in her Christian form, and while many of the apostles were yet living, we are told that, "Certain men which came down from Judea taught the brethren and said, Except ye be circumcised after the manner of Moses, ye cannot be saved." (Acts xv. 1) thus "adding to" the gospel as preached by Christ. It was to condemn this heresy that the "apostles and elders" came together in the council at Jerusalem. From the days of Abraham the Jews had occupied the position of God's peculiar people, and it was not without a fierce struggle that Jewish prejudice yielded to the clearly revealed truth that henceforward "in Christ Jesus neither circumcision availeth anything, nor uncircumcision, but a new creature." (Gal. vi. 15.)

2. In later times the "church catholic," as she delights to call herself, both Greek and Roman, has taught that the reception of the sacraments, especially that of baptism, is necessary to salvation, in so doing confounding that which God has made necessary as a duty with that which he has made a condition of salvation, in the proper sense of that expression. And along with this and as an inseparable part of it, she has taught the doctrine of "baptismal regeneration," *i. e.*, that regeneration, that great spiritual change which marks the beginning of the Christian life, is wrought "*en opore oporato*," by the application of water to the body, thus preaching "another gospel, which is not another, but a perversion of the gospel of Christ."

3. A perversion of the gospel, of greater practical importance for us Protestants to consider, is that which the awakened sinner often falls into when refusing to understand the gospel call in the plain sense of the words in which our Lord makes it, he insists that he must do

something to fit himself for coming to Jesus ere he can venture to approach him as the Saviour of sinners. The truth expressed in the words of Peter, addressed to the Jewish rulers, "Him," *i. e.*, Jesus, "hath God exalted with his right hand to be a prince and a Saviour, for to give repentance to Israel, and forgiveness of sins" (Acts v. 31), is very humbling to the pride of man's heart, and therefore hard for him to receive. Ordinarily, it is not until the sinner has tried, and tried in vain, to "fit himself for coming to Jesus," that he learns intelligently to say,

> "Just as I am, without one plea
> But that thy blood was shed for me,
> And that thou bid'st me come to thee,
>   O Lamb of God, I come.

> "Just as I am, poor, wretched, blind,
> Sight, riches, healing of the mind,
> Yea, all I need in thee to find,
>   O Lamb of God, I come."

III. IF THE GOSPEL OFFER IS SO FREELY MADE AND THE PROVISIONS OF GOSPEL GRACE SO FULL, THE QUESTION MAY BE ASKED, HOW COMES IT THAT SO MANY IN CHRISTIAN LANDS PERISH?

That many who have lived all their lives under the sound of the gospel faithfully preached, and have, at times, felt something of the power of that gospel, do perish, we cannot doubt, for our Lord expressly testifies, "Not every one that saith unto me, Lord, Lord, shall enter into the kingdom of heaven, but he that doeth the will of my Father which is in heaven. Many will say to me in that day, Lord, Lord, have we not prophesied in thy name? and in thy name have cast out devils? and in thy name done many wonderful works? And then will I profess unto them, I never knew you; depart from me, ye that work iniquity." (Matt. vii. 21–23.) How is this to be accounted for? and, more especially, how is this to be reconciled with the declaration, "God sent not his Son into the world to condemn the world; but that the world through him might be saved" (John iii. 17), and with God's sincerity when he says, "As I live, saith the Lord God, I have no pleasure in the death of the wicked; but that the wicked turn from his way and live; turn ye, turn ye from your evil ways; for why will ye die, O house of Israel?" (Ezek. xxxiii. 11.)

In attempting to answer these questions we must remember, (1), That the gospel is not a proclamation of universal salvation, but of salvation for "whosoever believeth in the only begotten Son of God"; and (2), That God's dealings with his creatures are always in conformity with the nature he has given them. Having made man an intelligent, free agent, he deals with him as such in matter which concern the salvation of his soul as well as in those which concern the well-being of his body. To the Jews, perishing under his perfect ministry, our Lord declares, "Ye *will not* come to me that ye might have life." (John v. 40.)

Not many months ago a man was hanged in our midst. He had been fairly tried, and convicted of cold-blooded murder. Under the laws of Virginia, as well as under the law of God, "He that sheddeth man's blood, by man shall his blood be shed." A murderer, this man but suffered the righteous consequence of his own crime. He was "hanged until dead" by authority of law and by a public officer representing the Commonwealth of Virginia. In view of these facts would any one think, for a moment, of impeaching the righteousness of his execution, or of calling in question the claim on the part of the government of Virginia to be a truly paternal government, seeking the highest good of its subjects, and with laws wisely designed to secure that end? The relation of God to the death of the sinner who perishes under this our gospel dispensation, is fairly illustrated in the conduct of our Lord, "God manifest in the flesh," when, for the last time, approaching Jerusalem, he wept over it, saying, "O Jerusalem, Jerusalem, thou that killest the prophets, and stonest them that are sent unto thee, how often would I have gathered thy children together, even as a hen gathereth her chickens under her wings, and ye would not! Behold, your house is left unto you desolate." (Matt. xxiii. 37, 38.)

IV. IS NOT THE DOCTRINE OF ELECTION, ESPECIALLY IN THE PRETERITION WHICH IT NECESSARILY IMPLIES, AS TAUGHT IN "THE CONFESSION OF FAITH," IRRECONCILABLE WITH GOD'S SINCERITY IN THE GOSPEL OFFER?

If that doctrine were such as it is sometimes represented, or, rather, misrepresented, to be by those who reject it, I think it would be. Not long ago I heard of a celebrated evangelist stating the case substantially as follows, viz.: "Suppose the case of a king making a great supper and inviting many guests, and then, at supper time, as the invited guests were all coming, causing his soldiers to seize them and tie them to trees in sight of the supper table; and when this was done, sending out his steward to ring his bell and cry, 'Come to supper, come to supper.' What would be thought of the sincerity of the king's invitation in such circumstances as these?" If this were a fair representation of the case, but one answer could be made to the question. But is it a fair representation? I answer, assuredly, no. There is just enough of truth in it to make it the worst of slanders.

1. It is true in so far as its representation of the help-less condition, by nature, of the sinner to whom the gospel call is addressed is concerned. The representations of Scripture on this point are stronger than that of this evangelist. According to Scripture, the sinner is, by nature, not tied to a tree, but "dead in trespasses and sins." (Eph. ii. 1.) God himself represented the work of preaching the gospel to his prophet, Ezekiel, in terms, if possible, more striking than those quoted above: "The Spirit of the Lord set me down in the midst of the valley which was full of bones, and caused me to pass by them round about: and behold, there were very many in the open valley; and, lo, they were very dry. And he said unto me, Son of man, can these dry bones live? And I answered, O Lord God, thou knowest. Again he said unto me, Prophesy upon these bones, and say unto them, O ye dry bones, hear the word of the Lord." (Ezek. xxxvii. 1–4.) I find no fault with the representation of man's helpless condition by nature as that of one tied to a tree. It certainly is not so strong as that of Scripture. But, then, there is a question which lies back of this which needs to be answered, viz.:

2. Who tied him there? His bonds, in part, at least, are the work of his own hands. Take the case of the drunkard, for example, and the Scriptures tell us that "no drunkard shall inherit the kingdom of God." (1 Cor. vi. 10.) His drunkenness, as long as it is per-sisted in, is an insuperable obstacle in the way of his "believing in the only begotten Son of God." Who made him the drunkard that he is? It is certain that God did not. His evil habit is his own work, and by its indulgence he is every day strengthening his bonds. And this which is true of drunkenness is true of all other sinful habits, *e. g.*, of covetousness, of unbelief,

and worldly lusts in all its forms.   In so far as these are
concerned, a man's bonds are unquestionably of his own
making.

But there is something back of all this, I will be told.
The man was sin-ruined from his birth, as David confesses with respect to himself: "I was shapen in iniquity, and in sin did my mother conceive me." (Psalm
li. 5.)   True; but in no proper sense of that expression
can it be said that God made him the sin-ruined creature
he was born.   We are all, not individuals only, but we
are all members of families, and peoples, and races as
well, and in many particulars God deals with us as such;
and man deals with his fellow-man on the same principle.   Adam, the federal as well as the natural head of
our race, God made originally "in his own image, after
his own likeness" (Gen. i. 26), "in knowledge, righteousness, and holiness," with ability perfectly to keep the
law.   But he, in the exercise of that free agency with
which God endowed him, sinned against God, and as
the righteous consequence of his sin, came under the
curse, and this curse he has transmitted as an inheritance to all his descendants by natural generation.   The
Scripture record is, "And Adam begat a son in his own
likeness" (Gen. v. 2), and so has it been with his descendants ever since.   In this way it has come to pass
that we are all "conceived in sin."   In view of these
facts, is it not a gross misrepresentation to speak of man
as one bound to a tree by the king's soldiers, and so,
virtually, by the king himself?

3. The statement we are examining contains a still
more radical misrepresentation of the truth in likening
the gospel call to that of the king's steward proclaiming
in the hearing of men bound to trees, "Come to supper,
come to supper."   Carrying out the figurative represen-

tation adopted, the steward's call, if it is truly to represent the gospel call, ought to be: ''Poor captive, let me loose thy bonds, that thou mayest come to the supper graciously provided for thee.'' One of the first records we have of our Lord's public preaching of the gospel is in the words: ''And when he had opened the book, he found the place where it was written, The Spirit of the Lord is upon me, because he hath anointed me to preach the gospel to the poor: he hath sent me to heal the broken-hearted, *to preach deliverance to the captives*, and recovering of sight to the blind, to set at liberty them that are bruised''—*the opening of the prison to them that are bound* (Isa. lxi. 1)—''To preach the acceptable year of the Lord . . . This day is this Scripture fulfilled in your ears.'' (Luke iv. 17–21.) At a later day, when discussing this very matter, he said to the Jews, in answer to their boast, ''We be Abraham's seed, and were never in bondage to any man, how sayest thou, Ye shall be made free? Jesus answered them, Verily, verily, I say unto you, Whosoever committeth sin is the servant (bond-servant, Rev. Ver.) of sin. . . . . If the Son therefore shall make you free, ye shall be free indeed.'' (John viii. 33–35.) As our Lord himself preached the gospel, it is not a call to a bound captive, ''Come to supper, come to supper,'' but, poor captive of sin and Satan, let me loose thy bonds that thou mayest come.

4. One of the most subtile, and therefore, most dangerous forms which self-righteousness assumes in the heart of the awakened sinner is that expressed in the words, ''I AM NOT FIT TO COME TO JESUS.'' We must not confound worthiness with fitness to come to Jesus. Worthiness has reference to man's deservings. Jacob, on the very occasion on which God changed his name

to Israel, because, "as a prince he had power with God, and with men, and prevailed," confesses, "I am not worthy of the least of all the mercies and of all the truth which thou hast shown unto thy servant." (Gen. xxii. 10.) Fitness has reference to what the occasion or circumstances of the case require. And never was there a more fitting occasion for Jacob to "wrestle" with God than the very occasion on which he confesses his unworthiness of the least of all his mercies, for then was he in an extremity in which God alone could help him.

Does Christ present himself in the gospel as a physician? And art thou sick? Then come to him that thou mayest be made whole. Thy very sickness makes it a fitting thing that thou shouldest come. Did Christ come "not to call the righteous but sinners to repentance?" (Matt. ix. 13.) And art thou a sinner? Then come to him, "For him hath God exalted with his right hand to be a prince and a Saviour, for to give repentance to Israel, and forgiveness of sins." (Acts v. 31.) Thy very need of "repentance and forgiveness of sins" renders it a fitting thing that thou shouldest come to him.

Do not mistake the nature of the gospel grace given us in Christ Jesus, and in thy folly attempt to do that which God alone can do, and which, for Christ's sake, he stands ready to do for you. You have within you "a heart of stone," i. e., a heart feeling no genuine contrition for sin, no faith in the Lord Jesus, no love to God; and by no determination of your own, by no effort of will, by no use of means can you ever change that heart of stone into one of flesh. If this work is ever accomplished, God must do it for you. And this is but a part of that which God proposes to do for you in the gospel, and what you need to come to him for. "A new heart, also, will I give you, and a new spirit will I put within you; and I will take away the stony heart out of your flesh, and I will give you a heart of flesh. And I will put my Spirit within you, and cause you to walk in my statutes, and ye shall keep my judgments, and do them." (Ezek. xxxvi. 26, 27.)

The repentance, faith and love; the contrite spirit, the believing mind, the loving heart, which, in their beginning at the least, make up the idea of fitness in the mind of him who says, "I am not fit to come to Jesus," are all "fruits of the Spirit." (See Gal. v. 22, 23.) They are not excellences to be wrought out by the sinner in preparation for coming to Christ, but "gifts of God," bestowed through Christ and for Christ's sake upon the sinner who comes to him. Believe, then, that our Lord meant just what he said, and all that he said, when he cried: "Whosoever will, let him take of the water of life freely."

"WHAT IS THE CHAFF TO THE WHEAT?"

BY REV. J. W. LUPTON, D. D.,
Pastor of the Presbyterian Church, Clarkesville, Tenn.

" What is the chaff to the wheat? saith the Lord."—JEREMIAH
xxiii. 28.

WHATEVER the Lord saith is worthy of the attention of men. The word the Father *writes*
in his letter is as important as the word he
speaks. If God, from the open heavens, should ask
each of us "What is the chaff to the wheat?" there
would be a thrill of activity running through us. He
does ask it, "What is the chaff to the wheat? *saith the
Lord.*" What is the outward hull of the body as compared with—the kernel—the deathless thing within?
What is that which goes into the flame or is driven before the wind as compared with that which is to be garnered in heaven or hell forever?

Let us try to answer God.

The most prominent thought springing from the text
in its relation to the context, is one for ministers of the
gospel. Let each one, as he sits in his study or stands
in the pulpit, weigh the question as it is related to verse
one of the chapter, "Woe unto the pastors that destroy
and scatter the sheep of my pasture! saith the Lord."
Or to verse eleven, "Both prophet and priest are profane ; yea, in my house have I found their wickedness,
saith the Lord." Or verse fifteen, "From the prophets
is profaneness"—margin hypocrisy—"gone forth into

all the land''; or verse sixteen, "They," *i. e.*, the prophets, "speak a vision of their own heart and not out of the mouth of the Lord." Read all the chapter and fit it to the text, and hear God ask his question, "What is the chaff to the wheat?" If we hear with the heart and not simply with "the hearing of the ear," a sense of dread responsibility would weigh us down and eliminate everything extraneous, and fire us with an unknown zeal to win for the eternal home all that is imperishable in man. A sense of the "woe unto me if I preach not the gospel" would be necessary to keep us in our places.

There were pastors who "scattered and destroyed the sheep of the pasture." The result was a land full of adultery, profanity and wickedness. Folly was in the prophets causing Israel to err. A general laxity from that high standard which the Lord requires was visible everywhere. And worldliness had eaten the church like a worm at its root. The Lord is represented as a holy and devout man, vexed beyond measure at what seemed a hopeless case, crying, "He that hath my word let him speak my word faithfully. What is the chaff to the wheat?"

Is prayer a necessity for ministers? Can the *people* afford to hear a sermon from him whom they have not commended to God? Should the cry, "What is truth?" ever be absent from a minister's lips? Should preachers earnestly seek the best gifts? Should sessions recommend and presbyteries license limp and cowardly men? Should he who regards the ministry as a mere profession be permitted to occupy the sacred desk? Are men still called of God as was Aaron? Should churches be so eager for men who will "draw," and for the purpose of drawing, should ministers preach short sermons, pleasant

sermons, easy sermons; sermons for the chaff and permit the wheat to shrivel and die?

If there be one thing worthy of the name of *supreme*
trifling among men, it must be found with that man
who, when Jesus had found his way to our apostate
world, and out of it through sufferings unequalled, and
then, that men might know his will, say, "Go, preach
my gospel," stands forth in some holy place in holy
time, and uses that place and time and opportunity in
tricking, amusing, or merely entertaining people for his
own ends.

If there be a deeper and darker place where God shuts
some off from future mischief, it must be occupied by
those of whom God says, "I have not sent these prophets yet they ran: I have not spoken to them yet they
prophesied." Usurpers. "Prophets of the deceit of
their own heart," "telling lies in the name of the Lord,"
and causing God's people to forget his name, and bringing myriad disasters upon the land.

Has this thing been done? Our answer comes through
references from the Scriptures of the Old Testament and
New; from ecclesiastical history; our own observation
as well as from what our fathers have told us; kings
who have usurped the theocratic throne as well as prophets and priests, have led the people away from God
after Baal, Mammon, and god's many and lords many.
Pharisees and Sadducees have done the same. So have
Antinomians, Socinians and Materialists, and men in
Popish and Protestant pulpits. Yes, and men who, in
the effort to exalt themselves and make their craft successful, have so carefully studied "the things that make
for peace" as to eliminate from their teaching all thought
that a God so holy that angels cannot stand before him,
can possibly have any charge against a man defiled from

the crown of his head to the soles of his feet. "All is done," "God is only love."

There is a high and broad way to heaven. Crowds are going. We hear but little of warnings of the necessity of repentance, consequently we see but little of conviction, and, if we may judge by the after life, but little of conversion.

When there is so much charity that dead men, however they have lived and died, can be carried to heaven on its wings as easily as Lazarus was by angels, men will live and die without regard to the word of the Lord. Hell drops out of the system. So does discipline. The newspapers tell the number of converts, worthless statistics pander to denominational pride, and a large, limp and deceived church starts on its way to the palace royal of the King, cleaving to the good things of this life, shunning the narrow road so difficult to find, and having so little company when found. Chaff gathered in, wheat left out. God and mammon are mingled. Rites take the place of religion; sin regarded as disease or misfortune only; Sabbath a holiday; Jesus Christ a mere man and but little better than other "holiness people"; bread and wine equal to faith and a spiritual life drawn from his body and blood; the Spirit of God a myth, and not unfrequently revelry, carnality and refined polite sensuality, a mark of liberty which souls, panting after God, have never found, and which regards with contempt people who strive to live within God's pavilion.

The minister who does not distinguish between the chaff and the wheat must answer for it in no small measure.

True, there are some things calculated to hold up fainting spirits when confronted with God's awful commands to his ambassadors, "I am a frail man like others''; ''I am not here from choice''; ''that woe keeps me at work.'' ''Friendships are sweet to me and it is hard to offend. I value the good opinion of my fellow-men, and I have faults and sins like others, and I am afraid of 'physician, heal thyself.' Then, too, temperaments differ, and it is right to reach results by pacific measures.'' ''Surely, then, the loving Master will not hold me to a strict account. He will take the blood of souls farther away from my skirts when he remembers the awfulness and the hardness of the work he has given me to do.'' He does not ask that a loving and tender regard for men, for ourselves or for him be forgotten, but that a constant remembrance of the value of the wheat above that of the chaff will keep us at our work in whatever way the Holy Ghost shall direct a prayerful and submissive Spirit. God's charges are not against frail men and loving spirits, but against men who keep his *truth* from the people. And this fully preached by any kind of spirit will produce the exact result Jesus foretold when his disciples asked, ''What shall we have?''

There can be but two reasons for fewer martyrs now than in a former day. Either God is curbing man's hatred and the powers of wickedness to give rest to his suffering people before the coming of those days of woe which, for the elects' sake, must be shortened; or the prophets prophesy smooth things, and the people love to have it so. The kind of preaching Jesus approved cost John the Baptist his head, took Jesus himself to the cross, and the disciples and a long line of martyrs to an untimely death, a blessed end as compared with that of him who overlooks the wheat.

Again—The question comes in practical form to all learners and teachers, especially parents.

What is the abundant cultivation of the intellect as compared with that of the heart? Why the excessive scholasticism sought by students and insisted upon by parents and teachers and the sad neglect of early piety? The Samuels, Josiahs, Daniels and Timothys seem to diminish in numbers.

It is not implied that the chaff is absolutely worthless, but only comparatively so. Independently considered, it is of great value, but only of value as it serves its part in furnishing the full grain for the garner. There is no intention to underrate careful intellectual training, still, the question comes back, what is exhaustive effort in this line as compared with the spiritual man? A man's Greek and Hebrew will greatly aid the soul in reaching a lofty maturity from the milk and meat of God's word. Observation, travel, thought, the study of great principles which underlie and hold up empires, will never be lost. Still, what is a man, however scholarly, his head bending under the weight of learning, his features chiseled into classic beauty, if the heart be starved and cold? As teacher, how can he warm a soul? as learner, how can he be receptive? or, what will Latin profit a lost soul, or music in a world of discord and with a tongue on fire? Will it avail anything to be able to curse God in Hebrew or in language the most scientific? Who cares to ask rocks, in geological language, to fall on them in the winnowing day? Will logic and rhetoric soften the description of woes eternal? or pure mathematics help to find the centre of a bottomless pit? What is the chaff of your child, your pupil, your hearer, yourself, to a deathless soul? What is the chaff to the wheat when both are on fire? Only the fuel which adds intensity to the flame. Culture to a lost man adds to his torment as he is beaten with many stripes.

And yet the truth stands out before us that the trend, even of the religious world, is largely in the direction of making everything attractive and easy. "Get the Bible out of the schools;" "the catechism is too hard;" "never whip your child;" never force him to church; let him attend family worship or not, as he wills; mind cultivated and soul neglected.

Again—The question comes in practical form to all readers and hearers. What is the body to the soul? the withering, dying thing, the hull, to the real man. "The Lord God formed man of the dust of the ground, and breathed into his nostrils the breath of life; and man became *a living soul;*" and the real man is that "living soul," and always will be. What is the dust to that? Gaze into the face of your friend; see there the eye out of which something looks; grasp a hand that has *life* in it; see lips open, out of which a *man* speaks, and that man links himself to the man within you by tendrils of love. Two bodies do not meet and attract or repel but two men—living souls. Look again; the eye is closed, your friend seems to sleep, no answer to your call. Open the eye; nothing looks out of the leaden-hued dead thing; you may get a word from the stone as readily as from that. It is unmoved by cries and tears or the worm approaching. In a few days lift the coffin lid, and you are convinced, if not before, that no living thing went in there, but something which made the heart beat against yours has gone and left the chaff, its wrapping, to perish; and we do the same, and leave it lying out in the cold and night and rain, or under the snow. In reality it is just what it was before, only the greenness has faded from the chaff; its form is changing, it is rapidly going to dust; still, if that be the real man, it needs your care all the more. Then why not dress it in holiday attire, seat it beside you, entertain it beneath the cypress trees with conversation and good fare? Alas, you would be called insane; those who spent their time among tombs were demoniacs. The world has made an advance since people, where affection is more than carnality, have ceased to throw themselves in abandon on dead bodies and wail, or to embalm them and bring them to annual feasts garlanded with flowers, and have learned to regard the body as dead and hence right that it should be "dust to dust" which they never will, nor wish, to see again as before. We are glad that flesh and blood, damaged by sin and the world, will never enter heaven. But where is that living thing that breathed and looked and loved, or where will it be when the garnered centuries of time are over? We are not infidels, in theory, at least. Our living souls press on to find the wheat when we are at our best, and we know right well where we shall see it again; but realizing how much we miss the precious truth, not only with regard to friends "loved long since and lost a while," but with regard to ourselves as we go on trying to solve the problem, "What shall we eat and drink, and wherewithal shall we be clothed" while neglecting the deathless thing which will soon leap out of its shell and live and grow forever.

No wonder God puts amazement in his question, "What is the chaff to the wheat?"

CHRIST'S PASTORAL PRESENCE WITH HIS DYING PEOPLE.

BY JOHN L. GIRARDEAU, D. D., LL. D.,

Lately Professor of Theology in Columbia Theological Seminary.

" Yea, though I walk through the valley of the shadow of death, I will fear no evil: for thou art with me; thy rod and thy staff they comfort me."—PSALM xxiii. 4.

IN this exquisite, sacred pastoral, the Psalmist of Israel celebrates, in touching strains, the constant and tender care which God exercises towards his covenant people. Under the beautiful imagery of a shepherd, leading his flock to green pastures and beside still waters, he is represented as conducting them to the rich provisions and the refreshing rest of the gospel. When, like wandering sheep, they deviate from his ways, he seeks them in love, collects them again with the pastoral crook, and guides them once more in the paths of righteousness and peace. When, in their waywardness and folly, they backslide from him, he still remembers his covenant, is faithful to his promises, and saves them for the sake of his own great name; and when they come to pass through the valley of the death-shade, his cheering presence dispels their fears, and his powerful grace proves their solace and support.

Though it be true that Jehovah, the triune God, is the Shepherd of his people, there is a peculiar and emphatic sense in which Christ is represented in the gospel as sustaining the pastoral relation and discharging its functions. The Evangelist John reports him as declaring,

"I am the Good Shepherd; the Good Shepherd giveth his life for the sheep." The Apostle Paul speaks of the God of peace as having brought again from the dead our Lord Jesus, that Great Shepherd of the sheep, through the blood of the everlasting covenant. The Apostle Peter reminds believers that whereas they were in their natural condition as sheep going astray, they are now returned unto Christ as the Shepherd and Bishop of their souls. And the same apostle exhorts presbyters to feed the flock of God in view of the reward which the Great Pastor would eventually confer upon them: "And when the Chief Shepherd shall appear, ye shall receive a crown of glory that fadeth not away." These passages make it sufficiently evident that the Lord Jesus is peculiarly the Shepherd of his people.

The pastoral relation is a comprehensive one, including the three offices which Christ, as Mediator, sustains: those of a Prophet, a Priest and a King. As it is the province of a shepherd to feed his flock, to rule and protect them from their enemies, and, if necessary, to lay down his life in their defence, the prophetical function, by which Jesus feeds his people, the kingly, by which he rules and protects them, and the sacerdotal, by which he redeems them through his death, are all embraced in his pastoral office. It touches the interests, the experience and the hopes of believers at every point, both in life and in death. It involves the application of a Saviour's power, love and mercy to their every emergency and their every need. With infinite tenderness compassion and vigilance, the great Pastor follows his sheep through every devious path of life, and extends to them his succor when they faint under burning suns, in the horrid wilderness, and amidst the glooms and terrors of the shadow of death.

I. In the first place, it may be remarked in attempting to expand the comforting truths suggested by the text, that the pastoral presence of Jesus is a protection to the dying believer from the fears of evil which would otherwise distress him. ''When I walk through the valley of the shadow of death I will fear no evil, for thou art with me.'' I have no objection to render to the view which makes these words applicable to those critical passages in the life of God's people, which may not inappropriately be described as the valley of the death-shade. This was evidently the interpretation of that masterly delineator of Christian experience, John Bunyan, in his immortal allegory. He represents his pilgrim as struggling with the dangers and conflicts of the valley of the shadow of death before he comes to the crossing of the last river. And it cannot be disputed that there are seasons in the experience of the believer, when, pressed by his besetting temptations, pursued by the malice of the devil, and fascinated by the enchantments or persecuted by the fury of the world, he encounters terrors which are akin to those of death itself. In these fearful exigencies, these periods of conflict, depression and anguish, he appears to be passing down into the darkness and gloom of the valley of death; and it is the pastoral presence of Christ in the hour of despair which dissipates the fear of evil and lights up the soul with returning joy and peace. But although this be true, I see no reason for disturbing the ordinary interpretation placed upon the words of the text—an interpretation which makes them specially applicable to the passage of the believer through death, and one which has proved a charm to dispel the apprehensions of ill from the bosoms of thousands of Christ's people amidst the doubts, the strifes, the agonies of the dying hour.

There are three great and notable epochs in the earthly history of the believer in Jesus. The first is that in which, at the creative fiat of the Almighty Maker, he springs from nonenity into being, and is confronted with the duties, the responsibilities and the bliss or woe of an immortal career. The next is that in which, by virtue of a second creation and through the wondrous process of the new birth and conversion, he passes from the kingdom of Satan and of darkness into the kingdom of grace and of light. From being a bondsman of the devil, a slave of sin and an heir of hell, he becomes, by a marvellous transformation, a subject of God, a citizen of heaven, and an inheritor of everlasting possessions and an amaranthine crown. It is a transitional process which awakens the pulse of a new life, engenders the habits of holiness, adorns the soul with the rich graces of the divine Spirit, and inspires the joyful hope of eternal felicity beyond the grave. The third, and it is the most solemn and terrible crisis of his being, is that of death, in which the believer passes through nature's closing conflict and the awful change of dissolution to the experience of an untried existence. The transition is suited to alarm. It is nothing less than one from time to eternity, and it is accomplished in the twinkling of an eye. At one moment he is surrounded by the familiar objects of earth, and looks upon the faces of his weeping friends who cluster around the bed of death, and in the next he opens his eyes upon eternal realites and the blaze of God's immediate presence. Nature, constructed originally for an immortal life, instinctively recoils from so violent and revolting a change as that which death involves. It shrinks back in terror from the vision of the coffin and the shroud, of the corruption and the worms of the grave. The circumstances attending the dying process are such as are suited to appal a conscious sinner, and fill him with consternation and dismay—the cruel rupture of earthly relations, the sudden withdrawal of accustomed scenes, the forced abandonment of wonted pursuits, the absolute loneliness of the passage, the dread neighborhood of the flaming bar and the rigor of the last account. My brethren, how shall we, without apprehension, encounter so tremendous a change? The text furnishes us an answer which illumines the gloom of the dying chamber, and lights up the darkness of the grave. The pastoral presence of the Lord Jesus is an antidote to the fears, and a preventive of the evils, of death. There are two modes by which this blessed result is accomplished:

1. In the first place the Great Shepherd accompanies the believer in his last passage as the Conqueror of Death. That which chiefly renders death an object of terror is the consciousness of guilt. The groans, the pains, the dissolution of our bodily organisms, are confessedly dreadful and repulsive; but the great poet was right when he intimated that it is conscience, a guilty conscience forecasting the retributions of the future, which makes cowards of us all. It is this which leads us to shrink from the dying bed as an arena of battle, and from the last struggle as a hopeless conflict with an evil which the startled imagination personates as a monarch and invests with power to destroy. Death becomes the king of terrors. Were there no sin, the change which might have been necessary to remove us from the present state and to adapt us to another would have been an easy and delightful translation, a euthanasia, disquieted by no apprehensions of the soul, and disturbed by no pains of the body. But sin has clothed death with its tyrannical prerogative as a universal and remorseless despot, con-

verted the world into a melancholy theatre of his triumphs, and transformed the earth into a vast graveyard, whitened with the monuments of his sway. The removal from the present state becomes a passage through a valley of tears peopled with shapes of terror, and encompassed with the darkness of the death-shade.

Christ has subdued this dreadful monster. He conquered death by conquering sin, and he overcomes sin by his dying obedience to law. This is the statement of the apostle in his argument touching the resurrection of the body: "The sting of death is sin." The power of death to inflict torture, to poison our happiness and blast our hopes, lies in the fact that we are guilty, and are, therefore, completely subjected to his tyranny. "The strength of sin is the law." The punishment of our guilt is penal. Our dying sufferings are the penalty of a broken law; and sin, in inflicting them upon us, throws itself back for the enforcement of its authority upon the irreversible sanctions of that majestic and eternal rule which we have outraged and insulted. Christ has stripped sin of this strength. He has unnerved the cruel monarch, and rendered him powerless to destroy his people. The glorious Redeemer, moved by compassion for our wretched estate, came down to our relief and stood forth as the champion of his church in her conflict with death. He assumed our guilt, took the sting of death in his own soul, underwent our penal sufferings and, in accordance with the law of substitution, relieved us from the obligation to suffer the same punishment, and has enlisted the divine justice on the side of our deliverance. Christ has died penally for his people. God accepts the vicarious sacrifice, and the believer cannot die in the same way. Justice cannot demand a double payment of the same debt. Death is divested of its

penal feature, and is transformed from a curse into a
blessing, from a passage to execution into a translation
to bliss.   In the tragedy enacted upon the cross, Jesus,
the representative of his people, engaged in a mighty
wrestle with Death.   He fell, but his fall crushed out
the life of his dread antagonist.   He died, but death
died with him.   He was buried, but he dragged death
down with him into the grave; and there, despoiling the
tyrant of his diadem, he unfurled over his crownless
head the ensign of his people's salvation, and, in their
name, took undisputed possession of his whole domain.
It is true that the believer must still pass through the
dying change, but the curse of it is forever gone.   It is
no more death in its true and awful sense as the penalty
of law.   "I," says the divine Redeemer, "I am the
resurrection and the life; he that believeth in me,
though he were dead, yet shall he live; and he that
liveth and believeth in me shall never die."   "He that
keepeth my sayings shall never see death."   It is true
that the believer must die; but in dying he is privileged
to suffer with his Master, that he may rise and reign
with him.   It is true that the believer must die; but
death now constitutes part of a wholesome discipline
which prepares him for glory; it is a process by which
he is purged from dross, casts off the slough of corruption, and is purified for his admission into the holy presence of God and the sanctified communion of saints.
It is true that he must walk through the dark valley;
but the Conqueror of Death descends into it by his side,
illuminates its darkness by the radiance of his presence,
protects him from the assaults of a now powerless foe,
and bearing in his hands the keys of death and the invisible world, peacefully dismisses the departing saint
from sin to holiness, and from the stormy trials of earth
to the joy and peace of an everlasting rest.

2. It may be observed further, that the pastoral presence of Jesus with his dying people is manifested by the tender ministration of his sympathy. There were two great ends which the Saviour contemplated in his sufferings and death—the one that he might redeem his people from sin and everlasting punishment; the other that he might be qualified by experience to sympathize with them while themselves passing through the afflictions of life and the pains of the dying hour. To achieve these results, he became incarnate, partook of our nature, and was made bone of our bone and flesh of our flesh. Not merely a legal substitute, but possessed of the sublime and tender spirit of a priest, he consented to be compassed with sinless infirmity that he might be capable of compassion for the weak, the wandering and the dying. An infirm human being, struggling under the burden of assumed guilt, and confronted by the terrors of divine wrath, is it any marvel that he looked forward to death not without fear? One of the most affecting and pathetic passages in the Scriptures is that in which the apostle, discoursing of the priestly sufferings of Jesus, tells us that in the days of his flesh he offered up prayers and supplications with strong crying and tears unto him that was able to save him from death, and was heard in that he feared. For it must be remembered, that the form of death which Christ encountered, while it included the experience of our sufferings, embraced incomparably more. In his own person, perfectly innocent, and in his character stainlessly holy, he merited intrinsically the admiration of his fellow-men, and the approval of his God. So far from deserving to die, he was entitled, on the naked score of retributive justice, to the highest and most blissful life. And yet condescending, in boundless mercy, to be treated as putatively

6

guilty for the sake of dying men, he underwent a form
of death, the least element of which was the pains of
dissolution—a death which involved the experience of
infinite wrath and the intolerable pains of hell. The
cup which was placed in the hands of Jesus in Gethsemane was one which was never offered to any other
human being on earth. The trembling and consternation of his human nature as he took that chalice of woe,
his thrice-repeated prayer to be relieved, if possible,
from the necessity of drinking it, and the bloody sweat
that swathed his body like a robe, attested an anguish
of soul which none but he was ever called upon to bear.
The Sufferer, who, for us, expired on the cross of Calvary,
endured a species of death which was as singular as it
was comprehensive and exhaustive. In body, he suffered the keen and protracted tortures of crucifixion; and
in spirit, reviled by foes, deserted by friends and abandoned of God, he descended alone into the valley of the
death-shade, which was not only veiled in impenetrable
gloom, but swept by the tempests of avenging wrath.
Furnished with such an experience, the Good Shepherd
ministers with exquisite sympathy at the couch of the
dying believer. He knows his doubts, his apprehensions, his fears; and, moved by a compassion which
naught but a common suffering could produce, he makes
all the bed under the expiring saint, smooths his last
pillow, and "wipes his latest tear away."

II. In the second place, the Psalmist beautifully por-
trays the consoling influence of Christ's presence upon
the dying believer when he represents the pastoral staff
as affording him protection and comfort. "Thy rod and
thy staff, they comfort me." The staff, the appropriate
emblem of the pastoral office, may be regarded in two
aspects. As a rod, it is a powerful weapon of defence;

and as a staff, it is an instrument of support. It is at once, therefore, the symbol of protecting power and of supporting grace.   When at even-tide the oriental shepherd had folded his flock, and missed from the number some crippled ewe or tender lamb, he failed not, albeit through night and storm, to go in quest of the wanderer as it strayed amid the jagged rocks of the mountain-side, or the terrors of the howling wilderness.   And when he had found it, he gathered it compassionately in his arms, laid it upon his shoulders, and took his way homeward rejoicing.   But often he was compelled to pass through some deep and gloomy gorge, infested by wild beasts and rendered dangerous by the swollen torrent dashing fiercely through it and making the passage hazardous and the foothold insecure.   Then, when from some neighboring thicket the young lion sprang forth and roared upon his prey, wielding his shepherd's staff as a weapon of defence, he protected the precious burden he carried, and beat back the assailant to his lair; or, as he stepped from one slippery rock to another, through the rapid current, he used his staff as a supporting prop, and stayed both himself and the feeble wanderer which he conducted to the folded flock.   Thus it is, my brethren, with the Great Shepherd and Bishop of souls, when, in the night of death, he leads the feeble and dying members of his flock through the valley of the death-shade to the heavenly fold.   There are two difficulties which the believer has not unfrequently to encounter when he comes to die:

In the first place, he is liable to the last and desperate assaults of the adversary of souls. Baffled by the power of the everlasting covenant in his attempts to compass the destruction of the believer, he meets him at the bed of death, and taking advantage of his helplessness, endeavors, if he cannot destroy him, to mar the peace and becloud the prospect of his latest moments on earth. He showers his fiery darts upon him, injects doubts as to his acceptance with God, conjures up from the past the apparition of his sins, and calls up before his appalled imagination the vision of an angry Judge, a fiery bar, and a night of eternal despair. But another and a greater than Satan is there. The Chief Shepherd is also in that chamber of death. Standing at the dying bedside, and lifting his pastoral staff as a rod of defence, he wards off from his agonized servant the incursions of the powers of darkness, and beats back the assaults of his satanic foes.

Another difficulty which is apt to disturb the peace of the departing believer is derived from his vivid remembrance of his sins, and his consequent fear that he is not prepared to meet his God. In the solemn and honest hour of death, his soul, conscious of its dread proximity to the judgment seat, takes a minute and impartial survey of the past. His memory, quickened into an energy which only death can impart, with lightning rapidity sweeps, as at a glance, the whole field of his earthly history. There is no glozing process then by which the hideous features of his sins can be painted or concealed; no apology for his crimes which will stand the scrutiny of the death-bed, or abide the breaking light of the eternal world. All his acts of youthful folly, all his broken vows, all his unredeemed promises to his God, all his fearful backslidings, all his sinful thoughts, words and deeds, now crowd into his dying chamber, throng around his dying bed, and threaten to go with him as swift witnesses against him before the final bar. The billows of a fiercer death than that of the body dash over his head, and, struggling in the torrent which threatens to sweep him through the last valley downward to a bottomless abyss, he cries in his extremity to the Redeemer of his soul. Never deaf to the appeals of his dying people, the Great Shepherd hastens to his relief with the succors of his supporting grace.   He whispers to the sinking believer that he died to save him, that his blood has cleansed him of all his sins, and that his perfect righteousnes, his atoning merit, is a ground of acceptance, a foundation that will not fail him when the wicked and unbelieving shall be driven from the divine presence like the chaff before the storm.   It is enough.   The dying believer, with the hand of faith, grasps the pastoral staff that Jesus thus extends to him, and, leaning upon it, passes in safety through the glooms and dangers of the death-shade, emerges into the light of heaven, and is satisfied with the beatific vision of God.

Fellow-travellers to the dark valley, let us believe in Jesus as our Saviour.   Let us put our trust in him as the Shepherd and Bishop of our souls.   So when we are called to die, no guilty conscience will break our peace, no condemning law will thunder upon us, no frowns of an angry Judge will deepen the awful shadow of death; but we will fear no evil, for Christ will be with us; his rod will protect us in our last conflict, his staff will support us in our latest pang.

THE PITILESSNESS OF SIN.

BY REV. J. B. STRATTON, D. D.,
Pastor (Emeritus) of the Presbyterian Church, Natchez, Miss.

"Then Judas, which had betrayed him, when he saw that he was condemned, repented himself, and brought again the thirty pieces of silver to the chief priests and elders, saying, I have sinned in that I have betrayed the innocent blood. And they said, What is that to us? see thou to that. And he cast down the pieces of silver in the temple, and departed, and went and hanged himself."—MATT. xxvii. 3, 4, 5.

THERE is a use to be made of this incident, lying outside of its direct bearings, which it may be well to glance at as we approach the study of it. That Judas spoke rationally and truly, in the confession which he here makes, cannot be questioned. According to the judgment of that arbiter which presides in the breast of every man, he took the right view of his conduct; he had an adequate ground for his self-condemnation and despair. He *had* sinned. He had not been *made* to sin. He had done freely, voluntarily, what he had done in betraying the innocent blood. It does not occur to him to say that he had been unfortunate; that he had been the victim of fate, or the irresponsible tool of a higher power. "I, I only, have sinned" is his confession; and any unbiassed mind which looks at his crime will endorse the confession. He stands guilty at the bar of every unprejudiced observer from the day that he appeared before the Jewish court, till now.

And yet, what Peter said, on the day of Pentecost, in

86

regard to the crucifixion of Christ, "Him being delivered by the determinate counsel and foreknowledge of
God, ye have taken and by wicked hands have crucified
and slain," he might have said of Judas' part in the
transaction. "The determinate counsel and foreknow·
ledge of God," which made the Redeemer's death certain,
included in them all the steps which led to the event.
And yet, no one doubts that it was with "*wicked* hands"
the Jewish rulers did their work; and no one doubts
that Judas "*sinned*" in the aid which he rendered them
in the doing of it.

You have here the problem of the coincidence of God's
sovereignty and man's freedom in his acts and his responsibility for them, solved by the spectacle of the fact.
The two agencies are seen, in this instance, actually co-
inciding—forming like two separate cords—the unity of
a knot. Speculative science, formal logic may say the
knot cannot be tied. In spite of all their affirmations, it
appears here, visibly tied. The philosopher's theories or
arguments do not make facts. Facts do not wait for
these, in order to command the acceptance of men. A
well-established fact, in the face of the dissent of science
and logic, may say the *difficulty is with you*. A fact,
inexplicable by your methods, is simply a truth standing
on an altitude above the reach of your ladders.

The fact, revealed to us here, in the case of Judas, is
a collateral light thrown upon a subject upon which the
minds of most of us are probably, often painfully, and
yet unnecessarily exercised.

There is still another direction in which this incident
may be used to lift from the religion of Christ a reproach
which is sometimes thrown upon it. The existence of
spurious members in the church is no impeachment of
the claim of the gospel to be a regenerating and sancti-

fying power amongst men. That there should have
been a traitor in the original body of twelve disciples,
and by the permission of an omniscient Master, may surprise us.   But the fact meets us.   It was so.   The great
Husbandman allowed tares to grow up with the wheat,
but the seeming anomaly does not prove that the wheat
was tares; but, on the other hand, makes it more evident that the wheat was wheat.   A wise foresight on
the part of its Head, of the condition of the material out
of which his church was to be formed, may be discovered
in this arrangement.   A Judas—a counterfeit disciple—
may have been admitted into the family of his followers,
in order that all the other members might be led to the
watchfulness which asks perpetually, ''Is it I?'' and to
the self-distrust which keeps them constantly mindful of
the Master's counsel: ''Follow me!'' Occasional instances of perfidy on the part of professed Christians is no
more a proof that Christianity is a pretence or a failure
than persecution is; and the Saviour may have allowed
a traitor to appear thus early in the history of the church,
as he did the persecutor, in order that his servants in all
ages might be forewarned of the perils which lay in their
path and of their need of divine grace to uphold them in
their steadfastness.

Passing now to the more direct teachings of the text,
I remark, first, that the case of Judas gives us a striking
illustration of the *power of a sinful lust, cherished in the
heart, to blind the mind to the character of the passion and
to the consequences which issue from it.* It is a matter of
common consciousness (though men seem very generally to overlook it) that the impressions we get of things
are due very largely to the condition of the organs
through which we deal with them.   A diseased eye will
give you a wrong idea of the color, form, or size of an

object.   There is more foundation than most people are
aware of for the apparently extravagant proposition that
every man makes his own world.   Certain it is that the
aspect under which the world presents itself to him will
be determined very much by his own subjective state.
Before your view of a thing can be accepted as right,
you must be sure that the instrument through which
you are looking at it is true, and that your medium is a
clear one.   Carry with you in your heart a vicious lust,
and it will be in you like a smoking furnace, the fumes
of which will becloud your intellect and immerse you in
an atmosphere of illusions.   It has in it a wizard's
power, and can, to your eyes, change darkness into
light, bitter into sweet, and evil into good.   What a
terrible disenchantment there was to Judas when he saw
his Master actually condemned to death!   His overwhelming distress shows that the possibility of such an
issue had never been distinctly realized by him; or if so,
that he had persuaded himself that Jesus, by some exertion of his power, could extricate himself from the hands
of his enemies.   But look at him now, when sign after
sign of humiliation is revealing the sufferer's weakness,
and forboding the fact that his innocent blood, through
his agency, was to be shed!   The spell which had be-
numbed his reason, is broken.   His silver has lost its
lustre.   His eyes have been open to the enormity of his
crime.   Do you wonder that he cast down his treasure
in the temple, and departed and hanged himself?

My friends, this is no poetic fiction—no dramatic picture af avenging justice.   It is a record of every day's
experience.   It is a fair exposition of the blinding and
stupifying effect of corrupt passion.   It is a representation of what I may call, the *pitilessness of sin*.   From
the first, its work is one of moral mutilation.   It steals

into the heart, and then puts out the eyes of the soul.
It is repeating, in a thousand instances, the same cruel
torture which Nebuchadnezzar inflicted upon Zedekiah,
the captive king of Judah.   Intent upon the gratification
of his desires, the victim of lust loses his capacity to
estimate the true nature of what he covets, or the ability
to look on to the end of his pursuit of it.   The forbidden
fruit seems fair to his sight and inviting to his appetite,
and in his eagerness to enjoy it, he ceases to regard the
deadly consequences which may lie behind indulgence.
"In the day that thou eatest thereof, thou shalt surely
die," may be written by the finger of God full in view,
but he does not see the threat, or he does not understand
the meaning of it.   If you have ever watched the operations of your own minds when under the influence of some
strong inclination, you will have observed how completely
they have been warped and biassed in favor of everything
which encouraged your wishes, and against everything
which opposed them.   The point of gratification has
been the point of attraction.   Everything in the way of
disaster or suffering lying in the rear of gratification has
been reduced in magnitude, or has been attenuated into
a filmy indistinctness, till it has hardly been seen at all.

Now, just this species of hallucination attends the
practice of sin in all forms.   How strong the passion
which engenders it is, may be inferred from the difficulty
there is in persuading men to give it up.   It is paralyz-
ing as the frost of winter and freezes the faculties of the
soul into motionless ice.   Thought, sensibility, sympathy, are congealed by it.   It encrusts the nature of its
subject with the hardness of the nether millstone.   It
pays its wages, "death," to its votary in advance—before his soul leaves his body, because it extinguishes
within him every instinct and element of a true and

generous manhood. Judas, under the influence of it,
could see more worth in a few pieces of coin than in
his divine Lord. The drunkard, under the infatuation
of his appetite, grows blind to the fact that his intemper-
ate courses are bringing his family to beggary and himself to shame and the grave. And this moral enfeeble-
ment, let me add, is just as real in the case of the decent,
respectable transgressor as in that of these more flagrant
offenders. It is the *love* of sin which makes the sinner,
whatever be the form in which that love expresses itself.
And love, in the nature of it, is devotion, servitude. It
takes captive its subjects. St. Paul calls all godless
men, "servants," or, as the word means, *slaves* "of
sin." They *are* slaves. They are fettered bondsmen,
whether their chains be the iron ones of the tenants of
the slum, or the golden ones of the worshipper of Mammon, or the silken ones of the devotee of pleasure. The
love of sin ensures the result that the man does not *want*
to be separated from the thing he loves, and has no
capacity to appreciate the reasons which would urge him
to separate from it. In the misty way in which the
admonitions and warnings of God's word appear to him,
he sees nothing in them to alarm him, or nothing which
a little ready sophistry cannot strip of its force. He can
relieve himself of all uneasiness by saying, that his form
of indulgence is a harmless thing, a light effervescence
of exuberant vitality which means no wrong; or he can
argue that God is too good and merciful to notice or
punish the petty frailties of his creatures; or he can con-
strue the threatenings of Scripture into poetical extrava-
gances, designed to intimidate the vulgar multitude;
and so he encourages himself in the pursuit of the things
he loves by dreams of security as false as those by which
Judas was beguiled.

But Judas, as we see in our text, awoke from his dreams, and in the light which fell upon his opened eyes, illusions vanished, and things stood before him in their naked reality. You know the result of the revelation. I have no heart, no power to analyze its contents. But does not the question press itself upon us: may not the sinner, in every case, awake from his dreams? Dreams cannot last always. The honest waking hour must come sometime. Oh, surely the fate of the traitor in that awful moment when he saw what he had been doing, ought to startle every man loving sin and living in the service of it, like a thunder-peal. The enchantments which evil lust throw around the soul must be dissipated sooner or later, for truth must win in its conflict with error. There *are* consequences to follow a life of ungodliness. The Bible says so, and its testimony is infinitely more worthy of the credit of a reasonable man than can be the biassed utterances of a heart debauched by the love of sin. The spectacle of Judas' anguish and despair at the close of his experimenting should settle that point forever.

A second fact, suggested by the text, is that *sinful affections, cherished in connection with favorable opportunities, for knowing and doing one's duty, may be expected to grow with rapidity and to attain to an extraordinary intensity*. We shall probably be safe in supposing that when Judas first began to follow Christ, the thought of betraying him to death for a sum of money would have filled him with horror. But after the lapse of three years he could do this atrocious deed. For during those three years, in spite of all the counsels of Jesus and the attractions of his holy example, leading him to self-denial and a low esteem for worldly possessions, we find him retaining unimpaired, what we may assume to have been his original greed for wealth. His opportunities for cultivating pious sentiments and principles were peculiar. But his ruling passion withstood them all, and in the course of time became strong enough to induce him to make the base proposal to the Jewish priests, "What will ye give me, and I will deliver him unto you?" And such a result was entirely natural. His propensity to avarice gained strength, his conscience became blunted every time he refused to give up his besetting lust under the admonitions and reproofs of his Master. He became a worse man rapidly by opposing the influences which were striving to make him a good man; and, finally, no extreme was too great for him to reach in the indulgence of his propensity. This tallies with common experience. Do you not know that you are adding to the strength of your limbs every time that you lift from the ground or throw down to the ground the bearrier that obstructs your way? Men who will hold on to their sinful passions and persist in leading a sinful life, in the face of the opportunities and facilities for repentance and amendment which the gospel affords, rapidly lose their moral sensibility and succumb to the mastery of their love of sin. They have resisted so much in prosecuting their evil courses, that the impulse acquired will carry them onward to the last point of indulgence. The gospel, thus, which they would not allow to be a savor of life unto life, becomes a savor of death unto death. The love of money, inordinately cherished, I doubt not, has operated in the case of many another man, just as it did in Judas'. It has led him, at first, to blind his mind to, and steel his heart against, the claims of religion, till he has gone a certain length, perhaps a moderate one, in the gratification of his desire to be rich. Then he has repeated the process, and again and again repeated it.

He has held on to his guilty purpose though the whole enginery of gospel motives has been laboring at his heart, to force it towards God and heaven. At the outset, probably, his feelings were tender on the subject of religion, and nothing would have shocked him more than to be told that he could ever sacrifice his Saviour for gold. But years pass on, in the heated pursuit of wealth and in obstinate resistance to Christ's warnings and counsels, and what is the result? His position is fixed. He has become petrified as Lot's wife. The last kindly thought of Jesus is gone. The last inclination towards religion has ceased to throb in his soul; and though he does not say it, and though he has never deliberately formed the purpose, yet the purpose *is* formed as positively and as inflexibly as though it were signed and sealed, to part with Christ for the golden equivalent for which his heart has lusted. And what is true of this craving for riches is true in regard to every sinful appetite which men have persisted in indulging, in defiance of the remonstrances and threatenings of the gospel. The result it is always preparing to bring them to is such an infatuated devotion, such an abject bondage, to the thing craved, that the abandonment of the Saviour, and the loss of the soul do not seem too great a sacrifice to secure the object. O ye, who are sitting to-day under the ministry of the blessed Jesus as he speaks to you in his word, and are yet putting off attending to the duties he urges upon you, through the solicitations of some sinful passion, will you not remember Judas? Your passion will master you before you are aware, as the traitor's did him ; and may present you before the judgment-seat, as guilty of selling your Lord, as he was !

And now I ask you in the third place to reflect *how miserably poor and mean all these objects of corrupt desire, supposing them to be possessed, must appear, when contemplated intelligently, in connection with the consequences to which the pursuit of them must lead you.* Let Judas again become your teacher here! Look at him as he throws his bribe, with loathing upon the temple floor! Was it not the very thing, the very sum, all told, in genuine coin, for which, a little while ago, he was so eagerly clutching, and for which he promised so eagerly to deliver up his Master? Why has that which seemed so precious then become so worthless now? Ah! Judas has got what he bargained for, but he has got something more. He has got his mind open to a distinct perception of the guilt and ruin which his prize has cost him. And hence the glitter of his silver has become dim, and its value has departed.

And so it must, sooner or later, be with all who consent, for any earthly gratification, to surrender the benefits of Christ and his great salvation. When the wrong they have done to the Saviour, and the utter bankruptcy they have inflicted upon their own souls by such conduct, become distinctly revealed to them, as they may be at a dying hour, and as they certainly will be at the judgment day, how will they, too, fling to the dust the accursed baubles which have beguiled them into such fatal madness!

And still further let us ask, *what comfort will the wicked draw in the hour of their distress from the objects which they have served in sacrificing Christ?* Judas, when remorse had seized him, came to the chief priests and elders, hoping, probably, that the sight of his contrition and agony might appeal, at least, to their humanity and secure some change in their treatment of Christ. But he was dealing with monsters. They had gained their purpose through his agency, and what cared they for

him? Vainly he made the hall ring with his protesta-
tions, "It is innocent blood which I have betrayed."
"What is that to us?" was the reply. "See thou to
that!" Your guilt is your own concern; bear it as you
can! And is this all the solace which the servant of sin
can expect from the master whom he has been so sedu-
lously serving? A multitude of Judases, whom no man
can number, answer, Yes. I can conceive of the slave
of drink personifying the vicious appetite to which he
has subjected himself, and in some moment of remorse,
appealing to it for pity, for release from its grasp, for his
wife's sake, for his children's sake, for the sake of the
innocent blood which it is causing him to shed; and I
can conceive of the cruel response which he would receive, "What is that to me? see thou to that. Your
position is of your own choosing. Make the best of it
that you can!" And there is no other reply which the
devil, or the world, or the flesh, or wicked men, or anything that the sinner may be said to have served by his
lusts, will ever give him. What response can the man
who has taken a viper into his bosom, and who is writh-
ing under the torture of its fangs, expect to his cries for
compassion but a hiss of derision? Oh! these passions
which lead the soul to deliver up its Saviour are pitiless
things! They first seduce their victim, and then mock
at his woes. They answer all his complaints and en-
treaties with the taunt, "What is that to us? See thou
to that!" And this will be all the comfort they will
ever offer him, either on earth or in eternity.

There is one truth more included in our text which I
must not overlook. It is this: that *there may be a repentance, consisting of a conviction of sin and of remorse
on account of it, which fails to bring to the subject of it any
relief from his distress, or deliverance from his despair.*

Judas, it is said, "repented himself." He had conviction and remorse; but he did not repent with that repentance which is "unto life." This is the gift of God by his Spirit; and Judas, in parting with Christ, had parted with the ground upon which, and the channel through which, all God's saving gifts are bestowed. And he had quenched that Holy Spirit by whose aid alone men can be renewed unto repentance.

My friends, we make a great mistake when we suppose that any uneasiness which we may feel at a retrospect of our sins, will bring us the boon offered to repentance in the gospel, or that repentance is such a thing of the will and the lip that it can be practiced whenever we choose. There is a sorrow for sin, the Bible tells us, which is "of the world," and "worketh death." It is the sorrow of nature, entertained under the coercion of shame, and suffering, and terror. The sorrow which leads to life is a "godly sorrow"—a sorrow born of a recognition of God in Christ, producing in the soul a sense of the intrinsic evil of sin, and a loathing of it as an offence done to God and his holy law, and a desire to be delivered from its vileness and guiltiness, and a dependence upon the grace purchased for sinful men through Christ's mediation and propitiation. Mere remorse, mere terror, do not produce such a sorrow. Judas had these, and yet Judas perished. It is not easy to get it, as it would be if it were merely the cancelling of a bargain when one finds it about to involve him in loss. It is gotten through a resort to the interposition of Christ and the Holy Spirit. And just as any man continues to separate himself from Christ by obeying his evil lusts, and continues to resist the Holy Spirit by asking a little and a little longer indulgence in his evil courses, he is making it more and more probable that the repen-

7

tance which is associated with pardon and reconciliation
to God he will never get. This solemn lesson Judas is
teaching us to-day. "Beware," we may hear him saying "of trifling with the patience and mercy of God till
there is no other repentance possible for you than that of
unassisted nature—the deadly sorrow of a soul that has
gained a sight of the guilt and the consequences of its
sin, and has lost the sight of its Saviour."

Here we must take leave of this painful theme. It
spreads before us a volume rather than a text. We have
drawn enough from its dark pages to know that their
contents are infinitely important. My dear friends, if
you will ponder them seriously as you ought, that lurid
beacon-light which the apostate's perfidy and doom have
kindled in the far gloom of the past will be for you a
salutary vision, a signal to point you to holiness and
heaven. May God help us all to be so startled and ad-
monished by it, that the torturing convictions, the unavailing regrets, the despairing lamentations, which
gathered around the suicide of Judas, may never be repeated at our dying hour!

THE HAPPY SERVICE.

An Expository Sermon Preached before the 18th Virginia Regiment, 1861.

BY R. L. DABNEY, D. D.

"Come unto me, all ye that labor, and are heavy laden, and I will give you rest. Take my yoke upon you, and learn of me: for I am meek and lowly in heart; and ye shall find rest unto your souls. For my yoke is easy, and my burden is light."— MATT. xi. 28-30.

THIS world, my brethren, is a weary one. If any of you think not so, I can but liken you to inexperienced youths, who are summoned in the morning to set out on a toilsome journey, and in their ignorance of its real character, suppose it to be a pastime, because the adjuncts of the hour of setting forth are pleasant. They are in raptures with the free motion, and the exercise of their own exuberant energies, with the perfumed breath of dewy morn, with the fields glittering with liquid pearls, with the eastern sky bathed in crimson and gold, and with the beams of the rising sun. They bound along the way in sport, wasting the vigor which they will sorely need ere nightfall. They forget the sultry hours of the afternoon, when this cheering sun shall have put on its fervid heats, the dusty, lengthening miles, the thirst, and hunger, the aching limbs, with which they must drag themselves at evening towards a goal which seems ever to recede.

But no man lives long enough to learn what life truly is, without reaching the conviction that this is a weary world. We "labor and are heavy laden." How pre-

cious and timely, then, is the promise of rest to such
beings? Many of you are weary and burdened with the
impossible endeavor to feed an immortal mind with
earthly food. Some perhaps are heavy laden with their
toils of self-righteousness, while they go about to establish
their own acceptance with God, grievously galled by an
uneasy, disapproving conscience. A few, I trust, are
laboring with the salutary burden of conviction for sin, and
conscious guilt. Some of you are wearying yourselves
in vain, with the effort to break your bondage under sin
in your own strength. God's people among you are oppressed with the "heat and burden of the day," while
they strive, painfully, yet with better heart and hope,
"to make their calling and election sure." Many are
crushed with sorrows and bereavements, or with anxieties and fears. All these are invited by the benevolent
Redeemer to come and find rest in him. Whatever may
be their burden, he promises a gracious relief. How
general, then, ought the interest in these divine words to
be; and how eager?

When we are invited, "come unto me," we understand, of course, that this coming is not a corporeal approach to Christ's local habitation, which is not possible
for us, in the flesh, nor necessary; but the embracing of
his redemption by faith. This usage of the word is too
well established in our Saviour's preaching to need
much illustration. When, for instance, he says (John
vi. 35), "he that cometh to me shall never hunger; and
he that believeth on me shall never thirst," the coming
is manifestly faith. The yoke which we are to take up
is the service of Christ. And when rest is promised to
those who believe, and who obey, it is not bodily indolence, or sensual ease, which the Saviour offers, but
inward peace. He himself defines it in the subsequent

words, as "rest to our souls." He may call us to
stormy trials for his sake; he assuredly will call us to
diligent, persevering labors for his cause; but he guarantees to us that sweet repose of soul, with which outward toils are light, and without which the ease and
prosperity of sin are but a mocking torture. The main
doctrine taught us, then, in this passage, is, that—

*First, Our Peace is to be found in embracing Christ and
his service by faith.*

At the threshold of the subject, we are met by this
inquiry: Who is it that makes this generous offer of rest
to all the weary and heavy laden of earth? Consider
how much is implied in it. To fulfil the obligation
which is thus assumed will require no small resources of
wealth, power, and love. To succor the multitudinous
evils of humanity is, indeed, a mighty undertaking. Let
us suppose that the mightiest emperor of earth, or the
most powerful angel in heaven, had ventured such an
invitation as this, and that it had been universally
accepted. Before this vast aggregate of the wants and
woes of men, his resources would seem to shrink into a
mite, and the greatest finite mind would reel and stagger
in the mere attempt to comprehend, as all created riches
would be absorbed a thousand times in relieving the
mighty mass. Who is this, then, that calmly stands up
and announces to his dying race the audacious proposal?
"Come one, come all, to *me;* and *I* will give you rest."
Is this the Nazarene, the carpenter's son; the man who
"had not where to lay his head"? How dare he pledge
to suffering mankind, he, in his beggary, a relief which
Cæsar, upon the throne of imperial Rome, with all the
legions of her armies bowing to his sceptre, and all the
nations of the civilized globe pouring their tributes into
his royal treasury, would not presume to undertake?

If he is only what he seems, well may scribe and Pharisee resent with hot indignation the insolence of such imposture; and say, this man at once blasphemes God, in assuming a prerogative of compassion which belongs to him alone, and mocks the miseries of man, by vainly offering to take them all upon his puny arm.

Be assured, my brethren, that the holy Jesus would have been incapable of using this language had he not been conscious that he was not only man, but God. It was because he could claim:[1] "I and my Father are one"; "It pleased the Father that in him should all fulness dwell." "He hath set him at his own right hand in heavenly places, and hath put all things under his feet, and gave him to be head over all things to the church." Unless the Son of man hath power on earth to forgive sins, and infinite attributes of omniscience and omnipotence, he cannot give peace to mankind. But he is both God and man. Unless the charge of insincerity and imposture can be brought against his character, this promise compels us to receive his proper divinity; and here, my brethren, is the foundation of our trust in him. Because he hath in himself all the fulness of the Godhead, therefore we can rely upon his love, power, wisdom and faithfulness, to make us happy in our dedication to him. Thus, the apparent paradox at the outset of his invitation is turned into a noble support of its solidity.

Second, We read assurance of our peace and blessedness in Christ in the nature of the yoke which we are invited to receive. "Take my yoke upon you, and learn of me; for I am meek and lowly in heart; and ye shall find rest unto your souls."

Here, again, there appears to the unbeliever a still greater paradox; he is invited to look for rest in assum-

---

[1] Jno. x. 30; Col. i. 19; Eph. i. 21-23.

ing a yoke! It is when the yoke is unbound and the wearied ox is released to follow his own will pastureward, that he finds rest. So the perpetual delusion of the unbeliever is, that he can find his preferred happiness in the emancipation of his soul from the dreaded restraints of Christianity, and in this alone. This error, we trust, may be dissolved by reminding you of a few plain facts. The first is, that there is no such possible alternative for you, as you vainly dream, between the bearing of Christ's yoke and entire immunity. No; the only real choice within your reach is that between the yoke of Christ and the yoke of sin, of which Satan is the master. Now, if this is so, manifestly, one may be reasonably invited to seek the relief of his toil by exchanging a cruel and unrighteous bondage for a mild and righteous service. But I repeat, no man is free, or can be; all who do not bear the yoke of Christ, groan under that of sin and Satan. Such is the testimony of the Scriptures. "Jesus answered them, Verily, verily, I say unto you, whosoever committeth sin, is the servant of sin." "Thou art in the gall of bitterness, and the bond of iniquity." They are "taken captive by the devil at his will."[1] I appeal to your own experience: Is the most reckless sinner really free from constraint? I speak not of the bonds of discipline; but in other respects, is he at liberty to regulate his actions by his own preferences? Nay; how often does his own passion and sin lay him under the most cruel restraint and self-denial? His delusive enjoyments in transgression are often purchased at a heavy cost, and then concealed at the expense of irksome sacrifices of inclination. These are but instances of the pinching of Satan's yoke. Here, then, is the choice which

---

[1] Jno. viii. 34; Acts viii. 23; 2 Tim. ii. 26.

you have to make, transgressor; not whether you may
repudiate every yoke and go free as the wild ass of the
desert described by Job; but whether it will most conduce
to the repose of your soul to bear the yoke of Christ,
your loving Redeemer, or of Satan, the soul-murderer.
The first is right and reasonable (your own conscience
avouches it), and your heavenly Master deals honestly
and graciously with you.   He lays it upon your shoulder;
but he assists you with his loving and almighty hand to
bear it; he solaces your labor with the sweetest foretastes
of an approving conscience and heavenly hope; he makes
it grow perpetually lighter by the growth of holy habi-
tudes of soul; and at the end he converts it into a crown
of glory.   But Satan, a ''liar from the beginning,''
brings his foul, unrighteous yoke to you, concealed with
frippery, and persuades you that it is but a toy.   Thus
he binds it upon your neck, and when he has befooled
you effectually, leaves you to bear it unaided, or mocks
you with sardonic malice, while it grows ever more
weighty; and having galled you like iron here, crushes
your miserable soul at last into perdition.   Under which,
now, of these yokes will you find rest to your souls?

The second fact is, that it is not apathetic indolence or
sensual ease which Christ promises, but rest for the
soul.   It consists of peace of conscience, harmony of the
affections, and the enjoyment of legitimate and ennobling
exercise for all the powers.   Man's true well-being requires activity.   Even an ancient pagan sage learned
enough of this truth to define happiness as ''virtuous
energy.''   This definition we may accept if we be permitted to take it in the sense of the normal and healthy
exercise of the soul's powers.   He who has no rule of
life, no worthy aim, no duty, can never be happy, because
he puts forth no virtuous energy.   He who bears the

right yoke, or, in other words, has assigned to him the proper activities, is the man who truly enjoys his existence.

Third, We may expect rest under the yoke of Christ because of the character of our Master. "He is meek and lowly in heart, and we shall find rest unto our souls." He is a gentle, kindly, tender master. A merciful master makes an easy service. His benevolence makes him watchful of the welfare of his servants, and considerate in dealing with their infirmities. His lowliness of heart ensures that he will never sacrifice the happiness and lives of his subjects in reckless and ambitious enterprises. He is not a tyrant to drag his wretched subjects, like an Alexander, or a Tamerlane, through frozen wilds and burning wastes, and to pour out their blood as a libation to the idol of his fame. He is the prince of peace, whose sceptre is truth and meekness and righteousness, and whose law is love. To his own people, he is the "Lamb of God," who loved them and gave himself for them. How, then, is it possible that he, in regulating the lives and services of his ransomed ones, should impose on them any other law than one which conduces to their truest well-being? To dread the yoke of Christ is guilty mistrust and unbelief.

But we shall not acquire the richest meaning of the passage, unless we include the connection of the clause, "learn of me," with the rest of the verse. Saith the Saviour, "Take my yoke upon you, and learn of me." What shall we learn of him? Obviously, we learn of his meekness and lowliness of heart, how to take the yoke and how to wear it. Thus shall we find true repose of soul. This is but teaching us, my brethren, that if we would have true peace, we must imitate the spirit with which our Redeemer fulfilled the will of his

Father, and bore his cross.   No more complete and ready
method of proof appears to establish this assertion than
to ask you to form to yourselves a conception of the inward life of such a man as the man Jesus.   Suppose a
servant of God, endued with just his affection and benevolence, with his unselfish disinterestedness, with his
purity, with his forgiving temper, with his magnani-
mity, with his elevated devotion, and moving among us
in the fulfilment of the duties of the Christian life,
under the impulse of these lovely sentiments, combined
with the social ties appropriate to our nature sanctified.
Does not this at once constitute a picture of a life than
which none can be conceived more imbuded with the
sweetness and sunshine of true happiness?   Would not
such a life glow with the very light of heaven's own
bliss amidst the gloom of our sorrows and sins?   Some
one may say, perhaps : Such was the temper of Jesus;
yet he was "the man of sorrows."   True; but it was
because he "bore our griefs and carried our sorrows."
It was the burthen of our guilt which pressed upon that
pure and holy heart.   Let us suppose that he had borne
no load of obloquy, of death, and of divine desertion for
us ; that he had enjoyed the friends and outward blessings with which our lot is crowned; and had experienced
no heavier chastisements than God's fatherly mercy ap-
points to his adopted children here, sustained by the
consolations of his grace.   Then, indeed, would his life
have been one of heavenly peace within.   And such
would ours be if we learned of him, his heavenly temper.   Reproach and opposition might still befall us, for
we should still be in a wicked world; but the serene spirit
of conscious rectitude and of forgiveness would sustain
our souls in a loftier atmosphere, high above the flights
of all the embittered shafts of malice.   Pain, fatigue,

sickness, would still visit us; but the spirit, baptized in peace, would sustain our infirmity. Our hearts would sometimes bleed with bereavements; for we should still be sinners, although pardoned; yet there would be no poison in the wound, for the assurance of the love of the hand which directed the stroke would medicate our pain. If, then, we would find rest to our souls, let us learn to imbibe the temper of the meek and lowly Jesus, and to bear his yoke with that devoted spirit with which he fulfilled his Father's will in living and dying for us.

Fourth, In the concluding verse our Saviour gives this crowning argument: "For my yoke is easy, and my burden is light; and ye shall find rest to your souls." But this reasoning the unbeliever repells with more incredulity than anything that has preceded it. The yoke easy, and the burden light! he exclaims. How can this be? Has not Christ himself said, "Strait is the gate, and narrow is the way?" Is not the commandment declared to be "exceeding broad"? "The righteous scarcely are saved." How, then, can it be argued that we shall find our true repose of soul in the service of Jesus Christ because the burden of it is easy?

The unconverted man has often a worse ground of incredulity than this: that of his own experience and consciousness. He says to himself: "I *have* endeavored to bear that yoke; I was earnest in my attempt, for was I not impelled to it by the infinite moment of the worth of an immortal soul, the sense of dreadful guilt, the terrors of an endless hell? I strove hard to live the Christian life. Often I renewed my struggle, even with almost despairing bitterness; but the task was too great. I have relinquished it, and again I am living the life of careless impenitence, conscious that the danger of perdition is not removed, but only veiled partially from my own eyes by my insensibility, well aware that my conscience is not cleansed, but only seared. So well have I learned, by my own miserable experiments, that this grievous yoke of Christianity would crush out every enjoyment of life for me, if borne in earnest, that I am now stubbornly braving the appalling risks of an unprepared death and a lost immortality, rather than face the burden again at present. And after all this, would the preacher persuade me that "the yoke is easy and the burden light? Alas! I know better!"

Such is the skepticism, and such its ground which most adult transgressors read in their own hearts, when they scan their contents honestly. Say, unbeliever, have I not given correct form to your inmost thought? And your most intimate conviction is at points with the express declaration of your Saviour. How shall I attempt to solve this crowning paradox for you, and to reconcile your unbelief to this gracious truth? This is a task which the Holy Spirit can alone accomplish with efficacy; and, thanks to him, he does not require the execution of it from his ministers. Nothing but a true conversion by his power, experienced in the heart, can enable the sinner to appreciate the nature of Christ's service. The blind man cannot be taught precisely what are the beauties of the spring before his eyes are opened. But yet something may be said to obviate your incredulity; something which, though it will not make you comprehend how this yoke becomes light, may yet enable you to apprehend that it is not unreasonable it should become so to the believer.

Remember, then, that the declarations which the Scriptures make of the straitness and difficulty of the Christian's way refer always to man's native unassisted strength. Relatively to that strength, the way is indeed arduous. It is impossible to exaggerate its difficulty; if we should persuade the unconverted heart that it is absolutely certain his unaided strength and resolution will fail before it, we should be strictly true. And now, I appeal to your own consciousness: Were not those ill-starred efforts to serve Christ, whose failure now so discourages you, made in your own poor strength? Did you not begin them unconvinced of your impotency? Was not this the thought of your heart: "Seeing the danger of my soul, *I*, as a rational being, will resolve; and *I* will fulfil what I resolve. I shall not be an inconsistent, half-way Christian, like these despised ones whose blemishes have so often been the butt of my contempt. I shall reform my life truly, and keep the law, and thus prepare and recommend myself for gospel forgiveness." Did you form those purposes of piety and make those efforts, in explicit, full dependence on a spiritual ability to be communicated to you by Christ, of free grace, so that your sole encouragement to attempt them was his faithful word of promise? Alas, no! And therefore your service of him was a mortifying failure. Now I beg you to weigh the real statement of your Saviour in the text. He has never said that the yoke would be easy, or the burden light to a soul which attempted to lift it apart from him. What he taught was this: that he who "cometh" to him, he who "learns of him" shall find the yoke easy. This you refused to do; you have never really tested the correctness of Christ's declarations; you have, in fact, no experience whatever upon the subject.

"But[1] when we were yet without strength, in due time Christ died for the ungodly." And one chief portion of his purchase for us was enabling grace, which is

---

[1] Rom. v. 6.

offered to our faith on the same terms with remission of sin. Hear now some of the blessed assurances of this fact:[1] "If any man be in Christ Jesus, he is a new creature; old things have passed away; behold all things have become new; and all things are of God."[2] "I am crucified with Christ; nevertheless I live; yet not I, but Christ liveth in me; and the life which I now live in the flesh, I live by the faith of the Son of God, who loved me, and gave himself for me."[3] "And he said unto me, My grace is sufficient for thee: for my strength is made perfect in weakness."[4] "A new heart also will I give you, and a new spirit will I put within you: and I will take away the stony heart out of your flesh, and I will give you a heart of flesh. And I will put my Spirit within you, and cause you to walk in my statutes, and ye shall keep my judgments, and do them."

If these precious promises are true, is it not clear that he who has them fulfilled in his soul may reasonably expect a wholly different experience from yours in bearing the yoke? Here new views of truth are given: a spiritual ability is awakened in the faculties hitherto misdirected to sin and sense; man's impotence of will for spiritual good is renovated by the almighty will of the Spirit. If, indeed, Christ does all this in him who comes and learns of him and takes his yoke, plainly that service may be easy and pleasant to him which before was intolerable. Sometimes the curious child, straying where the laborers have laid down their implements, takes up the axe or scythe adapted to a man's strength, and undertakes to use it. But his youthful limbs are unequal to the task; his toil is excessive; his breath heaves with panting, his heart throbs, and his joints

---

[1] 2 Cor. v. 17.   [2] Gal. ii. 20,
[3] 2 Cor. xii. 9.   [4] Ezek. xxxvi. 28, 26.

quiver with fatigue. As he lays it down, he concludes perhaps, thus : " How burdensome and repulsive must the life of the laborer be! Surely every pleasure of existence is crushed out by his excessive toil! Yet he is mistaken; he has judged their tasks by his measure of strength. They have the muscles of men; and when they come forth in the breezy fields or fragrant woods, refreshed with food and their veins rich with lusty blood, there is a positive joy in the vigorous swing of these weapons of sturdy and honest labor. Similar is the error which you have made, when you have attempted to bear Christ's yoke in your own strength, which is weakness; and overpowered by the burden, have inferred that Christ cannot make it light by his grace.

But there is another solution, which is, if possible, more important. It is found in the difference of motive and affection by which the service of the believer and that of the unbeliever are prompted. Those labors are easy and pleasant which are inspired by love, however absorbing they may be of time and strength. But if they are compelled by reluctant fear and rendered in hatred, the lightest exertions gall the heart. The man who is incapable of domestic love looks on the toils of the laborious father with disgust; he thinks his life that of a galley slave; and says to himself that no power nor price on earth shall ever bend him to so irksome a bondage. But does that careful parent think so? Nay, his labors, his crops, the glebe watered with the honest sweat of his brow, are dear to him; he cherishes them with all the affectionate interest of heart's treasures; they feed those whom he loves. As he pursues his busy tillage through the sultry hours, although he does feel the heat and burden of the day, he is happy in his endurance; because he has before him the peaceful home which is blessed

with the fruits of these labors, the board spread with
bounty by the work of his sturdy hand, with the smiling
faces around it, the welcome of pattering feet and gleeful
voices, and childish arms about his neck, which he ex-
pects to meet him as he returns at eve, heavy perhaps of
limb, but light of heart, from his daily tasks, and the
loving smile of the thoughtful mate, who keeps the
hearth bright for his coming.   Go now, to that man, and
tempt him to leave his fields for some scene of sinful
amusement; tell him that his daily labor is nothing but
a miserable drudgery, and that it is time for him to seek
enjoyment abroad.   Will he hearken?   No; his labor is
his enjoyment; those guilty and mischievous scenes
have no allurement for him, because love makes him
happy enough in his industry.

Or, if this instance is not enough, we may find a more
conclusive one in that which is the strongest and purest
of all affections found among sinful men, the love of a
mother for her babe.   And this, also, imposes the severest toils which any of the duties of common life require.
As the young female, a stranger as yet to this devoted
love, witnesses the sacrifices of some mother, lately her
comrade, amidst the perpetual watchings and sleepless
cares of the nursery, it may be that she looks on with
disgust and dread, and she says to herself, not for all
the world would I submit to such an abhorred burden.
But the time comes when the fountain of maternal love
is opened in her heart also.   Now see the recent vota-
ress of fashion!   How zealously does she forsake the
admiration of society, and sacrifice the bloom of her
beauty, lately so much prized, amidst the vigils of her
domestic tasks.   These cares are no longer repulsive.
Propose to her to resign her tender charge wholly to
some hireling, whose well-paid skill will probably far

surpass her inexperience in providing for its welfare, and to return to the delights of the ball-room. She will reject it, and as she presses her infant to her bosom, will declare that no joy of earth is so sweet as the care of this darling object. Whence this change? It is because a new love has been born along with her offspring. The yoke of love is ever easy, and its burden is light.

In like manner, if he who comes to Christ and learns of him, learns thereby to love, this new motive abundantly explains the fact to you, sinner, so incredible, that his yoke becomes easy. For, I take your own heart to witness, that in your former efforts to live a religious life, no love animated your resolve. The world and self-will were still sweet to you intrinsically. If you felt the sting and bitterness of any of your sins, it was only because self-love was terrified by the looming of the danger they incurred. The Christian life was abhorrent to your secret heart; and the language of your inner thought was that this divine Master was an austere man whose service you would defy if you dared. Poor, unwilling captive! No wonder your service, wrung by fear from a bitter, reluctant heart, was a galling bondage.

But now remember the blessed truth already established from the Scripture: that when a believing soul embraces the cross, Christ "crucifies the enmity thereby"; that he engages to take away the stony heart out of our flesh and give us a heart of flesh; that when he reconciles God to us by his atonement, he also reconciles us to God by our effectual calling, and sheds abroad his love upon our hearts. Then, as the regenerated sinner considers the amazing love and condescension of a Redeemer God, stooping to death to rescue him from unutterable ruin, a new-born gratitude conspires with

8

adoration for his excellences, and he begins to say, "I love him because he first loved me." Then the love of Christ constraining him becomes the spring of a joyful obedience; and he sings with devout delight, in the language of David, "O Lord, truly I am thy servant: I am thy servant and the son of thy handmaid. Thou hast loosed my bonds." This is the way, O sinner, the yoke is made easy and the burden light! Cannot you apprehend it?

Perhaps such a glimpse of the beauty and glory of the cross hath penetrated your heart (which may God grant), that you are almost ready to say: "Ah! if I could only claim that wondrous Saviour as mine, if I could believe that the divine blood was indeed shed for my sins; that the burning throne, whose just wrath now blights every look which my wretched soul turns towards God with fear and enmity, was changed for me into a throne of grace; that this dreadful God was indeed reconciled, and was become a tender Father, I, too, could love—I, too, could serve with hope and cheerful obedience. But how shall I know this? How read the secret verdict of heaven, which requites and adopts the object of almighty grace?

I will tell you how. But first let me warn you not to mistake the obstinacy of your own native opposition to God. If you think that the mere apprehension of your own interest in the cross, and of the excellence and love displayed therein towards you will be enough of itself without the invoking of the sovereign Spirit to renovate your obdurate heart, you will be disappointed. No doctrine, no moral suasion alone, not even that of dying love, will melt that flinty thing; nothing but the power divine which first created it. But if you feel that you could indeed love Christ, if only you were assured that he had first loved you, then it is my delightful commission to tell you that you may claim that privilege of loving. Christ invites you. His own words are: "Whosoever will, let him come." He tells us that the man upon whom God's secret verdict of the heavenly justification and adoption is passed, is he who is truly willing to embrace and to serve Christ. Are you willing? Then you are one of those for whom the invitation is sent. Come, then, thou weary, heavy-laden soul; "Come to Jesus and he will give you rest. Take his yoke upon you and learn of him; for he is meek and lowly in heart; and ye shall find rest to your souls. For his yoke is easy, and his burden is light."

Permit me, in closing this discourse, to point out two instructive lessons which are contained in these words of the Saviour.

One is, that faith always includes an immediate assumption of all known duty. Christ here explains "coming to him" in verse twenty-eight (which is his customary expression for believing), by taking up the yoke and learning of him in verse twenty-nine. The true believer, although of all men most impressed with his own impotency to live the Christian life aright, immediately sets about that very thing. It is because the gospel promise pledges Christ's strength to make the yoke easy; and the function of faith is to embrace the promise just as it is. Now, there is somebody here whose failure and distress are all explained by this remark. My brother, you think you comprehend and approve the plan for a sinner's pardon through Christ, and that you can trust it. But you have not found rest for your soul? It is because there is some yoke, some duty, which you have not assumed. What is it? You know; I do not. God does. Take it up like a man;

do it now, not self-righteously but believingly, and you will find the blessed rest.

Second, There is somebody else here who thinks he sees and craves the blessedness of the soul which has received the conscious assurance, in its own exercises, of being saved in Christ. He says, "Oh! if I could only feel in my heart these new-born affections and thus know my interest in him, how joyfully would I flee to him and embrace him with his service; and no toils nor sacrifices should tempt my happy heart for one moment to forsake his yoke. But alas! when I look within, all is cold and dark. How can I venture with this unrenewed heart?

The answer which Christ here implies is this: The conscious, inward experience of his grace is bestowed by your coming and when you come, not before. Hear him: "Take my yoke upon you and learn of me," . . . "and ye shall find rest to your souls." You must find it by taking the yoke, not before you take it. You must venture on his divine word, trusting that alone, and committing yourself to his fidelity in advance of your own experience. And does not he deserve this, who died for you? Cannot you trust him? If he saved you by the method you desire, your trust would be, after all, not on him but on your own experiences. How sandy a foundation!

But there is a more offensive form of this mistrust. Some anxious, convinced souls would fain have the peace; but they are loath to commit themselves irrevocably to Christ's yoke until they have made a sort of conditional experiment for themselves of the comfort and ease with which they may bear it. They cannot trust the word and oath of the Saviour who is the God, and who so loved them as to lay down his life for their souls.

No; they must be allowed to finger the yoke, to weigh it in their hands, to judge how it will wear, and then, if they like it, perhaps Christ will be permitted to bind it on permanently. Deluded soul! Of course the yoke, thus tried, will not wear lightly. And what is such mistrust but an insult to the majesty, the love, the faithfulness of Christ? He will not traffic with you for your deliverance on such terms as these. You must trust yourself without reserve to his fidelity, or he will turn with holy scorn from your insolent proposal, and leave your miserable soul to perish in its doubts. ''The fearful'' (they who are too timid to trust themselves to the faithfulness of their God and Saviour) ''and unbelieving and abominable . . . . shall have their part in the lake which burneth with fire and brimstone, which is the second death.'' (Rev. xxi. 8.)

SEEKING THE LORD.

BY J. W. ROSEBRO, D. D.,

Pastor of Tabb-Street Presbyterian Church, Petersburg, Va.

"Seek ye the Lord while he may be found, call ye upon him while he is near."—ISAIAH lv. 6.

THE fifty-third, fifty-fourth and fifty-fifth chapters of Isaiah should be studied together. They are closely and logically connected. In the fifty-third chapter, the great foundation truth of redemption is laid. The hope of Israel and of the world is in the suffering Messiah, who "was wounded for our transgression" and "bruised for our iniquities"; on whom the Lord hath laid the iniquity of us all.

The fifty-fourth shows us the church built on this great foundation. "I will lay thy stones with fair colors and lay thy foundation with sapphires." She stands as the House Beautiful with her chamber called "Peace" that always looked to the sun-rise. There can be no such church except as built on the suffering and death of him who made "his soul an offering for sin."

Then, in the fifty-fifth chapter, this glorious church flings her doors wide open in the world-wide invitation from her Lord, "Ho, every one that thirsteth, come ye to the waters." But there could be no such invitation, nor any church to give it if Jesus had not died. *The great invitation of the fifty-fifth is made possible* by *the truth given in the fifty-third.* Bear this in mind.

Our text gives us a *command*, a *promise* and a *warning*.

I. The *command* is, "Seek ye the Lord." It comes from one who has the right to command. Let not the fulness and freeness of the invitation lead you to think you have nothing to do. It is true Jesus says he came to *seek* as well as save the lost; yet he also declares we must seek if we would find. It is true, he stands at the door and knocks, yet must we knock if we would have it opened unto us. It is true, God opens wide the door of his grace and proclaims, "whosoever will may come"; yet must we "strive to enter in." He offers the water of life "without money"; yet must we "buy" it. God presses the gift of eternal life on us; yet is it true, "I will yet for this be inquired of by the house of Israel." God forces himself on no soul. He offers himself, and then it is our privilege, our duty to "seek the Lord." We cannot sit down and wait for salvation; we must seek the Lord, though he is not far from us.

Many of the young make the mistake of thinking that religion will come to them sometime in the future, and that they need not concern themselves to "seek." In every community there are a number of men of excellent character who hope that some day, through the prayers of their Christian wives, they will become Christians, yet never stop earnestly to seek for themselves. So the years go by and they drift farther and farther from the things they have heard. Hear all ye what God declares, "*Seek ye* the Lord." We must seek with all the heart. Then shall ye seek me and ye shall find me, when ye seek me with all the heart. Can you hope by a few fitful seekings to find the Lord? Seek as you do earthly prizes. What earnestness! What self-denial! What difficulties are struggled against and overcome! And for what? For corruptible crowns! Alas! for the incorruptible crown you are not willing to take a little time for serious thought and prayer.   The slightest hindrance will turn aside your purpose.   The difficulties in your way are but the test of earnestness.   When Jesus answered not a word to the prayer of the anguished mother pleading for her child; yea, when he cast her heathen origin in her face, and told her that heathen dogs had no right to the children's bread, she only drew the closer and put a deeper power in her appeal: "Lord, help me." When the crowd bade Bartimeus hush his cry, he but "cried out the more exceedingly."   When the press about the Lord prevented the four who bore the palsied man from entering the door, they climbed to the roof and opened a way and showed their faith.   Yet here are blessings, needed by you and offered to you, richer than ever blind begged for or palsied needed; yet, when Jesus is "near" to give these, and is "passing by" no more to return for some, you let any hindrance stop you. The fear of man, some business call, an invitation of pleasure, the faults of some Christian, any slight hindrance, is excuse enough for your neglect.   What is it you are thus lightly treating?   IT IS ETERNAL LIFE.

Oh! that it could be deeply impressed on you that while divine love has thrown wide open the door of life and written over it so all may see its words of welcome, "Ho, every one," still you must strive to enter.   Hear, then, God's command, "*Seek* ye the Lord."

II.   A *promise* is in the text, though it is implied, not distinctly stated.   If God *invites* us to come and *commands* us to come, there is surely an implied *promise* of acceptance, when we obey the command and accept the invitation.   He has filled his book with richest promises and holds up before us one illustration after another, that we may see how sinful souls came to accept his invitation and that none ever went away unblest. He assures us that the favor of God standeth sure, and that "*whosoever*" cometh to drink of this water shall receive it without money.

Now we may turn to consider the full confidence given us by the great truth taught in the fifty-third chapter. When our sins and fears arise and make us ask, "Can God accept and forgive me"? God answers by showing us one already "wounded for our transgressions" and "bruised for our iniquities;" the stripes due for our sin have been laid on him, and "with his stripes we are healed." Jesus has "made his soul an offering for sin," therefore he can be just yet justify you, ungodly as you are. That chapter assures us—

> " That love unknown
> Has broken every barrier down."

It is a glorious, amazing truth, that since Jesus died God is graciously bound to receive every soul that comes trusting in Jesus who died. See how beautifully this was illustrated in the case of Mephibosheth, Jonathan's son. You remember he was injured when a child and was always "lame on both his feet." When David came to the throne he sought the descendants of Jonathan that he might show to them "the kindness of God." But Mephibosheth thought David meant evil to him, and he was afraid and tried to escape and hide himself. When at last found and brought before David he came with fear and fell on his face. Yet did the king meet him with the gracious words, "I will surely shew thee kindness for Jonathan, thy father's sake." When Mephibosheth answered, "What is thy servant, that thou shouldest look upon such a dead dog as I?" What did David virtually reply? "I am not thinking of whether

you are comely as Absalom, or lame on both your feet;
I am thinking of Jonathan, of my love to him and of my
covenant with him. That covenant binds me to show
kindness to you, therefore you shall be as a king's son
and sit ever at my table.''

David and Jonathan had made a ''blood covenant''
together. The blood of each flowed in the other and that
covenant could not be broken. Therefore was David
bound to show kindness to Jonathan's son.

Oh, poor sinner! you have been running away from
God, and, when at last the Holy Spirit lead you to fall
before him, your sin makes you feel you are all unworthy
the least notice or favor. Why should he look on ''such
a dead dog as I am?'' With wondrous love God lifts
you up and says, ''There is a blood covenant between
me and my Son. By that covenant I am bound to show
the kindness of God to all for whom Jesus died and who
come to me by him. I cannot turn you away if I would.
You may feel all unworthy a place at the King's table,
but I make you as one of the King's sons and you shall
sit at my table forever.''

What absolute confidence is given to us by that invitation which says, ''Ho, every one,'' and then points
to the fifty-third chapter as giving us ''all the fitness he
requireth''! You see, you do not need to be cured of
your lame legs before he will show kindness. We are
ever putting the seventh verse of this chapter before the
sixth. We say, ''I will forsake my wicked ways and
give up my unrighteous thoughts, then seek the Lord.''
''No,'' God says, ''come to me first, then you shall be
strengthened to forsake your wicked ways. I put the
sixth verse before the seventh.'' What avails it to the
leper to cure a few of his sores when the fatal disease is
sent out from the heart in the blood? Come, ye lepers,

to the Son of man. Let his merciful touch make you clean. Wait not to rid your soul of one dark blot,

> "To thee whose blood can cleanse each spot,
>   O, Lamb of God, I come, I come."

Nor need you fear that you may be shut out because you are not of the elect. It is true that God chooses us and that we are "chosen before the foundation of the world." Yet he has left us the power "to choose whom we will serve." Paul does not hesitate to reaffirm the Saviour's teaching, that we owe our salvation to the sovereign electing love of God. Yet, side by side with this great truth he presses our responsibility. In the ninth chapter of Romans he presents the great subject of predestination in such a way that it gives some the cold chills to read it; yet he closes the subject by showing us in the last verse of the tenth chapter, God standing with outstretched hands of loving, earnest entreaty, and saying, "All day long I have stretched forth my hands."

We only "darken counsel with words" when we attempt to explain how God is sovereign in his electing love, and yet has left to us the power of choice. However we may fail to understand, we shall never fail to find it true that God's decree bars the door in the face of none who seek to enter. While election shuts a great many in, we know it shuts none out. So far from that being true, he has flung that door wide open and stands "*all day long*" stretching out his hands and saying, "*Whosoever* will, let him come." It is wonderful, wonderful! *All day long, all day long*. Does that look like God had shut the door? Nay, you must run away from God's loving entreaty and hide yourself from that invitation which follows you "*all day long*."

Thus, you see, the question with you is not will God

receive me when I seek him, but will I let him find me? The question is not will he hear me when I pray, but will I hear him beseeching me? It is not will he open to me when I knock and plead, but will I open to him knocking and saying, ''Rise and let me in?'' It is not will he give me eternal life in answer to my anguished prayer, but will I take the life which, with a father's love, he presses on me? Oh! every shadow of doubt is taken away from us, and we are stripped of every vestige of an excuse!

III. The *warning* of the text. The preacher would not be faithful to did he not press on your thoughts the warning in this text. Do not the words, ''while he may be found,'' ''while he is near,'' warn us that there is a time when he may *not* be found, when he is *not* near? For one hundred and twenty years God was near to the people in the days of Noah, and through the open door of the ark God was to be found. At last he shut the door. Then it was too late to seek. The door was shut and there was no more refuge to be then found from the beating storm and whelming waters. Were there not five virgins who gave little heed to invitation and warning, and who stood at last outside and the door was shut? It was the voice of the Bridegroom, no longer near, who bade them depart.

> ''Too late! too late!
> Ye cannot enter now.''

There is a time for the husbandman to sow. If he sow not neither shall he reap. Ask the Holy Spirit to burn into your soul the words in Proverbs i. 24–32: ''Because I have called, and ye refused; I have stretched out my hand, and no man regarded; but ye have set at nought all my counsel . . . . when distress and anguish cometh upon you. Then shall they call upon me, but I will not answer; they shall seek me early, but they shall not find me.'' When infinite patience gives us up, to whom shall we look for help? When the Spirit of grace, long grieved and resisted, takes *his* sad flight, what is left us but the darkness of eternity's night?

Delude not yourself with the thought, '' God will be too merciful to let me suffer.'' He solemnly declares he must. Delude not yourself with the hope that you will have another trial in the world to come. There is no *second probation*, as if God had not given you a fair chance here. If you lose now, all is lost. The appeal of the rich man in hell to Abraham in heaven, and the answer given back to the lost man, forever settles it as a tremendous fact, that when once we cross the river of death, there can be no changes in our destiny. A great gulf rolls between heaven and hell, and they ''that would come from thence '' will find that it is forever impossible. It must be forever true, '' He that believeth on the Son hath eternal life, but he that obeyeth not the Son, shall not see life, but the wrath of God abideth on him.''

Was it any wonder that when David thought of the ungodly going to such a doom that horror should take hold upon him? That Paul could not speak of it without weeping? That tears of divine pity should have fallen from the eyes of Jesus, as he beheld the city nearing destruction? That the cry should be wrung from the heart of God, '' How can I give thee up? '' Can you then treat such a warning lightly?

The hour of your spiritual death may come long before the day of your bodily death. Have you never seen strong trees standing on the hillside, around which the axe had cut a broad girdle, severing the current of its life? This was done in the late spring. All summer these trees waved their green leaves as full of life as any that stood on the hillside. Yet all who looked at that white girdle knew those trees were dead. So may men go in and out among us, they may be active in their pursuits, and may possess much that is attractive in their lives, but the seal of spiritual death is on them. Achan died when he stole the wedge of gold, before his body was broken with the stones of justice. Ananias and Sapphira died when they lied to the Holy Ghost, days before their bodies fell at Peter's feet. Herod died when he put away John the Baptist's warning words, long before his body so miserably perished.

> " Spurn not the call to life and light;
>   Regard in time the warning kind;
>   That call thou mayest not always slight,
>   And yet the gate of mercy find.
>
> " Sinner! perhaps this very day,
>   Thy last accepted time may be;
>   Oh! shouldst thou grieve him now away,
>   Then hope may never beam on thee."

Oh! God is near us now. Souls are seeking him, and finding him near; are calling on him, and he is found of them. Shall this house of prayer be the place where you shall decide against him, and shall it be in this hushed assembly that the destiny of your soul shall be fixed?

Several of us lads went one day to see a railroad bridge, which the workmen were then building, and which was said to be the highest in western North Carolina. We were standing at the foot of the highest pillar, guessing its height. The foreman came to us, and pointing to some bloody marks on the ground said, "There is where one of the workmen fell yesterday. He was under the influence of drink and would not be warned. He fell from the top of that pillar, and here is where we picked up his crushed body." We started back from the place. It was a solemn spot to us, that marked where the man had died.

But there may be made in this church, while we are hearing God's invitation, a spot far more solemn ; one that shall mark the place where an immortal soul perished; one over which you will weep in eternity, and say: "There I refused to hear God, and there I lost my soul."

Oh! while the Spirit is whispering in your heart, "To-day, if ye will hear his voice, harden not your heart," while Jesus once more invites, while God is near, *come!* COME! Provoke not that state in which it will be impossible to renew you again to repentance. It were better for you, if you had never been born.

Begin now to seek the Lord. Stop and think. You cannot stop and think of your sin and ingratitude against such love and patience without coming to repentance. You cannot think of Jesus bearing your guilt, of his suffering and death for you, without learning to love him who thus first loved you. "My people will not consider" is the mournful charge God brings against us. Therefore does he entreat us to—"Come now let us reason together." "Harden not your heart," but "seek ye the Lord while he may be found; call ye upon him while he is near."

OUR REDEEMER'S PRAYER FOR CHRISTIAN UNITY.

BY REV. NEANDER M. WOODS, D. D.,

Pastor of the Second Presbyterian Church, Memphis, Tenn.

"That they all may be one; as thou, Father, art in me, and I in thee, that they also may be one in us: that the world may believe that thou hast sent me."—JOHN xvii. 21.

A RECENT writer, referring to the prayer of Christ recorded in the seventeenth chapter of John's Gospel, says, "We have here the words which Christ addressed to God in the critical hour of his life— the words in which he uttered the deepest feeling and thought of his spirit, clarified and concentrated by the prospect of death." Melancthon, the great Reformer, speaking of it, says, "There is no voice which has ever been heard, either in heaven or in earth, more exalted, more holy, more fruitful, more sublime, than this prayer offered up by the Son of God himself." In recent times more than one devout commentator has expressed the sentiment that when we stand within the precincts of this profound passage of God's word we are on holy ground, yea, in the very Holy of Holies. It becomes us, therefore, as we enter upon the consideration of a portion of this wonderful prayer, to take off the shoes from our feet, and to invoke the Spirit of all grace to bestow upon us that deep humility and reverence of mind we would need in coming into the very presence of God. As we proceed, let us also bear in mind the fact that this prayer is a part of Christ's official ministration as our divinely authorized Intercessor and High Priest before the throne of God. The prayer consists of several distinct portions, and I shall now ask your particular attention to those four verses (20–23) which relate to the oneness or believers.

Never, perhaps, since the apostolic age, has there been manifested throughout Christendom at large so deep an interest in the subject of Christian union as has been witnessed during this latter half of the nineteenth century. The indications to which I allude are such as the following, to-wit: the growth, among Christians of widely separated faiths, of a larger tolerance of each other's divergencies of belief; an increased readiness on the part of various denominations to seek closer fellowship with brethren from whom they have long been estranged; the marked falling off in the number and acrimony of polemical discussions; and a more general desire for the obliteration of all separating walls not actually demanded by loyalty to essential truth. Whilst candor obliges us to admit that much which passes for zeal in behalf of Christian union has no better foundation than gross ignorance of the grave issues involved, or culpable indifference to sound doctrine, it is still true that the prevailing sentiment of the Christian world to-day in regard to the sin of schism is in closer accord with the mind of Christ than was that of former generations. Nevertheless, the moment one attempts to locate the blame for the numberless divisions now marring the body of Christ, or even to suggest a remedy, a storm of discussion arises at once, revealing only too plainly that the day for the complete healing of Zion's sorrows is yet far in the future. This fact, however, should not discourage those who pray for the peace of Jerusalem, for the real pro-

9

gress already noted within the last half century is full of promise for the coming years, and it may well stimulate the hope that Christ's prayer will surely be realized at last.

The first question to be considered is: What is the precise character of that oneness which our Saviour here has in mind? To what extent, and in what sense, does he desire all his followers to become one?

1. Whatever the oneness was to which he had reference, it was something which, at the moment he spoke, had not been realized in full perfection among his then living disciples. This seems to follow, not merely from the fact that he did not assert that it was then in existence, but because he asked his Father to create or bestow it. At the time Christ offered this prayer he had some hundreds of genuine disciples in Palestine, who for months or years had been savingly converted. These persons, from the very instant of their renewal by the Holy Spirit, and by virtue thereof, were unquestionably one in several vital respects. They were all one in their regeneration by the same divine Spirit; one in their union by faith with the same Redeemer; and one in their possession of an indefeasible title to the same inheritance of everlasting life. Surely, all these unspeakable precious features of a true spiritual oneness belonged to each and every one of those disciples before Christ offered this prayer; and by no possibility could that oneness be diminished, much less lost. There were other features of oneness, however, which they certainly did not yet possess, and which they would have to have before they could all be perfectly one. We know that at that moment the Christians then in the world did not even enjoy that oneness of external organization which our Lord gave them a few weeks later by the hands of his

inspired apostles. Not until after the day of Pentecost
were the Christians welded into one body called the
Church of Christ, having one set of officers and one set
of rules and ordinances to serve as a common bond of
union. But more than this, the Christians then living
were very far, indeed, from being entirely one in their
apprehension of the doctrines of the gospel. Neither
were they completely one in harmonious, brotherly fellowship. Not to mention the unseemly self-seeking and
contention among the apostles themselves in regard to
the places of honor in Christ's kingdom, which he had
had to rebuke, we learn from the sacred records in Acts
and the Epistles that in a little while two factions arose
within the bosom of the infant church, the one composed
of Jewish and the other of Gentile converts ; and before
the first century is half gone we find the apostles consuming much of their time reproving schismatics, and
trying to reconcile alienated brethren in various portions
of the church.   One need only peruse the several books of
the New Testament in order to discover the humiliating
truth that good Christian people can take diametrically
opposite views of almost every doctrine of the Bible, and
can divide the church into rival sects and factions until
sensible men of the world are puzzled to understand how
all these warring elements can possibly be one in any
vital sense whatever. In view of these admitted facts,
whilst we are unable to see why our Redeemer should
take up the closing hours of his earthly ministry in begging his Father to make believers one in those respects
in which they were already and necessarily such by virtue of their new birth, we can see abundant reason why
he should pray that they all might be made one in their
understanding of all the doctrines and precepts of the
gospel, one in every essential particular of their church

life, one in their harmonious, brotherly fellowship, and one in their plans and labors for the evangelization of the human race. Therefore, it becomes us to view with distrust all those interpretations of this great intercessory prayer which represent our Lord as asking his Father to bestow upon believers something they already possessed, and yet making no special requests for other important elements of oneness without which they could never hope to bring the world to his feet.

2. A second characteristic of the oneness for which Christ prayed is that it is the exclusive possession of regenerate persons. None but believers can either share this oneness or fully understand it. Our Lord wants men to know that true Christian unity is something divine and sacred. God may and does use men as his instruments in bringing it to pass, but it is a work of divine grace. Hence no man can bring himself into the charmed circle of Christian unity merely by uniting with a Christian church. Now, unless this simple truth is clearly seen, we are certain to fall into confusion of thought when we come to deal with the matter of Christian union. One great trouble arises from the well-known fact that the purest Christian churches on earth contain a good many spurious members. It is also true that in some of the most corrupt churches there is only a very small proportion of really regenerate persons. It is easy, therefore, to understand that mere oneness of outward organization might have no real connection with true Christian union. Hence the attempt of some good men in our day to bring together, in one grand world-wide church, all the scattered and opposing Christian bodies, regardless of their wide divergencies as to faith, polity and worship, is the very wildest of dreams. Such an enterprise, if carried out, would probably do no more

to further true unity than would the consolidation of a Christian denomination with some great political party. In order to unite two or more bodies to any good purpose, a large majority of the members thereof must be, in the judgment of charity, real Christians; they must be substantially agreed as to all essentials of the Bible; and there must be such a general degree of harmony in regard to the details of church life as gives promise of good results. The practical significance and use of this condition attached to true oneness which confines it within the circle of believers, is not to prohibit the union of now separate churches merely because some spurious members are on their rolls, but to admonish us that oneness of outward organization is not the synonym of Christian unity. This outward oneness is, at best, only one means to the true inward oneness, and it will even prove worthless in that respect unless, in our attempt to heal division, we are loyal to the whole truth of God, and exercise sound common sense.

3. The third and most wonderful characteristic of that oneness which Christ prayed the Father to bestow upon all true believers is an absolute completeness which has its analogy in the perfect unity existing between the Father and the Son. The language our Lord here employs to set forth the intimacy and divine perfectness of this unity of believers is altogether remarkable in its varied iterations. First, he prays for believers in every age of the world—"that they all may be one; as thou, Father, art in me, and I in thee, that they also may be one in us." Then a little farther on he varies the expression somewhat—"that they may be one, even as we are one; I in them and thou in me, that they may be made perfect in one." Of course all will agree that there is a mysterious sense in which creatures could not

become precisely like the Godhead, but it would seem
perfectly clear that these words of our Redeemer contemplate a oneness of believers in respect to all the
things of salvation which in its utmost reach must exclude all divergency of doctrinal belief and Christian
practice, and everything akin to rivalry or division.   Can
we conceive of the Father and the Son as having opposite views of the plan of salvation, of church government, or of the methods for the evangelization of the
world?   Do they find two different sets of truths in the
Bible?   Is it even thinkable that they should ever come
into the slightest collision in respect to any feature of
church life?   Surely not.   But Christ's request is that
his disciples shall be one even as he and his Father are
one.   More than this he could not ask.   He does not
ask that his people shall merely bear a general family
likeness or be one in some essential respects, but that
they shall become as completely one as the Father and
Son are one.   He does not ask merely that Christians
of various bodies may learn to exhibit kindly tolerance
of each others diverse beliefs, for his prayer contemplates
the abandonment of all wrong beliefs, so that there will
be no opposing beliefs needing our tolerance.   But what
view did the inspired apostles of Christ take of this matter?   Did they make apologies for the differences they
witnessed among Christians so long as they did not
utterly subvert the fundamental doctrines of grace?
Did they speak or act as if it were no sin to organize
separate churches so long as the differences related only
to the form of government, or the forms of worship, or
the mode of baptism?   Listen to the way Paul talked to
the Corinthians who were disposed to array themselves
in parties under the names of even inspired apostles:
"Now I beseech you, brethren, by the name of our Lord

Jesus Christ, that ye all speak the same thing, and that there be no divisions among you; but that ye be perfectly joined together in the same mind and in the same judgment.'' (1 Cor. i. 10.)   A little farther on (1 Cor. iii. 1–4), referring to the same differences at Corinth, he says: ''And I, brethren, could not speak unto you as unto spiritual, but as unto carnal, even as unto babes in Christ. . . . for whereas there is among you envying, and strife, and divisions, are ye not carnal, and walk as men?   For while one saith, I am of Paul; and another, I am of Apollos; are ye not carnal?''   It is but just to affirm that the differences to which Paul here refers were of no graver kind than some of those which now divide various evangelical denominations of Christians in our own land.   That he would have condemned as ''carnal'' the persons who are responsible for these modern divisions as he did those schismatics at Corinth seems absolutely certain.   And it seems equally certain that this blessed prayer of our Redeemer contemplates the complete obliteration of all these divisions to the end that his people may become one even as he and his Father are one.   He did not specify the date at which he expected the complete realization of his heart's desire for Christian union ; but we feel sure it will be realized in absolute perfection in heaven, and that the realization of it then will be the culmination of a long series of prayers and labors running through ages of faithful use of means on the part of his dear people, whom he hath made coworkers together with himself.   In this vast enterprise, as in the matter of our own sanctification, and in that of the conversion of the world to Christ, the work is of God, and must advance by gradual steps; but each Christian has an important part to perform, and there can be no surer evidence of our own renewal than a constant, longing desire to see Christ's people made truly one.

4. A single other feature of the oneness Christ prayed for will be mentioned, namely: It is not something concealed in the hearts of believers, but it is something which, like the fragrant ointment, bewrayeth itself; like the city set upon a hill, which cannot possibly be hid. The unbelieving world will be forced to take knowledge of it, and it will have a marvellous efficacy to convince men that the religion we profess is from God. Thus it will avail to achieve what ages of arguments and preachments have signally failed to effect—it will be a gigantic object lesson which shall be read of him that runneth. The plain inference is that the one hundred and fifty sectarian divisions of Christianity which we have in our own land to-day are fearful obstacles to the conversion of the world. Is it not a striking confirmation of the justice of this inference to note the fact that all the missionaries of the various churches who go out into the heathen world to persuade benighted men to turn from their corrupt faiths to Christ are generally embarrassed when intelligent heathen demand the explanation of all these distinct and rival organizations, and ask why it is that the servants of the one Redeemer must needs carry such diverse flags? And it is no matter for surprise that we find, in some instances, ministers, whose brethren at home stoutly oppose closer relations with other bodies of similar faith and order, driven by the very exigencies of the foreign work to trample their theories under their feet so as to hide from the keen eyes of perishing pagans the differences which, at home, may be even cherished as too precious to be allowed to vanish. Out there on the frontier the true soldiers of Christ see that in union there is strength; and the lesson which we at home need

to learn is that if the millions of unevangelized people in this so-called Christian land are ever to be savingly impressed, the church must present an unbroken front as the one army of the living God. In this republic, to-day, we have seventeen millions of voters. This, of course, leaves entirely out of view all the female part of our population, and all males under twenty-one years old. The later census shows that on the rolls of all the various churches, Catholic and Protestant, there are less than four and a quarter millions of these voters. That is to say, after generations of effort, and with all our church machinery, not much more than one-fourth of the people of this land are even church members. Christ teaches us that the oneness of Christians can answer the scepticism of men as nothing else can, provided it be visible and unmistakable. Our reliance, then, is not to be mainly on oratory, or learning, or fine churches, or even that "generous rivalry" of the several denominations of which we hear so much in so-called union meetings, but of which we find not one word of approval in the Bible—our reliance, I say, is not to be mainly on these things, but on that glorious heaven-born unity of the followers of Christ which is able to silence the voice of scepticism and usher in the millennial day.

Having endeavored to set before you a faithful representation of the Christian unity our Lord prayed for, I now desire to point out what seem to be the principal means we should employ in coöperating with God to bring that unity to pass. I assume, as beyond all dispute, that in this gigantic undertaking, as in that of extending Christ's kingdom to the ends of the earth, you and I and all other Christians are solemnly bound to use the means within our reach. It is not the sword of the Lord, much less the sword of Gideon, that is to smite to

the earth the confederated hosts of bigotry, pride, ignorance and hate, but it is " The sword of the Lord and of
Gideon "—a sword which our puny hands must wield,
but all whose efficacy is due to the power of Almighty
God.

1. I sincerely believe that the very first important
means of furthering this glorious oneness is to bring ourselves to see clearly that schism in all its forms is a high-
handed sin against God.   When can we be fairly said to
be guilty of the sin of schism?   We commit this sin
whenever we teach or sanction ruinous error, or lay
unjust burdens upon the consciences of our brethren, so
as to drive them out of our communion.   We commit
this sin whenever we withdraw from the church and
create a new sect by reason of our having cherished un-
christian feelings towards brethren, or adopted unscrip-
tural opinions.   We may also commit this sin by throwing
our influence against an honorable settlement of differences which could be healed but for our obstinacy or
resentment.   The sin of schism is distinctly pointed out
and condemned in the New Testament.   This is true
even where the errors referred to did not involve the
surrender of fundamental truth, but consisted mostly of
the display of a spirit of strife and dissension.   Paul refers to this sin in his closing exhortations to the church at
Rome (Romans xvi. 17, 18).   He says: "I beseech you,
brethren, mark them which cause divisions and offences
contrary to the doctrine which ye have learned; and
avoid them.   For they that are such serve not our Lord
Jesus Christ, but their own belly."   In his enumeration
of "the works of the flesh" (Galatians v. 20) Paul men-
tions some of the very evils which have been at the
bottom of almost every division that ever occurred since
the ascension of our Lord, namely, "hatred, variance,

emulations, wrath, strife, seditions, heresies, . . . they
which do such things cannot inherit the kingdom of
God.'' Sin or culpable ignorance, one or both, have
been the causes of all the divisions now disfiguring the
Bride of Christ. The degree of guilt greatly varies, we
doubt not, but somebody's folly or sin has in every case
been responsible for the creation of new sects. Yet we
often hear the prevalent divisions of Christendom spoken
of in terms of great praise, as if they were in themselves
quite desirable. We are told that for men of different
tastes and diverse mental structure, etc., rival denominations are beneficial. If it were only contended that so
long as men remain blinded by sin and prejudice these
divisions are far better than compelling all men to join
one outward organization, we could agree to the statement. The trouble is that much of the talk we hear
directly encourages schism by depriving sectarian separation of its repulsive ugliness. This argument, however, proves too much. If the one hundred and fifty
existing divisions of Christians in America be desirable,
and if it is unwise to have any one remain in a church
because he happens to cherish some views unlike those
of his brethren, then each of the existing denominations
could profitably be subdivided, and instead of a paltry
hundred and fifty sects we could easily have a thousand,
with their multiplied machinery and consequent waste of
energy. Here, as often elsewhere, it behooves us to
turn away from the theories of men to God's word, and
to inquire how this matter was practically handled by
the inspired apostles whom Christ chose to organize the
church a few weeks after his departure from this world.
We know that the apostles at Pentecost and soon after
had thousands of new converts to deal with, representatives of both Judaism and Paganism, and from every

nation under heaven.   There were men of all races, and
classes, and civilizations, and religious antecedents.   If
ever there was a motley crowd on earth it was that one.
If ever there was an occasion when the beauties of separate denominational lines would have been visible, it
was then and there.   But those earnest apostles pro-
ceeded to organize but one church for the whole world,
and as the work of organization and moulding went on
they built up in all parts of the vast Roman empire
churches with but a single creed, and precisely alike in
every essential particular.   Nor was this all: they jealously guarded this one church to preserve it intact; and
as soon as the apostles discovered signs of schism, they
boldly denounced the guilty parties as the enemies of
Christ, and urged all the brethren to hold fast to the
faith once delivered to them, and remain in the church
Christ's apostles had founded.   That was the apostolic
method, and it was as unlike the methods of modern
schismatics as the day is unlike night.   I grant that
fidelity to essential truth does demand separation, and
the innocent parties are not schismatics.   Our Saviour
did, indeed, say: "It is impossible but that offences
will come," and yet he added, in the same breath, "but
woe unto him through whom they come!   It were better for him that a millstone were hanged about his neck
and he cast into the sea."   Until Christians shall have
made vast progress in both knowlege and holiness the
church is going to be marred and crippled by denominational rivalries and divisions; but the only consistent
view to take of these divisions is that they are, at best,
necessary evils—necessary only for the guiltless ones
who could not heal these divisions without compro-
mising essential truth, and excusable even as to them
only so far as they maintain their blamelessness by

standing ever ready to do everything consistent with loyalty to truth in order to come into closer relations with all brethren from whom they now are separated.

2. A second means of advancing the cause of true oneness among Christians is to school ourselves habitually to think of every believer under the whole heaven as our brother and fellow-heir, entirely regardless of his church relations. No matter where men live, and no matter of what race or religion they may be, if they do really love our Saviour they are united to Christ |by indissoluble bonds, and we are unspeakably near to each other, and are to spend eternity together in loving fellowship in the perfected kingdom of God. They and we may be far apart as respects our training, habits, feelings and religious activities, but we are completely and forever one in several most vital particulars, and the time is absolutely certain to come when we shall look into each others faces with joy, and wonder how we could ever have had any other than the utmost tenderness of feeling towards each other, or been unwilling to bear patiently with each others blindness and follies. I love to think that even in the most corrupt communions of Christendom there are those who are looking for eternal life to that very Jesus who is the only hope of my own sinful self, and who rejoice with me in the hope of that same glory which is to be revealed when he comes again. The very thought of this blessed tie, binding us to all others who believe, will help us to stifle the ungracious and spiteful words which sometimes press for utterance, and cause us to welcome every occasion when we may, without dishonor, get closer to them. The prevalence of such feelings in the hearts of Christians generally would soon awaken longings for the removal of every needless wall of separation, and prove the harbin-

ger of a more glorious day for the church of Christ on earth.

3. Among the most powerful of all the means we can employ for the furtherance of true Christian union is prayer. The inspired Psalmist exhorts us to pray for the peace of Jerusalem, and adds the promise that they that love her shall prosper. In one of the Beatitudes our Saviour has declared the peace-makers to be peculiarly blessed, for they shall be called the children of God. The transformations which must precede the realization of true oneness are so vast that as we contemplate them we are led to exclaim, "Behold, if the Lord would make windows in heaven, might this thing be?" But the ear of our God is not dull of hearing, neither is his arm shortened that it cannot save. When Carey, the great Baptist missionary, took leave of England a century ago to attempt the conversion of India to Christ, even good brethren shook their heads as though the task were too great even to be considered at all. But lo! what hath God wrought in one century, even with his church all disabled and hampered by endless divisions and unbelief! That almighty power, which has already moved mountains in the foreign field, can cause mountains here in Christian lands to depart and be removed into the midst of the sea; and when we reflect that above and behind us stands the Great Intercessor perpetually offering that same prayer for the oneness of his people, and pleading the merit of his infinite sacrifice, our hearts may well take courage. Let us accustom ourselves to pray often and earnestly to God for the enlightenment and sanctification of his people in every one of his churches; that every false conception of the truth and every mistaken policy may be abandoned; that all of us who are in the wrong may not only have eyes to see it,

but the grace and courage to confess it; and that all of us may, when constrained to contend earnestly for what we sincerely believe to be the faith once delivered to the saints, seek to be scrupulously fair, and always speak the truth in love.   Who can believe that such prayers as these would be in vain?   No doubt the changes which must pave the way for the reunion of Christendom will be gradual, and all of us now living must die without being permitted to witness the full consummation of our hopes, but it could surely add no thorns to our dying pillows to reflect that we had loved the church for which Jesus died, and had done what we could to make her a praise in the earth.

I might, if time permitted, dwell upon yet other means of advancing the cause of true oneness; as, for example, joining heartily in every worthy Christian and philanthropic enterprise with our brethren of other denominations, in which no compromise of principle would be made; recognizing, as far as we consistently can, the ordinances and churchly character of all evangelical bodies; and abstaining, as far as possible, from all ungracious interference with the enterprises of other churches.   But I must conclude this discourse with two needful cautions, to-wit: The first caution is that we should never, for one moment, imagine that the interests of Christianity can be furthered by hiding our colors or obscuring any doctrine of the gospel for fear that some whom we wish to conciliate may be offended.   Be assured that when at last unity shall be perfectly realized in heaven it can have no other basis than the truth of God as we have it in the Bible.   And the attempt to keep in the background any doctrine of the Holy Scriptures would not only be a cowardly artifice, but would, in the end, prove an obstacle to real oneness.   You might as well seek to harmonize the solar system by blotting some of the planets from the universe; you would only introduce new complications, ruinous in their results. Whatever we do, let us, with the apostle, shun not to declare the whole counsel of God with frankness and fairness, and out of loving hearts. The other caution, close akin to that, is to beware of allowing our desire for Christian union to render us lifeless and half-hearted in our efforts in behalf of the denomination to which we belong. It has been the observation of many pastors that the amiable people who say they love one church as well as another, soon reveal their emptiness by loving no church well enough to be willing to render it much service. It is possible to be warmly devoted to one's own church and at the same time to love the whole of God's scattered family. The ancient Spartans had this motto: "Sparta is thy portion; do thy best for Sparta"; and so long as yours is, all in all, the best church you are acquainted with, you will do well to make that motto your own. In all our labors, however, in behalf of the church of Christ let us never lose hope in regard to the final realization of Christian unity. The faint streaks of light already visible give promise of the coming day. The Great Intercessor ever lives to plead; and as sure as God's promise stands fast, every wall of separation must crumble, and all the followers of Christ be made one.

THE

DIVINENESS OF THE FAMILY BOND.

BY REV. W. U. MURKLAND, D. D.,

Pastor of Franklin-Street Presbyterian Church, Baltimore, Md.

"I thank God, whom I serve from my forefathers with pure conscience."—2 TIM. i. 3.

O F the social order which is to rule in heaven only
one glimpse has been disclosed. The structural
unit of the new Jerusalem, as of human life on
earth, is not the individual, but the family. For this
cause I bow my knees unto the Father of our Lord
Jesus Christ, from whom every family in heaven and on
earth is named. The church of the First Born in heaven
is bound together by personal relations, even the relations which make home and kindred on earth. And for
aught we know, the innumerable company of angels
who have kept their first estate, albeit descending from
no common head and unbound by ties of flesh and blood,
may yet rank themselves in households. As across the
breast of the ecliptic the stars group in zodiacal signs,
which borrow shape and name from earthly figures, so
the celestial society, the unquenchable stars that shine
forever in the spiritual firmament, move in the clearly-
defined circles of the Home. In the Father's house are
many mansions in which the family bond remains un-
changed. From the Father every family in heaven and
earth is named. We cannot in our English speech reproduce the fine play of thought and expression which
leaps from word to word, binding up in a common root

10   145

the divine Father and the heavenly family. *Pater—Patria*. They are forms of the same word. The family has a right to the name, because it draws its being from the father, and both by descent and name the family bond is entitled to be called divine.

I thank God, whom I serve from my forefathers, for the sacredness, the divineness of this, the strongest bond on earth.

Let us emphasize the divineness and far-reaching power of this bond. For in it rest the pillars of our social order. On the recognition of its inviolability depends the future of the nation and of the world. On it reposes the grandeur of the House of God. The vigor and aggressive power of the church are conditioned by the moral tone of the family. The vitality of the congregation is measured by the vitality of its households. "If the foundations be destroyed, what can the righteous do?" I take it that these are the most vital, the most pressing, the most imperative questions of the church of God to-day. "I thank God, whom I serve from my forefathers with pure conscience."

When a man can, he ought to thank God for his forefathers. For each of us is planted at birth within a sphere of necessity created by his descent. The infant is born to-day, but he is the creature of yesterday. A child is born into the world with wings upon his shoulders, or with gyves on his wrists. He is a thrall to the conditions of the household. He belongs to a family, and the character of that family may enfranchise or fetter his whole life. He did not choose his parents; they were chosen without his knowledge or consent; and yet he is born, linked to circumstances that lift him up as wings or press him down to the lowest earth. His whole life is bound up indissolubly with his parents and kindred. Race, and language, and religion, and social position, and earthly estate, and health, and mental power are forced upon him. He is planted in a circle of necessity that for years, if not for his whole life, may cause his heart to burn with gratitude and pride or crimson his cheek with shame.

Jesus Christ was born to poverty and to the social condition of a mechanic, because he was the reputed son of Joseph, the carpenter; and he was met in the rising success of his public ministry with a sneer, designed to crush his influence. "Is not this the carpenter's son?" "Can there any good thing come out of Nazareth?" But there comes a time when a man and woman are going to weave the same net-work of necessity for others. They marry, form a new home, create a new household, in which children are born and nurtured and impressed for all their lives. What is to be the influence of that new circle upon the children? Will they grow up to manhood and womanhood thanking God for their forefathers? Will there be recollections of a beautiful childhood, a pure youth, a faith and love transmitted as an hereditary possession, a devotion and service of God with a pure conscience, to be renewed and to reappear in their own lives, the traditions of a godly household bound up with the record of unbroken service, to be handed down to the generations which are to follow after?

The bond which creates and perpetuates the Family relation is the marriage bond. It is an institution divine and human, and its sanctity and inviolableness are distinctly the fruit of Christianity. The idea popularly held and often proclaimed, that marriage is only a civil contract, to be kept or terminated at the pleasure of the parties, like any other contract, is untrue as well as destructive. Marriage is more than a human contract or

convention. It is a divine institution. It belongs to
the race from the morning of creation. He created man
male and female ; he made one wife for one man when
he could have made a hundred. Says the prophet Mala-
chi : ''Did not he make one ? Yet had he the residue of
the spirit. And wherefore one ? That he might seek a
godly seed.'' It is the only human institution for which
Jesus Christ directly legislated. He reaffirmed its divine
origin and integrity ; he cleared it from the perversions
and glosses of his day ; and he asserted its indissolu-
bility by man except for one reason, the one sin which
kills love and makes the one flesh twain again. And
then, to glorify wedded life, he made it the symbol of
unbroken union between himself and the church, for
which he gave his life. The noblest epithalamium ever
chanted by human lips was sung by Paul, unfolding this
divine mystery : '' Husbands, love your wives, even as
Christ also loved the church, and gave himself for it, . . .
that he might present it to himself a glorious church, not
leaving spot, or wrinkle, or any such thing ; but that it
should be holy and without blemish. So ought men to
love their wives as their own bodies.'' And his praise
of unwedded life was not for its superior saintliness, but
for its superior ease and comfort in troublous times, and
its fitness for special service of God, to which some are
called.

I do not think we always recognize the debt of happy
homes and wedded lives to Christianity. The theory of
the Jews in Christ's day, however invaded by the practice of loving hearts and households, was that divorce
was practicable on almost any ground and for every
cause. Said the son of Sirach : '' If she go not as thou
wouldest have her, cut her off from thy flesh, and give
her a bill of divorce, and let her go.''

The teachings of Hillel allowed everything which made the company of a wife distasteful as sufficient ground for repudiation. If a woman had spoiled her husband's dinner, "burned his mess"; if she found no favor in his sight; if he liked another woman better; if a wife was quarrelsome or troublesome; if she was of ill-repute; if she was childless for ten years, she might be put away.

But Jesus Christ drew the line at one sin, a line so straight and rigid that even his disciples said, "If the case of a man be so with his wife, it is not good to marry."

In the great Roman world, and in the capital where Paul wrote the words of our text, the marriage bond had lost its sanctity. The Cæsar in whose reign Jesus Christ was born divorced one wife after another, and then quickly divorced the young Livia from her husband Augustus, to whom she had borne one child, and was about to bear another, and took her to be his own wife. The domestic life of the Cæsar in whose reign Paul was writing was simply infamous.

The chief orator of the world divorced his wife, married another for her dowery, and then, when he had paid his debts with that fortune, divorced her. Another distinguished citizen married a beautiful girl and almost immediately divorced her, only deigning to remark, "My shoes are new and well-made, but no one knows where they pinch me." On the other hand, illustrious and high-born women counted their years not by the consuls, but by the number of their husbands. The poet satirist tells us of a woman who had eight husbands in five years. Cicero speaks of a gentleman who, coming home from a journey, was told by his wife that their relations were dissolved, and that she was going to wed

Deo Brutus. The earlier constancy of wedded life had
given place to that laxity into which even conservative
states and cities are drifting.

The position of the children in these Roman homes
was that of a slave. The law gave, and had always
given, the father almost absolute power over wife and
children. The sons were only free when they had been
sold three times. They were then "emancipated," and,
when emancipated, lost all claim upon the estate or care
of the father. While in the family they were the chat-
tels of the father. He could sell, scourge, and slay his
sons. He could drag a gifted son from the tribune, where
his eloquence was enchaining the people, before the con-
sul, the tribune, the multitude, to his own house to be
scourged.

Into such domestic corruption and darkness came the
teaching of Christ and of Paul. We are all children of
God. The marriage bond was created by him. The
family is called from the divine Father. "Children,
obey your parents in the Lord." "Husbands, love your
wives as Christ loved the church." "Fathers, provoke
not your children to wrath." They were the rays of a
new sun, the seeds of a new life ; they regenerated the
family ; they saved Society.

I do not mean to deny all domestic virtue and happiness to that old Pagan world. The inscriptions on some
tombs thrill us with their tenderness and beauty : "She
was dearer to me than my life." "She never caused me
a pang but by her death." "To my dearest wife, with
whom I lived for eighteen years without a complaint."
These were gracious flowers springing out of that rank
soil ; but their root was simply in chance nature, not in
principle or in duty. They knew not the high note of
origin and of destiny struck by the Christian prisoner in

the dungeon of the Prefecture. "God created man male and female." "What God hath joined together let no man put asunder." "The divine Father, from whom every family in heaven and earth is named."

It is when the divineness of the family bond is recognized and obeyed, that the mysterious necessity which envelops us in the dawn and nurture of our very life is lighted up and glorified. There is a moral inheritance which belongs to every child as his birthright, whose spiritual issues are immeasurable. There are lines of blessing, threads of light and love, strands of golden hope, woven through and through the texture of our early life, which appear in the consummate fabric of noble character.

"I thank God, whom I serve from my forefathers with a pure conscience." The purity of motive, the devoted service, the radiant hope, the fervent love, the unconquerable purpose, which made the life of the Christian Paul reflect most fully of all men the example of Christ himself, were the inheritance of Saul of Tarsus from God-fearing ancestors, all touched by the grace of God. He had exalted and continued the traditions of his house. And the other home in Proconsular Asia, upon which he turns his eye in the very act of thanksgiving, was a signal witness of the same fact: "When I call to remembrance the unfeigned faith that is in thee, which dwelt first in thy grandmother Lois, and thy mother Eunice; and I am persuaded that in thee also." The ancestral faith unfeigned—oh! how true is this faith that comes down through the blood of godly parents!—which flowered and fruitened in Timothy, the noblest flower of the apostolic age, had descended from generation to generation. There is a law of spiritual heredity running through the line of family descent. It

is recognized in the very heart of the moral law, graven
in stone by the finger of God himself: "I, the Lord thy
God, am a jealous God, visiting the iniquity of the fathers
upon the children unto the third and fourth generation
of them that hate me, and showing mercy unto thousands
of them that love me and keep my commandments."
It enters into the very description of God given by himself: "The Lord, the Lord God . . . keeping mercy for
thousands; . . . visiting the iniquity of the fathers upon
the children, unto the third and to the fourth generation."
It is expressed by name in every great covenant relation
into which he enters with men: for life and death, with
Adam; for succession of the seasons, with Noah; for
ecclesiastical privilege, with Abraham; for kingly position, with David; for a new church, proclaimed at Pentecost and afterwards.   Grace does not run in the blood,
and a man is spiritually born, not of man, nor of the will
of man, but of God.   Yet the mental and moral qualities
which lie at the basis of all character; the lines of thought
and feeling along which character is built up; the tendencies which are moulded by grace and fixed into
habits; the sensibilities and moral fibres which underlie
conscientious service; the knowledge of God instilled in
half-conscious infancy, and the familiarity with Scripture
terms which express the faith and hope of Christian
men; the atmosphere of holy feeling and reverent movement which fills the Christian home, inhaled at every
breath; the unconscious moulding of an ever-present
Christlike life, and the education of mind and heart by
conscious and unconscious instruments—these are a
splendid portion of the spiritual inheritance into which
we are born, and in the midst of which, as in a citadel of
unworldliness, character is securely built up.

The nurture and discipline of the Lord in which chil-

dren are brought up is the means of grace employed by
the Spirit of God, who works when and as he wills, who
uses Christian nurture, as he uses Christian truth, to
regenerate the soul, and decides by Christian influences
the destiny of the soul, as by the conditions of the household he determines the worldly future of its members.
The family life, therefore, is the spiritual force which
we cannot afford to overlook, and I take it that one great
reason why the church seems now to be shorn so largely
of its aggressive power, is the low vitality of Christian
households.

It is this conception of family life and growth which
runs through the Old Testament as well as the New.
What a noble outline of the advancement and expansion
of the House of God is given in the exquisite prayer of
the old Psalm: "That our sons may be as plants grown
up in their youth; that our daughters may be as corner-
stones, polished after the similitude of a palace"!   The
imagery is as rich in suggestion as it is in beauty.   "Our
sons as plants grown up in their youth."   The seed
planted in the garden of the home, by the living water,
springs up in all native vigor and beauty.   The child
rises into manhood as the tree into the air, free, gracious,
strong, full of leaves and full of fruits, unfading and
perennial, because it is the garden of the Lord, and the
roots go down to living water.   As the gentle English
prelate said: "If a gentleman is to grow up, he must
grow like a tree: there must be nothing between him
and heaven."   The image of the daughters is radiant
with beauty, and suggests the noblest mission and work
of woman.   "Our daughters as corner pillars sculptured
to grace a palace."   For the woman, wife and mother, is
the corner-stone which binds together the family from
which she springs and the family to which she comes,

uniting both by her native beauty and exquisite polish, sculptured and polished to grace the palaces of man and of God. On her fidelity rests the family, society, the church, which is the house of God.

It is through these olive plants around the table; through these arrows in the hands of a mighty man, this heritage and reward of the Lord, that the Lord builds the house of the Happy man and of God. The unit of increase is the Household. The growth is by multiplication. The law of increase is unfailing, and the building up is symmetrical, continuous, silent, glorious. " The Lord doth build up Jerusalem; he gathereth the outcasts of Israel." He doth restore the prodigals and exiles to the Father's house. He brings the wanderers home again. But the great expansion is from within. As then, as in the days of Pentecost, so now the promise is unto us and to our children, and as many as the Lord our God shall call. This is the natural law of building the House, and it ought to be as certain as the processes of nature. The influences in the natural world are silent and gradual, but unceasing and unfailing. The spiritual forces which the Lord employs in the silent growth of his kingdom are unceasing and unfailing, too. The nurture of the Christian home! who can portray its power? The children are born within the house of God; the air they breathe is charged with heavenly influences; the conditions which envelop them are the mould of Christian thought and feeling; the power of holy example presses like the atmosphere on the whole surface of their being; while the unique, transcendant authority of the parent, that holds in its hand life and death, name and position, culture and religion, is paralleled by a love which is the only measure of the love of God. Oh! it is a sight that touches men and angels, when a strong

spirit that has tried to solve, unaided, the problems of
doubt and eternal hope, wounded, baffled, broken, comes
back at last, like a tired child, to repose upon the bosom
of his father's peace and his mother's comfort.

What, my friends, is the dominant influence of your
homes? "To impart a knowledge of the law to a child
conferred as great a spiritual distinction as if the man
had received the law on Mount Horeb," was a saying of
old among the Jews, and they added, that every other
engagement of a man should give place to this pre-emi-
nent duty. Is the church and the kingdom of God first
in the thoughts and speech of your family circle? Is
the teaching, the law of the home, that its services are
to be attended as an act of solemn worship, its obligations to take precedence of all others? Is there a true
confession of Jesus Christ before children, guests and
servants? The imperious prescription of the godless
social world has done so much to mutilate and destroy
the worship of the Sabbath, barely yielding to the Lord
the time for morning service, and stealing the afternoon
and evening of the Lord's own day for social diversion,
until even the more obscure in a community have decided it to be their duty to follow fashion in its war upon
worship. It ought to be true of every Christian home,
"the church in thy house "—that which is the Lord's in
thy house, or simply, "the Lord's in thy house."
There is a wealth of meaning in that old English word
Church. It comes to us transliterated through our
mother tongue from Paul's own word *kuriakon*, "that
which belongs to the Lord"; and it holds its place in
all modern languages, hardly changed in sound. When
we add, "in thy house," the abode of our dearest life,
the most sacred spot on earth, we have the very core of
heaven. For what is heaven but the church in our

Father's House? The walls of our little homes melt away into the immeasurable expanse of the city of God. The family circle widens into the household of the divine Father, from whom every family in heaven and on earth is named !

There is one sacred bond of the home life which binds the members together, and all to the throne of God, relaxed and sometimes cast aside by Christian households. It is the worship of the Family; the grouping of the whole band—father, mother, children—around the Family Altar in united prayer; the pillar of cloud, and guiding by day; the pillar of fire, lighting and guarding by night those who seek its sanctuary.

It was not a preacher, it was not a Christian man, who wrote *The Cottar's Saturday Night*. It was a man who drank himself to death in the meridian of life. But he was one of the poets of the century, and he wrote what he had seen and known, what had helped to make him intellectually great. And as he tells the story of the godly peasant home, the meal, the uncovered head, the big Bible, the reading of the Old and of the New, he sings—

> "When kneeling down to Heaven's Eternal King,
>   The saint, the father, and the husband prays;
>   Hope 'springs eternal on triumphant wing,'
>   That thus they all shall meet in future days;
>   There ever bask in uncreated rays,
>   No more to sigh or shed a bitter tear,
>   Together hymning their Creator's praise,
>   In such society, yet still more dear,
>   While circling time moves round in an eternal sphere.
>   From scenes like these old Scotia's grandeur springs,
>   That makes her loved at home, revered abroad;
>   Princes and lords are but the breath of kings;
>   An honest man's the noblest work of God!"

Will our children sing the same note, our friends, our households? What influence shall I exert on those who live with me, and on those who come after me? Shall unfeigned faith descend from father to son, from mother to daughter, to flower in some elect Timothys, whose lives shall witness, and whose speech shall confess, the glory of divine grace and truth? Oh! to send down to a thousand generations the unbroken traditions of a Christian ancestry, and the unbroken service of a pure conscience. For this we may well thank God on earth and in heaven too!

"I thank God, whom I serve from my forefathers," cry many of us to-day with grateful and exulting hearts.

> "My boast is not that I deduce my birth
> From loins enthroned, the rulers of the earth;
> But higher far my proud pretensions rise,
> The son of parents passed into the skies."

"The glory of children are their fathers." "I was my father's son, tender and only beloved in the sight of my mother." As I speak to-day, does not, for some of us, the old home come to life again, clear-cut and definite, every room projected before our eyes, as if we were once more children, and the shadow of the sun upon the dial had turned backward twenty, forty degrees? Come back, O prime of my youth! Come back, O image of my father, strong-hearted and gentle, who taught me also, and said unto me, "Let thy heart retain my words: The fear of the Lord is the beginning of knowledge. Forsake not the law of thy mother." Come back, sweet-faced and patient mother, on whose brow that law gleamed as on the mitre of the high-priest, holiness to the Lord. Thank God! the bond of the family is not broken by death. It leaps over the grave. It abides for aye in the

Celestial City. "In my Father's house are many mansions." From whom every family in heaven . . . . is named!

"I thank God that I do *not* serve him as my forefathers did," may, alas! be the boast of some here to-day. "I have outgrown the old faith, the old creed. I break with the traditions of the past. The old Bible, the old church, the old purity, are dead and buried. I am emancipated from the old superstitions."

Why does one despise the religion that is old? He does not reject the stores of the past in learning, in invention, in civilization. They are incorporated with the riches of the present. But some despise Christianity because it was the religion of their childhood. Because their fathers believed in the whole Bible, they are avowed infidels. Because their mothers lived and died and sang all the way in the faith of Christ, they will abandon it. They cut loose from the past heritage, and sever every heavenly cord.

It is possible to cut off the spiritual entail, to sell one's birthright for a mess of pottage; but, oh! it is a suicide, where more than blood is spilt, for, once accomplished, this man can find no place of repentance, even though he seek it with tears.

Do you remember the story of the Italian nobleman who, in his insane passion for gambling, had sacrificed nearly all of his ancestral possessions? One night, maddened by drink, he began to play desperately with a cool antagonist, who had before won a large portion of his wealth. The noble would win all or lose all. He staked his money, cattle, land, credit, and lost all. At last, in wild despair, he staked his name, a name which had been honored for centuries in his own and other lands. He lost that! Then the degradation and terror

of the man knew no bounds.   He had forfeited his ancestral name !   He fell upon his knees ; begged piteously
for its return—not for his wealth, or his lands, or his
cattle, only for his *name !*   But the pitiless winner would
not yield, and the wretched bankrupt rushed forth into
the darkness to disappear forever, a man without his
name.   What a fight the soul must make to lose its
spiritual birthright, of which the Christian name is the
symbol !   Over how many obstacles must the child of a
godly house leap to perish !   How much it sacrifices to
be lost !   How much !   Behold the shadowy forms which
stand weeping around the grave of a disinherited soul,
disinherited by its own suicidal hand !   The generations
of Christian forefathers, Christian parents, Christian
friends and kindred, Christian faith, Christian hope,
all surmounted, all sacrificed, for a sunless, Christless
grave!

I cannot close with this sad note.   I strike another
key.   It is the music of the divine home ; of a Father's
house in which is bread enough and to spare ; of a
Father's heart that sees a great way off, and is full, so
full, of compassion for every wanderer.

When, a few years ago, I sailed down the upper
Danube, the place which stirred me most was the castled
height of the river where Richard the Lion-hearted had
been entrapped and imprisoned on his return from the
Holy Land.   No one in England knew the place of his
captivity.   But his faithful minstrel, Blondel, journeyed
from city to city, from castle to castle, playing and singing under stone walls the strains which Richard knew
and loved; and, lo! as he played by this unknown
castle, the music stole into the prison of the king.   The
king made sign of his presence, and, once found, the
ransom and deliverance followed fast.

I play an old melody to-day. I touch the strings which sing of home and early faith; of a mother's love, of a father's God. O friend! does not the song find thee? Make signal of thy captivity. Come out of thy prison. There is a Friend without the gate. The ransom of a king is in his hands. Exiles from God and hope, or captives in sin, within the stone walls of an ill-spent, wasted and sorrowful past, I say unto you, there is joy in heaven over one sinner that repenteth!

Why Believers Should "Not Fear."

BY REV. A. W. PITZER, D D.,
Pastor of Central Presbyterian Church, Washington, D. C.

"Fear not, I am the first and the last : I am he that liveth and was dead : and, behold, I am alive for evermore, Amen : and have the keys of hell and of death."—Rev. i. 17, 18.

THE Apostle John was a prisoner on the island of Patmos for the sake of the gospel when he received this wondrous revelation of Jesus Christ to the churches. His companions in the apostolate had all passed away, and in a little while he, too, must go hence. From the rocky crags of Patmos, he could look across the beautiful waters of the Ægean, and see the coast line of Asia Minor, and almost to the sites of churches planted by apostolic hands. For him, the outlook was dark and dreary, and doubtless this last of the apostles had his seasons of fear and despondency.

He was in the spirit on the Lord's day, and in the midst of the seven golden candlesticks he saw one walking like unto the Son of man. He was clothed in full priestly garments, and his countenance was as the sun shineth in his strength. The vision was so majestic, so overpowering, that John fell at his feet as dead; then the glorified Redeemer laid his right hand on his servant, and said unto him, "Fear not." And through John he has said to every believer, and says to us to-day, "Fear not."

Years before, this august being had appeared in visible bodily presence, and with audible voice had spoken to Saul of Tarsus, and had chosen him to be a witness unto all men of what he saw and heard. Now once more he appears to the beloved disciple, who leaned upon his breast, and delivers a message, not only to him, but, through him, to all believers until the end of the age, when he shall return in glory from the skies. "Fear not," he says to John; "Fear not," he says to us.

Finite, incomplete, and dying, with eternity before us in such a world as this, we cannot pass through life without many fears.

One person has an intense dread of physical pain, he shrinks with horror from the mere thought of being laid upon a bed of sickness to be racked, week after week, with pain. Another is haunted with apprehensions of poverty; he fears that he will lose his place, his office, his occupation; that his income will be cut off; that he will be left, in his old age, helpless and penniless. Another is constantly looking forward with the most dismal forebodings to the hour of death. How shall he meet that dreadful enemy? How shall he pass safely through the gloom of the grave? or else, he is thinking of the dread issues of the invisible realm, and the awful realities that lie beyond the vail.

Let the weak, fearful, desponding child of God take courage; to every dread and anxiety and apprehension there comes to him from his Lord and Master, from his Friend and Brother, from him who has encountered every enemy, who has endured every possible human agony, and who has come off conqueror and more than conqueror over them all, "Fear not: I am the first and the last: I am he that liveth and was dead: and behold,

I am alive forevermore, Amen, and have the keys of hell and death.

In every congregation there are some weak and wearied ones, some tried and tempted ones, some heavy-laden, burdened ones, some doubting, desponding ones. To all such the Lord himself sends a word of cheer and comfort; and then he gives the reasons, and they are all found within himself, why believers should "fear not." Let us state and analyze the four reasons given by our Kingly Priest why his people should be of good courage:

I. *"I am He that Liveth"*; or, *I am the Living One.* These words do not simply mean that he who spake to John was at that time a living person, for this he must have been to be able to speak at all. They mean infinitely more than this: it is a claim made by this august person to the possession of an underived, an independent, and an eternal life.

Of all the mysteries in the universe, nothing is more inscrutable and mysterious than life. What it is, who knows? or, who can tell? Of its essence we know absolutely nothing. Life in the flower that to-day is and to-morrow dies; life in the animal, the man, the angel. We know something of the manifestations; nothing whatever of the essence. Attempt to grasp, to hold, to analyze it, it eludes you and disappears.

Science tells us that all life comes from life, *"omne virum, ex vivo."* There is no such thing known in the domain of science as spontaneous generation. Out of the dead there never has come life. All life, therefore, that we see and know in this sphere must come from preëxisting life in some higher realm and sphere of existence. Our lives are finite and dependent; there must therefore be some fountain of life, uncreated and independent, out of which all streams of life do flow.

In this Scripture, as elsewhere in the Word, Jesus Christ asserts his preëxistence and his eternity, "I am the first and the last and the living one. Before Abraham was, I am. Abraham rejoiced to see my day: he saw and was glad. In the beginning was the word, and the word was with God, and the word was God. All things were made by him, and without him was not anything made that was made." In him was life, and here we reach the infinite and eternal fountain of all finite and dependent life.

The names, titles, attributes, and works that are proper to God, and that are ascribed to God, are also given to Jesus Christ; if the Scriptures of both Testaments do not clearly teach his supreme Godhead, then language is incapable of expressing that thought. He is the origin and end of all things; the creator and upholder of all beings and all worlds; the life and the light of men; the resurrection and the life: the Alpha and the Omega; the first and the last; the prince of life, who is, and who was, and who is to come.

This glorious being, with knowledge that is omniscient, with power that is omnipotent, holding all forces, all agencies, all beings, and all worlds in his hand, says to every timid, frightened, weary and heavy-laden child of God, "Fear not, I am your friend, your brother, and all the exhaustless treasures of heaven and the Godhead are pledged for your safety; I will make all things work, I will make them work together, in harmony, in co-operation, for your good." Surely if God be for us, we should not fear anything that may be against us.

II. *And was Dead, or became Dead.*—This is the second reason why the believer should not fear. It is not merely that his Saviour is divine, and therefore able to keep him from falling, and to present him faultless before the throne; but this power of almightiness is directed by inextinguishable love, a love higher than the heights, deeper than the depths, that even death could not chill nor destroy.   It is as if the Son of man said to John and to us, I, who am divine, who have all power, have loved you unto death, in death, and through death. I became dead for you, because I loved you.

The Godhead of the Son could not die, and so the word became flesh and dwelt among us.   Godhead united to itself a true body and a reasonable soul, and in the God man Christ Jesus, this human soul and body could be separated one from the other, and this was done, and this was death, and thus the living one became dead.   He said I have power to lay down my life and I have power to take it up again.   It was because he was God that he could offer up himself, lay down his life and take it up again; because he was man, he could die.

Did this most remarkable person, this living one really become dead?   This is a question of fact, and must be decided by the testimony of the witnesses.

The witnesses say, he gave up the ghost, or literally he breathed out his soul.   Father, into thy hands I commend my spirit.   As God, he separated his human soul from its body, and sent it to his Father God.

When the soldiers came to hasten the death of the three condemned men, who hung upon the cross, they found Jesus already dead, at which they marvelled, and did not break his bones.   When one of the soldiers thrust his spear into his side, near the heart, then came out not blood only, but water and blood.   His body was taken down from the cross by his friends, who prepared it for burial, which they would never have done, had not life been extinct.   The whole New Testament record affords the most conclusive evidence that the

Christ of gospel history did indeed become dead. He that liveth was dead.

But why should this death rather than any other death afford grounds for courage and comfort? Why should the death of a powerful friend be given as the reason why the believer should fear not? Ordinarily, we feel far more secure in the presence of a living than a dead friend. The live man can help, comfort and sympathize with us. The dead man can do us no good whatever; a living dog is better than a dead lion.

It would have sounded strangely to the ears of Israel if it had been said to them, "Moses is dead; fear not." How bewildering to the seven thousand in Israel who had not bowed the knee to Baal had Elisha said, "Elijah is dead; fear not." How incomprehensible to the Corinthians had Titus said, "Paul is dead; fear not." What encouragement to the Hollanders to announce to them the death of their beloved William; or, to the French the death of the great Napolean; or to Americans the death of Lincoln; or to Confederates the death of Jackson? These words, as applied to any other person than to Jesus of Nazareth, would be filled with bitter mockery. Not so when he uses them as a ground of comfort to his disciples.

I died for you; I took your place; I bore your sins in my own body on the tree; I paid the price; I endured the penalty; I magnified the law; I obtained redemption. The accursed cross, the sacrificial death, the atoning blood—these give peace, and comfort, and courage, and strength to the soul of the believer. To every whisper of Satan's malignity, to every thunder of the law, to every alarm of conscience, to every foreboding of the future, to every apprehension of the judgment, to every fear of hades, the Lord Jesus lays his pierced hand on the believer and says, "Fear not; I am the first and the last and the living one, and I became dead for you—died that you might live."

III. "And *Behold, I am Alive Forevermore.*"—This presents a third reason for the believer's confidence. This Son of man who speaks to him, not only became dead, but he passed through the gates of the grave with the tread of a conqueror; he went down into the regions of the dead, and bound the strong man armed, who had the power of death and who kept his goods. He spoiled the principalities and power of darkness, and came forth from the realms of the dead clad in the radiant glories of the resurrection life.

His Godhead wrought in the grave and lifted his mortal body up into immortality and brought back his sinless human soul from his Father's bosom to reinhabit his glorified human body, and thus he became the first-fruits of all them that slept. "And now, Christ being raised from the dead, dieth no more; death hath no more dominion over him." The person who speaks to John is not merely the Living One, the first and the last, not merely the Son of Mary, but the glorified Son of man, with his now exalted humanity united eternally to his Godhead. He can, indeed, sing, "Oh, death, where is thy sting? Oh, grave, where is thy victory?" for his corruptible has put on incorruption, and his mortal has put on immortality. After death has reigned with resistless power over the race for four thousand years, his conqueror has at last been found—the great victor has at last appeared. Man is, indeed, redeemed, and the resurrection is no longer a hope, but a fact and a reality.

Alive again, and alive forevermore. The dead who had been brought back to a mortal life in the flesh were not alive forevermore, for they had not experienced the transforming power of the resurrection. The daughter of Jairus, the son of the widow of Nain, and Lazarus, died again; they were not made alive forevermore. But here is one who can never die again, because he has conquered death, and, therefore, over him death hath no power.

The hand laid with such regal majesty and yet with such infinite tenderness on the believer, is one that bears the print of the nails—a hand that was nailed to the cross, but it is also a hand that burst the bonds of death, and is now clothed with all power in heaven and on earth. Surely, we need not fear when guided and defended by him, who not only died, but who is alive forevermore.

IV. "And *have the Keys of Hell and Death*," or, as in the latest revision, "the Keys of Death and Hell."—This is the fourth reason given why the believer should "not fear."

The key is the symbol of ownership, of possession, of legal power and authority. Ordinarily, the person who has the key of a house is the owner of the house—has rightful possession and authority in it and over it. He can open and shut the doors, go in and out as he pleases, admit or exclude persons according to his own good pleasure. When a contractor builds a house and his work is completed according to the agreement, he delivers the keys to the lawful owner. The key is evidence of ownership. The Lord Jesus Christ, as risen and glorified Son of man, has the keys of death and the grave. He is the rightful owner of the whole invisible world, because he humbled himself and became obedient unto death. God hath highly exalted him and given him a name above every name, and invested him with power and authority over all worlds visible and invisible. Why should the believer fear when his Lord and Saviour has supreme authority over death and all realms of the unseen world?

There are two objects of fear to almost every human being; there is the dread of death and the dread of the issues that await us after death. Let us look at these in the order of nature or in the order of the Canterbury version. Death first, then hades, the world of the dead. Death is emphatically the king of terrors; there is something fearful and repulsive in death. He always comes with a sting, and is seldom, if ever, a welcome visitor. Men may deny the fact of sin; they cannot deny the fact of death; and yet God always connects the two. Men die because they are sinners. Sin is the cause of death. That which invests death with such appalling horror is sin; the sting of death is sin.

To leave this world forever, to look no more upon the glad sunlight that fills and floods the heavens and the earth; to see no more the sky bending in beauty over us; to hear no more the song of birds, the murmur of the sea, the happy voices of childhood; to leave these homes of ours forever and forever; to say farewell to the loved ones of earth; to leave these bodies of ours, these tabernacles of our souls, in the cold and silent grave. This, this is death. Can we say less than that it is an enemy, and the sum and culmination of all earthly ills? The grave is chilly, cold, cheerless, damp, dark, dismal, and yet it is the home for these bodies of ours. What millions and tens of millions have gone down into its silent embrace! The mighty kings and warriors of old who filled the world with terror and alarm; statesmen who led their people in paths of greatness and renown; poets who sang so sweetly that all men rose up to call them blessed. These, with the unknown and unnumbered multitudes, the old and the young, the rich and the poor, the noble and the base, all, all have passed away into the grave and to the pale realm of shades. The vast procession, that started in Eden with the death of Abel, has moved on without a halt or a break, silently and sadly, to the tomb. It is moving to-day, and at each tick of thy watch one soul passes into the unseen.

It is vain to say that we do not fear death. Some say they do not, and, perhaps, they may not, but surely such a dreadful event in human existence should not be lightly esteemed, and should produce in all thoughtful minds salutary dread. But the Christian need not fear to die! There is one who is his friend, who has overcome death and who holds the keys of the grave and the unseen world, and who says to him: ''Fear not.''

The gates of death cannot open for you one moment before the appointed time, and he, who has the keys and opens the doors, will go with you into the darkness and conduct you safely into the light and glory on the other side.

It is appointed unto men once to die, and after death the judgment. It is not death, only, that men fear, but what is beyond—hades, that vast and eternal world into which all shall enter, where each one shall dwell forever.

Hades with its unearthly inhabitants, its disembodied spirits, its angels and demons, and spirits of the just made perfect, its eternal retribution, its worm that never dies, its fire that is never quenched, its ceaseless torments, its accusing conscience, its hopeless and helpless despair. Who will befriend us there?

To every alarm of the believing soul there comes the re-assuring word, ''Fear not, I have the keys of all

the doors of this vast and unseen world." His feet as
burnished brass tread down his and our enemies, his
voice as the sound of many waters compels the obedience of the unearthly inhabitants of that infinite realm,
and from the glory of his countenance, shining as the
sun in his strength, none can escape.

Angels, principalities and powers are subject to him,
and he is King of kings, and Lord of lords, and this
glorious person is our steadfast and unfailing friend.   He
loves us with an intense, a divine, a personal love, and
with his almighty hand laid upon each believer, he says,
"Fear not." My Christian brother, this is the message
sent you, nay brought to you, by your Lord himself.
Why should you fear, when all things are yours, whether
Paul, or Apollos, or Cephas, or the world, or life, or
death, or things present, or things to come; all are
yours, and ye are Christ's, and Christ is God's. You
may have come this day to your Father's house, weary
and heavy laden, pressed down with many anxieties,
and doubts and fears. Listen, I beseech you, to this
voice from Patmos, "Fear not; I am the first and the
last: I am he that liveth, and was dead; and behold, I
am alive for evermore, Amen; and have the keys of hell
and of death."

Perhaps you can sing with Mrs. M. C. Edwards her
little hymn, entitled "God Cares for Me:"

" I sat in the door of eventide,
    My heart was full of fears,
And I saw the landscape before me lie,
    Through the mist of the burning tears.
I thought to myself the world is dark,
    No light, nor joy I see,
Nothing but toil and want is mine,
    And no one cares for me.

" A sparrow was twittering at my feet,
　　With its beautiful, auburn head,
　And it looked at me with dark mild eyes,
　　As it picked up crumbs of bread:
　And said to me in words as plain
　　As the words of a bird could be,
　'I am only a sparrow, a worthless bird,
　　But the dear Lord cares for me.'

" A lily was growing beside the hedge
　　Beautiful, tall, and white,
　And it shone through the glossy leaves of **green**
　　Like an angel clothed in light;
　And it said to me, as it waved its head
　　On the breezes soft and free,
　'I am only a lily, a useless flower,
　　But the Master cares for me.'

" Then it seemed to me that the hand of the loving **Lord,**
　　Over my head was laid,
　And he said to me, 'Oh! faithless child,
　　Wherefore art thou dismayed?
　I clothe the lilies, I feed the birds,
　　I see the sparrow's fall,
　Nothing escapes my watchful eye,
　　My kindness is over all.' "

THE RULER'S QUESTION.

BY REV. J. H. BRYSON, D. D.,

Pastor of the Presbyterian Church, Huntsville, Ala.

"Good Master, what good thing shall I do, that I may have eternal life?"—MATT. xix. 16.

THE interesting incident, to which the words of the text refer, is given by three of the evangelists. This short discourse with the young Jewish ruler evidently made a very profound impression upon the minds of the disciples. They were made to see the spirituality of the divine law, and the severity of its demands, in a light which they had never contemplated. Their eyes were opened to the fact, that the law required something more than a mere external conformity to its precepts, that its claims embraced the inward affections of the heart, and that no obedience could be perfect which did not originate and rest upon the principle of love. The divine Master takes this occasion to expound the true nature of the law of God, and show the broad sweep of its demands ; and he does so in a way that the important truth cannot possibly be misapprehended. The exposition, which he gives, is a startling disclosure both to the young ruler and to the disciples. They see, perhaps for the first time, that all acceptable obedience must be founded in love, and that love to God is the chief and great requirement of the law. The painful discovery is made, that human actions may conform to the letter of the law, and yet be devoid of the very element which gives them merit.

The doctrines taught by Jesus Christ in this interesting interview with the young Jewish ruler are of general application; we are all alike concerned in the principles brought to light in this discourse. "*What must I do to inherit eternal life?*" is a question which has claims upon us, which we do well to consider. It is of the utmost importance to know what is the true solution of this problem. How is eternal life to be obtained? By what process is the inestimable boon to be secured? Where is it to be found? By what pathway is it to be reached? What course of conduct must be adopted, that will ultimate in its possession? Such inquiries justly deserve the most serious attention. No blessing can be compared to that of eternal life. Before it all else sinks into insignificance. It is the one matter of chief concern which should put every other question in the background. We can place before ourselves no more serious inquiry than that contained in the words of the text: "*Good Master, what good thing shall I do, that I may have eternal life?*"

Our discourse upon these words will be divided into three parts—

I. *The facts of this interesting incident.*

II. *The solution which the Master gives.*

III. *The result of this interview.*

Notwithstanding the general prejudice against Jesus Christ, we find a number of intelligent Jews came to inquire of him concerning the doctrines he taught and take counsel of him as a wise teacher in spiritual things. We have two cases presented by the different evangelists of particular interest; the one was that of Nicodemus, a distinguished rabbi, who came to Jesus by night at the beginning of his public ministry; the other, that of a wealthy young ruler, who came to Jesus at the close of his labors in Perea. The two rulers seemed to be alike desirous of being instructed by Jesus Christ. Both wanted more light, and were honestly and earnestly seeking after truth. The two cases gave a favorable opportunity to the blessed Master to bring to light very important doctrines. Nicodemus opened the way to announce the profound doctrine of regeneration by the power of the Holy Spirit; that it was a fundamental change wrought upon man's moral nature, and that it was an indispensable requisite to admission to the kingdom of God. The young ruler, in his inquiry as to what he must do to inherit eternal life, gave a most suitable opportunity to exhibit the spirituality of the divine law, that its claims extended to the motive which prompted the act, as well as to the act itself.

The case of this young man, who came running to the Master, and earnestly inquired, "*What good thing he must do to have eternal life*," is one which deserves our most careful study. Human actions, performed under the most favorable circumstances, are here brought to the severe test of a perfect law; an infallible judge presides, and there can be no possible mistake in the conclusion.

The incident referred to in the text occurred near the close of the public ministry of Jesus Christ as he was passing through Perea and approaching Jerusalem for the last time. This young man who came to the Master to inquire what he must do to inherit eternal life, was of high standing among his people; he was a ruler, a member of the chief council of the nation. He had great wealth, and was distinguished for his intellectual and social culture. "Better than this, he was both amiable and was virtuous; he had made it, from the first, an object of worthy ambition to be just, and to be generous, and use the advantages of his position to win, in a right way, the favor of his fellow-men. But notwithstanding he was successful in all the aims of his past life, there was a restlessness, a dissatisfaction at heart, a deep consciousness that he had not yet obtained that for which his better nature was longing." He had heard Jesus speak of eternal life, something evidently far higher than anything he had yet attained, and he wondered how it might be secured. To his mind, there appeared but one possible way to secure this great blessing, and that was to do some work of extraordinary merit; and so he comes to Jesus with the pointed inquiry, "*Good Master, what good thing shall I do that I may have eternal life?*"

Jesus knew the prevailing thought in this young man's mind, that eternal life was to be merited by some extraordinary work which might be performed; that he regarded it as the reward of some higher virtue which he might yet attain. The very form of the question shows that the young man was fully possessed of this idea, that the title to eternal life could be secured by his own effort. He wanted this great blessing, and if he only knew what would secure it he was, as he supposed, ready and willing to do it. The disciples and the multitude gathered around, were anxiously waiting to hear what answer Jesus would give to the question which the young ruler had so earnestly asked. Perhaps, to their surprise, he said, "If thou wilt enter into life, *keep the commandments*," and the young man immediately responded, Which? not conscious that any of the commandments of which he had any knowledge had been neglected. Jesus then said, "*Thou shalt do no murder. Thou shalt not commit adultery. Thou shalt not steal. Thou shalt not bear false witness. Honor thy father and thy mother; and thou shalt love thy neighbor as thy self."* The young man listened to the Master as he detailed the various precepts which the law enjoins, and promptly, without the slightest misgiving, he answered, "All these have I observed from my youth. What lack I yet?" He was perfectly honest and sincere in making this reply. He was satisfied that his obedience to these commandments during his past life was everything it should be. To his fellow-men and to himself there would seem to be no defect in his character; he was honest and upright, just and generous to all. To this noble character and virtuous life, he exhibited an amiability of temper and disposition, that drew forth the admiration of all who knew him. Indeed, so attractive did this young ruler appear as he knelt at the feet of Jesus, declaring that he had kept all the commandments from his youth, that it is said, *"Jesus beholding him loved him."* As a certain writer has appropriately said, "It was something new and refreshing to the Saviour's eye to see such a specimen as this of truthfulness and purity, of all that was morally lovely and of good report among the *rulers* of the Jews. Here was no hypocrite, no fanatic; here was one who had *not* learned to wear the garb of sanctimoniousness as a cover for all kinds of self-indulgence. Here was one who had thus far escaped the contagion of his age and sect, who was really striving to keep himself from all that was wrong, and endeavoring to be towards his fellow-men all that he understood the law of God required." And as Jesus looked upon this noble young ruler of wealth and distinction, humbly kneeling at his feet asking the way of eternal life, *"he loved him."* Here is the highest tribute that has ever been paid to that moral goodness which is attainable by human effort. None can ever hope to surpass it; few ever equal it. To be so upright, so just, so amiable,

12

as to win the love of the Saviour, is an attainment few, if any, will venture to claim for themselves. And yet, if it were true that any one could be classed with this young ruler, it will be seen that eternal life is not secured, and the deep cravings of the heart are not satisfied. This very fact ought to have led that young man to suspect that there was something wrong in himself. If his morality was sufficient, why did he come to Jesus at all? He was a rigid moralist, but his soul had never felt the first pulsations of a new life; his heart was not happy with a sense of the divine love, and he knew not the meaning of forgiveness. "Beneath all the pleasing show of outward moralities, there was in that young ruler's breast a lamentable want of any true regard to God, or any recognition of his supreme and paramount claims. His heart, his trust and his treasure were in earthly, not heavenly things. He needed a severe lesson to teach him this fact and to lay bare at once the true state of things in his soul." He had yet to learn what true obedience to the law of God was. He had yet to discover the pure spirituality of the law, and have its claims flashed upon his naked soul, demanding that love to God shall be the prime motive of every act of obedience. It was a critical moment in this young man's history. He was at the feet of the divine Master, who knew what he was, and whose searching eye read the hidden thoughts of his heart. And when he said, I have kept the commandments, and asked the question, "*What lack I yet?*" Jesus said unto him, "*If thou wilt be perfect, go and sell that thou hast, and give to the poor; and come and follow me.*" "*And when he heard that saying, he went away sorrowful, for he had great possessions.*" The one thing lacking was not the mere renunciation of his property and giving it to the poor; it was a supreme devotedness to God, and clearly indicated duty which he lacked—a willingness to give up anything, yea, everything, if God required it, when the holding of it was inconsistent with fidelity to him. Jesus Christ struck directly at the idol of this young ruler's heart, and he required the instant and absolute dethronement. The demand was refused. He would neither give his property to the poor, nor would he follow Christ. He could not bear the test. He was not what he was supposed to be. This thought brings us to the second part of our discourse—

II. *The solution the Master gives of the case of this young man.*

We have here a most signal exhibition of the fact that amiability of character and a rigid moral life furnish no assurance that the heart is right with God. This young man had the outward appearance of keeping the law; he was honest, he was upright, he respected all the rights of his neighbors; but he did not love God supremely; he had never given his heart with all its wealth of love to God; he had never brought himself to the point to say that the divine will should be his will. Although he knew it was his duty to dispose of his property to the poor and follow Christ, he was not willing to take the step; he chose to do the very opposite, to keep his possessions and go away. Such was the temper and spirit of this young man, whose moral character a little while ago appeared so attractive. It was his boast that he had kept the law from his youth up, and yet his obedience was wanting in the particular element which alone can render any obedience acceptable, and that is supreme love to God. The specific demand of the law is, "Thou shalt love the Lord thy God with all thy heart, soul, mind and strength." Every precept of the decalogue is inlaid in this principle; and no obedience can be perfect that is not prompted by this love. Here is the fatal rock on which this young ruler, with all his morality and amiability of character, was wrecked. He had large possessions which he loved more than God, and he would rather keep them than part with them to follow Christ.

It is not to be understood that the Master is here laying down a *universal condition fo Christian discipleship*. No such thing is intended; he puts no premium on poverty, and he puts no penalty on wealth. It is a particular treatment which he adopts for a specific case. If the difficulty in the way of following Christ had been the love of pleasure, or the love of power, or any other object, the test which the case needed would have been framed accordingly. We are not forbidden to love any object that is properly worthy of our love, but we are to allow no object, whatever it may be, to stand in the way of our following Christ. God is justly entitled to the highest place in our affections, and no idol can ever be allowed to usurp that sacred throne. This is the very difficulty that stands in the way of many persons becoming Christians. I may be addressing some one to-day who is stumbling just here. You perhaps have said, "I would like to be a follower of Jesus," "I would like to become a child of God," "I would like to join the church," but there is this difficulty in the way, and I cannot do it.

I beg you to consider most seriously what you are doing. Your case is precisely that of the young man who came to Christ. You are allowing some particular object to come between you and your recognized duty to God. You have something which you are not willing to give up, something which you are not willing to sacrifice, to follow Jesus. So long as this is true you never can become a Christian. You may be amiable and lovely, you may be honest and upright, you may be generous and benevolent—all this will not give you eternal life. God must be enthroned in your affections, your heart must be given to him before you can be saved. Whenever the sinner comes to the point that he is willing to give up all for Christ, every difficulty disappears at once, and he finds himself, he scarcely knows how, in possession of a new life and a blessed hope.

How different would it have been with the young Jewish ruler, if he had been willing to give up all to follow the Master. He was, perhaps, unable to see how such a step could give *eternal life*, but God required it, and it was his duty to obey. To him eternal life was not possible in any other way. And so it is now we have the unequivocal word of the Master: "*If any man will be my disciple, let him deny himself, take up his cross and follow me.*" On no other terms can salvation be found. And yet there is a particular something which keeps many a sinner from becoming a follower of Christ. Each individual has his particular [hinderance, which prevents him from doing what he knows he ought to do. These difficulties, whatever they may be, will be sure to stand between the sinner and his Saviour just so long as he chooses to let them be there. But can he consent that any difficulty, whatever may be its magnitude, shall keep him back from discharging that highest of all duties, *giving his heart to God*? Let no one be deceived here. The hinderances that keep the sinner back from the Saviour are hinderances only so long as he *chooses to make them such*. All difficulties vanish so soon as the sinner makes up his mind to trust all to the Saviour; and there is no obstacle to this trust but his own will.

The third part of our discourse was to consider—

III. *The result of this interview between the young ruler and Jesus Christ.*

When the question was asked so reverently at the feet of the Master, "*What good thing shall I do, that I may have eternal life,*" it was natural to suppose the young man would willingly do whatever might be required of him to obtain this blessing. Such, however, was not the case. When "eternal life" was offered to him on terms so different from what he had supposed, he declined it. He would willingly have undertaken to do some extraordinary work, if thereby he could merit, or be entitled to eternal life, but he would have it on no other condition. He wanted the blessing, but he must have it on his own terms and in his own way. The case of this young man is a fair illustration of what is daily taking place under the preaching of the gospel. Persons are asking what they must do to be saved, but they are unwilling to do what that gospel requires; and salvation is not possible in any other way. It is true eternal life was once offered to our race as the reward of perfect obedience, but that opportunity was lost forever when Adam sinned and fell. Obedience to law is not now the source of spiritual life to our sin-cursed race. The law has no life-giving power. Under the "covenant of grace," however, a new order of things is introduced. *Eternal life* is now offered as "the gift of God through Jesus Christ our Lord." It is no longer a question of doing, it is a question solely of faith, faith in a particular person. Believe on Jesus and thou shalt be saved. It is an astounding procedure, filling heaven and earth with amazement. Still, it is true. Faith, humble, child-like faith, is all that is demanded of the sinner that he may have eternal life. Whatever may be the mysteries about faith, it is the sinner's own individual act, for which he is held responsible, and he should not delay to put its virtue to the test. He, who believes, is saved, saved immediately, saved for ever. *"He that believeth on the Son hath everlasting life; he that believeth not the Son, shall not see life, but the wrath of God abideth on him."*

Morality, amiability of character, and uprightness of conduct, are all very good, they are qualities which challenge our admiration and love, but they are insufficient to deal with the fearful questions of *sin* and *guilt*, and *death*. Faith is the mighty power the sinner needs. It opens to him the vast treasures of a Saviour's love. It wipes out all the disastrous consequences of sin, and fills his new-born soul with joy and rejoicing. It readjusts his relations to the divine law in a harmony that can never be broken, and it transforms his whole nature into the divine image, which he shall wear for ever. This is the precious message of the gospel: *"God so loved the world, that he gave his only begotten Son, that whosoever believeth in him should not perish, but have everlasting life."*

THE CHILDREN OF THE COVENANT:
THEIR PRIVILEGES AND RESPONSIBILITIES.

BY REV. S. W. DAVIES, D. D.,

Pastor of the Presbyterian Church, Fayetteville, Ark.

"Ye are the children of the prophets, and of the covenant which God made with our fathers, saying unto Abraham, And in thy seed shall all the kindreds of the earth be blessed. Unto you first God, having raised up his Son Jesus, sent him to bless you, in turning away every one of you from his iniquities."— Acts iii. 25, 26,

WHAT is the covenant here referred to? In what sense were the Jews whom the apostle addressed, and in what sense are all baptized persons now, children of this covenant? And what are the benefits and duties resulting from this relation?

The covenant here referred to, as the terms used to describe it indicate, is the covenant which God made with Abraham, sometimes called the the Covenant of Circumcision, from its original sealing ordinance. The record of its institution is contained in the seventeenth chapter of Genesis. This covenant marks an important epoch in the history of redemption. From it dates the origin of the church as a visible, organized body, distinct from the family and the state. It was made with Abraham as the representative of the faithful of all ages and nations (Rom. iv. 11, 12, and Gal. iii. 29); and its design and effect was to organize believers and their children into a visible society or church; separating them from the unbelieving world, at first by the outward

rite of circumcision, and afterwards by baptism.   The
component elements of the church existed before this
covenent.   There was a revelation of the Saviour and of
the way of salvation through him ; there were believers,
and there were institutions and ordinances of divine worship, for the instruction, the strengthening and comfort
of believers.   But there was no visible church organization, separate and distinct from the family and the state.
On the other hand, from this time forward, through the
entire Scriptures, the visible church can be distinctly
traced as a separate organized society, with a government
and officers established in it; as a body externally called
to the privilege of receiving the oracles of God, of being
under the charge of Jehovah, as his peculiar people, and
of being the special beneficiary of the blessings of the
covenant.

If starting with the church *as an existing institution*,
you undertake to find its origin by tracing its history
backward to its source, you will search in vain for it
anywhere short of this covenant with Abraham.   All are
agreed that it has not originated since the age of the
apostles.   And if you examine the Acts of the Apostles
and the later books of the New Testament you will find
abundant references to ''the church'' as an existing
institution, but there is no account of its organization.
The gospels, in like manner, are absolutely silent on this
point, a fact which cannot be accounted for, if, as some
would have us believe, the church was organized by the
Lord Jesus, or by his great forerunner, John the Baptist.
So through all the ages back to Moses we can trace the
existence of the church.   And even Moses found it in
existence when he began his mission ; for it was to the
assembled elders of Israel, the representatives of the
church as an organized body, that he was directed by the

Lord to present his credentials. But when we take a step further back in the history, and come to Abraham, we find no longer any references pointing us still backward; but here stands this peculiar transaction, constituting him "the father of many nations," under "an everlasting covenant," with a special "seal," marking and separating him and his seed from the world. Here then, we are warranted in concluding, we have found the object of our search; since no where else, as we have traced the history backward, have we found anything like a divine charter or covenant creating this singular and evidently divine institution.

We are justified, therefore, in asserting, that the covenant with Abraham, to which the apostle refers in the text, is the divine charter of the church, as heretofore and still existing; and that there has never been but one church, in the broad sense in which we here use the term. There has not been an Old Testament church and a New Testament church, a Jewish church and a Christian church, in the sense of two separate, independent and in some sense antagonistic organizations; but only an Old Testament *form*, and a New Testament *form* of the one only church of the living God. Its outward ordinances and modes of worship have been changed under different dispensations to suit the requirements of the changing times and circumstances. But the church itself has not been dissolved, nor its divine and everlasting charter annulled. It was in this church that God "set some apostles, some prophets, and some pastors and teachers under the new dispensation." It was from this church that the unbelieving Jews were cast out after they had rejected their Messiah; and it was into this same church that the believing Gentiles were grafted, when they believed the gospel and turned from their iniquities unto God. (Rom. xi. 17–20.)

By this covenant, made with Abraham and his seed, as the representatives of believers and their children in all ages, not only are they organized into a body distinct from the world, called the church ; but certain privileges and blessings are guaranteed to them. These are expressed in the declarations, "I will be a God to thee and to thy seed after thee," and "in thy seed shall all the nations of the earth be blessed." In which God indicates his purpose to be a God to this peculiar body of people in a special sense ; to dwell among them, to manifest himself to them and to bless them, as he does not the world, and through them to make known his grace and salvation to the nations. They are his peculiar people, the special objects of his favor and care ; and among them he dwells and manifests the glory of his grace. To them are committed the oracles of God. Theirs are the covenants and the promises. For their gathering, edification and comfort the ministry of the word is ordained, and the ordinances of divine worship instituted and maintained ; and they are God's chosen and commissioned agents for disseminating the knowledge of his truth and salvation among their fellow-men.

Now of this covenant with the fathers, organizing the visible church, and guaranteeing to it these precious privileges, the Apostle Peter, in the text, tells the unconverted Jews of his day that they were "the children" or heirs. By which he means, that they were parties to the covenant and interested in its provisions. In other words, they were members of the church and participants in its privileges. And inasmuch as the covenant with Abraham has never been annulled, and the church of to-day is the legitimate successor, the actual continuation of the church which was organized under that covenant, the baptized children of believing parents

sustain a similar relation to the church and its privileges.
They are not made members of the church by their baptism any more than the children of Israelitish parents
were made members by their circumcision. But the
latter were circumcised, and the former are now baptized,
because of their being members. It is in reference to
this that believers are called *saints*, and their children are
said to be *holy*. By this it is not meant that they are
sinless, but that they are consecrated to God. They
belong to the Lord, they are separated and set apart to
the service of the Lord. And as the parents are holy, so
also is their offspring. "The believing husband sancti-
fieth the unbelieving wife; and the believing wife sancti-
fieth the unbelieving husband; else were your children
unholy; but now are they holy." That is to say, the
children of believing parents are consecrated to God,
members of the church, and sharers in its privileges, by
virtue of their relation to their parents; and their baptism
is simply the outward sign and symbol of their membership.

But when we affirm that the children of believing
parents are members of the visible church and partakers
of its privileges, we do not mean to be understood as
holding and teaching that they, in all respects, stand on
exactly the same footing in the church as their believing
parents. Our little children are citizens of the state,
subject to its authority, and entitled to its protection.
And they are such by virtue of their relation to their
parents; but they are *minors*. They do not enjoy the
privilege of transacting business in their own names, of
voting or of holding office. Their citizenship is compassed with certain limitations until they reach a certain
age. So in the church, the children of believers are
members, but not in full communion. They are not

admitted to the Lord's table, nor to the privilege of voting and holding office in the church. There is this difference, however, between the minor in the state and the minor in the church : the minor in the state is admitted to the rights and privileges of full citizenship when he attains to a certain age ; but in the church the minor is invested with the rights and privileges of full membership as soon as he gives evidence of personal piety, and not until he does give such evidence. Hence the children of believing parents, who do not give evidence of a change of heart and personal faith in the Lord Jesus Christ, are members of the church in a state of spiritual minority, even though they may be mature men and women.

But though justly and properly debarred from the special privileges which I have mentioned, unconverted children of the covenant, by virtue of their connection with the church, enjoy many peculiarly precious and exalted privileges. Their church membership, though often undervalued and despised, is far from being a mere nominal thing. Among the precious privileges secured to the children of the covenant by their connection with the church, may be mentioned—

1. The example, training, instructions, and prayers of pious parents. How much depends on early training. How infinitely important to men's temporal and eternal interests that this early training should be of the right kind. And what an inestimably precious heritage are the prayers of consecrated fathers and mothers. Is it, then, a matter of small consequence that you were born in a godly home, and of parents who themselves feared God; and who recognized their religious obligations to you, who pledged themselves by solemn vows to train you up in the nurture and admonition of the Lord, and

who not only continually prayed with and for you, but
taught you to pray for yourselves? Have you ever re-
flected, you who have had pious parents, how different
is your condition, and how great have been your advantages over those whose parents are pagans, or like many
that you know around you, unbelieving, irreligious, and
wicked; who never pray with or for their children, never
teach them to pray, or to read God's word, or to go to
God's house on the Sabbath, but suffer them to grow up
in ignorance, irreligion, and vice? Whatever advantages
you enjoy in these respects, you owe them to the fact
that you are children of the covenant.

2. Another benefit which you derive from your connection with the church, through your pious parents, is
the oversight, the instruction and the pastoral care of
the officers of the church. This is a privilege by no
means to be despised. It throws around you safeguards,
and affords you advantages, for securing your own personal salvation not enjoyed by others. It is a very great
advantage to have been taught to respect the Sabbath
and the house of God, and from childhood to have known
the Scriptures. But as experience proves, the instructions and example of pious parents need to be followed
up, and reinforced by the affectionate oversight, the wise
counsels, and the tender warnings and appeals of the
faithful officers of God's house, and the sanctifying, re-
straining and elevating influences of the instructions and
worship of the sanctuary. These are, under God, most
powerful and effective means of bringing men to a saving
knowledge of God, and a personal consecration of themselves to his service. And it is to this circumstance
that their connection with the church, brings them
directly and constantly under these influences, that we
are to attribute the significant fact, that the great majority

of all true converts come from among the children of the covenant.

3. But the benefit of greatest value involved in your hereditary connection with the church, is the intimate and peculiar relation into which it brings you with God himself. As children of the covenant you stand in a different relation to God from the children of unbelievers. He stands pledged to be a God to you in a sense in which he is not their God. You are his people in a sense in which they are not. You are lambs of his flock. His name is upon your brows. You are under his special guardianship and care. You are objects of his most tender interest and regard. "However wayward you may be; however forgetful of him and of your duty to him, the Great Shepherd does not forget you." He thinks of you as a wanderer from his fold. He pities you in your wanderings, and longs to see you turn from your iniquities and come back to him. This is what Peter meant when to the Jews, who like you were "children of the covenant," and had like you received the seal of the covenant in infancy, he said, "Unto you first," as those in whom he felt the deepest interest, and for whom he had the most anxious solicitude, "Unto you first, God having raised up his Son, sent him to bless you, in turning away every one of you from his iniquities." For though, thank God, the Saviour and the gospel are for all men, and "whosoever will may come and take of the water of life freely"; yet there is a sense in which they are specially for his covenant people. For when God sent forth Jesus his Son, he sent him *first*, not to the Greeks, or to the Romans, or to any other Gentile nation, but to his own covenant people. And so still, when he comes by his word and Spirit to bless and to save, it is to you, the children of the cove-

nant, *first*, that he comes, and afterwards to others. You are permitted therefore to feel, without presumption, that you are nearer to him. "You may go to him with more freedom in prayer. You have special promises that you can plead. Like the psalmist you cannot only say, "O Lord, truly I am thy servant"; but you can also say, "I am the son of thine handmaid." You can plead out only the promises that are made to those who penitently turn to God; but you can plead the promises that are made to "the children, and to the children's children of such as love him and keep his commandments." You are therefore under special and peculiar obligations to love and obey the Saviour; and the sin of despising and neglecting him is, in you, peculiarly heinous.

I need hardly remind you that these distinguished privileges are bestowed upon you, not for your sakes alone, not to encourage in you spiritual pride, or arrogance, or carnal security; but that in you, and by means of you, all men might be made partakers of his grace and salvation. All your privileges, great and precious as they are, will not save you, if you do not personally accept Christ as your Saviour, and turn from your iniquities unto God. Not only so, but they will increase your guilt, and fearfully aggravate your condemnation if you despise or abuse them. Esau and Ishmael were children of the covenant. Both of them received the seal of the covenant, and were dedicated to God in infancy. But they despised their birthright and neglected to improve their privileges, and for their unbelief and sin were cut off from the congregation of the Lord; and they and their children excluded from the blessings of the covenant. And many of the very persons to whom the words of our text were originally addressed refused to believe and obey the preaching of the apostles, rejected the Saviour, and perished in their sins.   Take heed, therefore, lest a similar or worse thing befall you.   Many of you are yet young it is true; but you are old enough to understand and appreciate your privileges and re-sponsibilities.   You are old enough and you know enough to love and trust and obey the Saviour; and yet some of you are not doing it.   For all that the gracious Saviour has done for you, your love and gratitude and obedience are due in return to him.   Not to love him, not to trust him, not to turn from all sin to him, is a great sin, even in those who have only heard of him with the hearing of the ear; but in you it is grievous and inexcusable wickedness.   Let your earnest and daily prayer be, "Gracious Saviour, teach me to know thee and to love thee.   Reclaim me from all my wanderings. Bless me with thy light and thy salvation.   Let me abide forever under thy gentle control, as one of the sheep of thy pasture—one of the people of thy care."

Some of you, on the other hand, have long passed the period of childhood.   The claims of the loving Saviour have often been pressed home upon your hearts and con-sciences, and as often been neglected or resisted.   How much longer do you intend thus to trifle with the patience and forbearance of God?   Will his Spirit always strive? Are your birthright privileges in the kingdom of God matters of so little value that they may be bartered away for some momentary sensual gratification, or trifling earthly advantage?   Let the melancholly experience of poor Esau, his early folly and profane contempt for his high spiritual privileges, and his subsequent remorse and anguish and hopeless unavailing grief and regret be a warning to all who sustain similar relations to the church and the blessings and privileges that belong to

13

its true and faithful members; and let them by sincere and timely repentance and turning to God save themselves from a similar or worse fate.

We are, it will hence be seen, not without a sufficient and satisfactory answer to the question, which many regard as a fatal objection to the doctrine of infant baptism and infant church membership, viz. : What good do they do? Of what practical benefit are baptism and membership in the church to infants, who can neither understand their significance nor design? Our reply is, that their benefits, like those of membership in the family, and citizenship in the state, are not dependent upon the child's understanding of them. The little ones, by the ordination of the beneficent creator, are born into the family, because they need its love and care, and into the state, because they need its protection, and not because they understand anything about these things. So they are born into the church, and receive baptism, the sign and seal of membership, not because they understand the meaning and purpose of these things, but because, from the very beginning, they need the spiritual guardianship, instruction and care of the church, which is charged with the religious oversight and training of both parents and children. The vows which the church exacts of parents, when they present their children for baptism, binding them by the most sacred obligations to train them up in the nurture and admonition of the Lord, she exacts by virtue of this double oversight and authority; and in proportion as she is loyal to her divine Master, and faithful to the charge which he has commited to her, she will see to it that these vows are fulfilled. And as from the beginning, "God having raised up his Son Jesus, sent him *first* to bless the Jews in turning them from their iniquities," so still the church's mission is first to her own baptized children and then to the world.

MAN INSPIRED OF GOD.

BY REV. G. R. BRACKETT, D. D.,
Pastor of the Second Presbyterian Church, Charleston, S. C

"There is a spirit in man: and the inspiration of the Almighty giveth them understanding."—JOB xxxii. 8.

ALL things sustain necessary and vital relations to their Creator. In him they "live, and move, and have their being." "In whose hand is the life of every living thing."

One of the most wonderful discoveries of modern science is the correlation and conservation of forces. The forces of light, heat, chemical force, and electricity are transmuted into each other, but the sum of the original force is never diminished. Moreover, it has been discovered that the sun is the source from which all these forces originate, so that it is "one and the same force, but under a vast variety of modifications, which warms our houses, and our bodily frames, which raises the steam and impels the engine, which effects the different chemical combinations, which flashes in the lightning, and lives in the plant. It furnishes the most striking manifestation of God; the one God, with his infinitely varied perfections; and we should see the one power blowing in the breeze, smiling in the sunshine, sparkling in the stars, quickening us as we bound along in the best enjoyment of health, efflorescing in every form and hue of beauty, and showering down daily gifts upon us."

Again, we read: "The Spirit of God hath made me.

and the breath of the Almighty hath given me life.'' The word ''spirit'' literally means ''breath,'' and ''inspiration'' the act of inbreathing. In a physical sense, all life, motion, activity depend upon the constant inspiration or inbreathing of the Almighty, but in a higher, spiritual sense, the spirit of man is inspired by God.

The Spirit of God is said to exercise a peculiar efficiency in all the rational and moral actions of men. He inspired men to rule and govern his ancient people, and with courage and skill in the day of battle. Nor is this influence confined to the people of God. Even ungodly men have been providentially raised up, and specially qualified to execute divine judgments. Cyrus, a heathen prince, is called the ''Lord's anointed,'' and Jehovah inspired him with wisdom, courage, and military skill. Only those who received the ''unction of the Spirit'' were said to be anointed, and when the anointed Cyrus had accomplished the divine purpose, in the destruction of Babylon, Jehovah said to him, ''I have girded thee and thou hast not known me.''

When the Persian Empire rose like a mountain before Zerubbabel, apparently an impassable barrier, to the work assigned him of rebuilding the temple, the prophet said, ''Before Zerubbabel, O mountain, thou shalt become a plain; not by might, nor by power, but by my Spirit, saith the Lord of hosts, and the Spirit of the Lord came upon Joshua, the high priest, and upon Zerubbabel, the civil ruler, and upon all the people,'' and also worked in the minds, and hearts, and counsels of their enemies, bringing them to confusion.

When the Spirit of God came upon Gideon and Jephthah, they were mighty men of valor. The Spirit of the Lord came mightily upon Samson, inspiring him with bodily strength, and when the Spirit of God departed from him he became as weak as other men.   Bezaleel and Aholiab were inspired with artistic and mechanical skill for "cunning workmanship" in beautifying the tabernacle.   In some sense all men are inspired by the Spirit of God.   The redemption of Christ has placed the world under the dispensation of the Holy Spirit, who directs, controls, and restrains the ungodly, and whose universal presence and agency is the source of all those virtues that are the bond of society.

How the Spirit of God works in and through the "spirit in man," without disturbing our free agency, we do not know.   Neither do we know "how the light shines through the transparent crystal, or how matter conducts electricity, or how an opaque body becomes luminous without the least change in its organization."

But passing from this general view of the subject, let us consider more particularly the kind of inspiration indicated in our text, whereby the "spirit in man" receives such an "understanding" as qualifies for the knowledge, love, and service of God.

1. It is as a spirit that man is capable of divine inspiration, and as a spirit he is related to God, and bears his likeness.   God is the "Father of our spirits," and "we are his offspring."   The soul of man is a spiritual substance, manifesting all the properties of pure spirit.   It is immaterial, invisible, indivisible, intelligent, self-conscious, and voluntarily active.   He who can say, "I am," is the image of the "Great I Am."   He who can say, "I think," is the image of the Supreme Intelligence. He who can say, "I will," is the image of the Omnipotent Sovereign.   He who, in the consciousness of personal identity, can say through all the vicissitudes of life, "I have the same unchangeable personality," is the image of the immutable God, who is "the same

yesterday, to-day, and forever." He who has but to
will it, and his imagination calls into existence new
worlds, and peoples them with its own ideal creations,
and his fashioning hand creates new forms of matter in
endless combinations, and by his miracles of art "mocks
his own Creator's skill," is in the image of the all-wise
Creator. He who feels the pulse of immortality beating
in his soul, which is incapable of death by dissolution,
bears the image of the ever-living God. "The eternal
years of God are hers." He who sits upon the throne
of the lower creation, and feels, notwithstanding his lost
"dominion," that he is still lord of all, "subduing time
and space," controlling the mighty forces of nature, and
rendering all things animate and inanimate, subjects of
his royal authority, and compelling them to glorify his
name, and who rules among the kingdoms of the earth,
is the image of "the sovereign and only potentate, the
King of kings and the Lord of lords." Thus, as another
has expressed it, man bears the "traces of God's incom-
municable perfections." All this is implied in the term
"spirit," which is the image of the Infinite Spirit, considered as the natural image of God.

But man was created for moral and spiritual ends, of
which this natural image is the mere servant. It is only
as this spiritual nature, with its faculties of understanding, affection, and will are crowned with the glory of
holiness, that man reflects the image of God's moral perfections. In the epistle to the Colossians we learn that
"the new man is renewed in knowledge after the image
of him that created him"; and the Ephesians are exhorted "to put on the new man, which after God is
created in righteousness and true holiness." Holiness
in the soul is what life is in the body. It is the principle which pervades all its faculties and powers, and

determines their character and direction. Holiness in the understanding imparts to all our information the character of true knowledge and wisdom. We know with the certainty and clearness of God's knowledge as we become like him in holiness. Holiness in the heart, purifies the affections and draws them up into the fellowship with God, and our love responds to his love. Holiness in the conscience, reveals the law of righteousness, the image of God's moral rectitude. Holiness in the will, brings it into gradual harmony with the will of God, and produces the image of the divine freedom.

Thus holiness is the bond of union between the soul and God, and between the various powers of our nature, securing their perfection and harmony. If we were perfectly holy, knowledge would always nourish our love, and love would always move the will, and the will, guided by the law of the conscience, would always yield a spontaneous and joyful obedience. As by an irresistible attraction, holiness draws all the powers of the soul to God, as the centre and inspiration of all their movements, which realizes its perfection and blessedness in the divine favor, fellowship and service. For as holiness is the life of the soul, love is the life of holiness, and communion and obedience are the life of love.

All this is implied in the term "spirit." The "spirit in man" is the image of the spirit in God. Man was created in his likeness that he might be capable of divine inspirations. He was made to receive all the fulness of those attributes of spirit which can be communicated to a creature. And inasmuch as the spirit in man is capable of infinite and eternal expansion, he bears no dim traces of those infinite attributes which belong only to God. Through the endless ages of eternity, he will be forever approaching the infinite, outstripping all present angelic glory, and the "rapt seraph that burns and adores" before the very throne of God.

2. The spirit in man! Here is the true measure of its dignity and grandeur, and the magnitude of its spiritual wants:

Man's arts and inventions; his scientific and philo-sophic achievements; his wisdom, penetrating the se-crets of the telescopic and microscopic universe; his power, controlling and mastering the tremendous forces of nature, chaining the lightning, harnessing the steam, and making the winds and the waves to obey him, are but dim prophecies and shadowy intimations of the glorious possibilities of eternity, when our perfected and enlarged and ever-expanding faculties shall work without let or hindrance, in a sphere that is unlimited, in a light that is clear and cloudless, and overflow with the ever-lasting influx of infinite wisdom, perfect holiness, and boundless love.

O brethren! what must be the wants of such a being, so allied to the infinite, eternal, and ever-blessed God, reflecting his divine attributes, and capable of being filled with all his communicable fulness! Created in the likeness of God, can the spirit in man find anything outside of its Maker to suit its god-like capacities? All our faculties turn to God as their ultimate end, and find in him their highest activity, their complete develop-ment, and their full satisfaction. Matter and spirit have nothing in common. Earthly things are material and have no affinity for the soul. They are only instruments and occasions of the soul's felicity.

Our lower nature has affinities for material things. God has given us a nature that responds to the beautiful in the physical world, and to the pleasures of wealth, honor, learning, and social relationships. These lower objects were made to be loved, and only as they are loved and enjoyed, according to their nature and design, can we fulfil the end of our being, and glorify our Maker. But God, himself, must ever be the supreme Portion of the soul. The spirit in man must hold communion with the infinite Spirit. The sweet and blissful amenities of human society can never satisfy a capacity for love God made for himself to fill. Again, man has a capacity for knowledge, which the knowledge of all created beings and of the whole created universe could not satisfy. He has, also, capacious activities which find an adequate scope for their development and exercise only in the service of an infinite being. Virtue is indeed its own reward, and there is a pleasure in holy energies. There is a delight that flows from a mere sense of duty. The self-denials and sacrifices we make in the service of others is attended with a high and noble joy. But not until we recognize our relations to God, and 1ealize that we are doing his will and accomplishing his purposes, do our faculties reach their highest limit of power, and the fountain of our joy touch the skies.

1. In the light of this subject, we see wherein consists the essential misery of our fallen state. Said an old divine, "The fall of man was the departure of the Holy Spirit from him." Disobedience broke the communion between the "spirit in man" and the Spirit of God ; and though the Holy Spirit continues to exercise his creating, sustaining, and controlling agency, he no longer dwells in the unrenewed soul, as the source and inspiration of its life. "To be severed eternally from God's inspira- tion," says Dr. Bushnell, to whom we are indebted for some thoughts of this discourse, "is enough, as we are constituted, to seal our complete misery. What is called hell in the Scripture is the world of misery constituted

by the complete absence of God. It is the outer darkness because it is that night of the mind which overtakes
it when it strays from God and his light.''

Dear brethren, does not this account for all the misery
of this life; for the mysterious sadness of those who are
''smothering their affinities for God ' '; for the ''sublime
unhappiness '' of great souls whose spiritual faculties
are closed against the inspirations of God; for the rest-
less undercurrent of dissatisfaction, when the sea is calm,
the sky clear and cloudless, and favoring breezes fill
the swelling sails ; for the feverish excitement of men of
business ; for the intoxicating mirth of the votaries of
pleasure ; for the mad ambition that never rests so long
as there is another height to gain ; for the sickening disgust with earthly vanities; for the corroding cares, the
gnawing envies, the burning jealousies? There are so
many ways the hungry, famishing soul has of saying it
is not satisfied without God.

2. Again, we see the true glory of the gospel. The
curse of sin is lifted from the guilty conscience, and the
broken law, that the redeemed and regenerated soul may
be brought into living, conscious relations to God, that
the Holy Spirit may return to his deserted habitation,
and abide with us as the source and inspiration of all our
energies. An unpardoned soul cannot be inspired by
God; therefore it must be redeemed. A soul that does
not love holiness cannot receive divine inspiration ; therefore it must be ''born again.'' In Christ we are restored
to our relation to God as justified sinners. In Christ we
receive the gift of the Holy Spirit, and with him the
restoration of the lost image of God ; and as the work of
sanctification progresses, all our faculties are opened,
more and more, to the inspirations of God.

How unreasonable and utterly vain are all our efforts

at self-restoration!   All our works are dead works, until
our spiritual life is restored.   If we are constitutionally
related to God, and made to live in his inspiration, then
we must live as we are made to live, if we will be happy,
and this inspiration extends to the humblest duties of
life.   He who "abides in his calling with God," will
find God abiding with him, inspiring him to do all things
rightly and wisely.   Thus the whole "spirit in man"
becomes like an instrument of music, filled with the
breath of God, and whether we press the higher or the
lower keys the music is all divine.

"HOW LONG HALT YE BETWEEN TWO OPINIONS ?"

BY REV. J. R. BURGETT, D. D.,

Pastor of the Government-Street Presbyterian Church, Mobile Alabama.

"And Elijah came unto all the people, and said, How long halt ye between two opinions? if the Lord be God, follow him: but if Baal, then follow him. And the people answered him not a word."—I KINGS xviii. 21.

IT has often been remarked that they who have been most successful in their efforts, and who have acquired greatest eminence in any particular department of life, have been men of one idea. By this is meant that the purpose, which they were seeking to accomplish, was always before their minds, absorbing and enlisting all their thoughts and energies. Their attention was not directed to a multiplicity of objects, which could not but tend to confusion of thoughts and waste of strength. On the contrary, they labored with an eye single to the accomplishment of some one thing, which was most dear to their hearts. This is what may be called living and acting with singleness of aim or purpose. The man of wealth; the man of high attainments in scholarship; the man of honors, whether political or military ; the man of eminence in art or science all alike have won their way to such celebrity and renown, by adopting this principle and giving constant and exclusive attention to the direction of their aim, the accomplishment of their purpose. A hundred such could be named, who, on the pages of history, stand out foremost in their chosen spheres of action. Newton, Bacon, Locke, Humboldt, in science or metaphysics; Luther, Calvin, Wesley, Whitfield, in theological attainments, and preaching ability and power; Webster, Clay, Calhoun, William Pitt, in statesmanship; Napoleon Bonaparte, and others, both ancient and modern, in military science, illustrate the great advantage of singleness of aim in the pursuit of any object. In fact, it is what is sometimes called "decision of character"; and our text, with its context, is intended to enforce the lesson of its necessity and importance.

The metaphor "halting" is taken from the unequal walk of a lame person, who is sometimes fast, and sometimes slow; sometimes on one side of the way, and sometimes on the other. To a spectator it is uncertain whether he will persevere to the end of his journey or leave the path with the vain hope of finding one that is easier and better. No reliance can be placed in such a person as to the object or purpose for which he sets out. Now what is thus true in the physical is equally true in the moral and religious world. Multitudes fail of the success they desire, and come short of the enjoyment they would otherwise experience, just because they are vague, uncertain and vacillating in their aims and efforts.

This was the conduct of the Israelites in their relations to God and the duties growing out of them. They wavered in opinion and varied in practice, sometimes worshipping Jehovah, and at other times worshipping Baal, just as their convictions or interests prevailed. They sought to make a compromise between the two, and to mingle their worship so as to accommodate both flesh and spirit. Baal's prophets would, in all probability, have yielded very readily to such a plan, but they could never have gained God's consent, for he rejects *in toto* all worship or service which does not exalt him as supreme in the heart. Elijah, therefore, in a spirit of the most scathing rebuke, condemned their unmanly and wavering conduct: "*How long halt ye between two opinions?*" he demands—thus placing before their minds, by a metaphor which they all understood, the contemptible manner of their walk before God, and the wicked folly of persisting in it. Then he called upon them without further delay to determine whether of the two was the self-existent and eternal God, the Creator, Governor and Judge of the world; and to follow him alone. They were to consider diligently the proofs and arguments respectively by which the claims of God and Baal were sought to be established; determine on which side was the stronger claim, the preponderance of proof; and show at once by their action that they submitted to its convincing power. If the Lord was God, they were to follow him alone; or, if Baal, then they were to follow him. What he demanded was that they must be wholly on one side or the other, and must persevere as thus they decided so as to be harrassed by no conflicting doubts.

Let us attend to the lessons which these words suggest, and try to profit by them:

1. There are three classes of persons who are not included among those thus addressed; who are not to be regarded as "halting between two opinions," or undecided on the subject of religion. One is the openly skeptical and profane, who bear the mark of the beast; who make no pretensions to religion, but have made up their minds to reject it as a foolish superstition unworthy of belief; and many of whom hate it, oppose it and persecute it.

Another class is the decidedly sincere, some of whom are very zealous, useful and spiritually strong; and others of whom are weak and feeble, but fully decided as followers of Christ, and so positive in their convictions that no one can doubt as to where they belong. Sincerity is the test; and where such aim at loving and serving the Lord in truth, the Lord owns and blesses them as his people.

The third class are those who are in an awakened condition, and earnestly seeking the Lord; whose faces are turned Zionward, and longing to be consciously within its gates and among the true and accepted worshippers of God; who are actually standing in the way, and inquiring for the good old paths, and ready to walk as they may be divinely directed. They are like the Philippian jailer, who, under deep conviction and longing for the peace and rest which conscious forgiveness gives, cried out: "Sirs, what must I do to be saved?"

None of these three classes are among the undecided; those who are halting between two opinions. The skeptical and profane blasphemer of God, of the Bible, of the plan of redemption as there revealed in and through Christ Jesus, and of all sacred institutions, have made their choice, and are *so* wedded to it in word and act that there is no mistaking where they belong, or as to their attitude toward the Christian religion. The decidedly sincere of all grades are equally positive in *their* choice of *God*, Christ and the great salvation on the terms offered; and utter no uncertain sound in giving their testimony. Those who, under the influence and guidance of the Holy Spirit, are seeking to be saved in God's own way, are ready as soon as they see and know what that way is, to accept and walk in it as the only way. They seek the Lord not with a divided but whole heart; and, according to divine promise, they will therefore surely find him.

2. The *undecided*, or such as "halt between two opinions," may be divided into four or five classes. There are those, for instance, who are among the people of God and class themselves with them, but who are not of them. Some are there merely through the influence of education; others from the fears of conscience, which will not allow them to neglect the church and its ordinances. Yet all such are only *hearers*, and not *doers* of the word. They do not hunger and thirst after spiritual things, but are afraid to wholly neglect or cast them aside; and thus they are "halting between two opinions." There are those, also, who avoid open impiety, and yet do not sincerely and with their hearts serve God. They would be horrified at the very idea of being notoriously wicked; and yet God is not at all in their hearts. They are not at all spiritually minded; and they have never really felt their sins to be a heavy burden, from which they would gladly be delivered. There are those, also, who try hard to unite the world and the church, to worship both God and mammon. They call themselves industrious, prudent, and sociable; but the truth is their hearts are exclusively and idolatrously set on the world in all its variously attractive forms and phases, such as are calculated to fascinate and please the natural, unrenewed man. They are covetous, and pleasure-seekers. They love gold, and are intent upon the accumulation of wealth for its own sake and for what it can do in gratifying their selfish aims and desires. They love amusement for its own sake, and hunt for and enjoy it as one of their chief occupations in life. But along with all this, they wish to be found in the company of the sincerely devout and pious, and to be classed with Christians; because, as they think, their temporal respectability and standing will give them influence in the church.

Then, again, there are those who labor to unite works and grace, in effecting their salvation. They do not *fully* trust *in either*, but in *both partially*, and therefore come short of fully realizing that salvation which comes through Jesus Christ only, and by an exclusive trusting in and resting upon his all-sufficient righteousness. There is still another class of the undecided, the halters between two opinions, whom I ought to mention. They are those who would privately but not publicly profess Christ. They fear the cross connected with a public profession; the ridicule, reproach, scorn, and trials of many kinds which are apt to follow. They fear being laughed at by their old associates; and pointed out and spoken of, in a spirit of ridicule, as having become pious, etc. They fear the power of temptation, and that they will not be able successfully to hold out against it; and so they decline a *public* profession of religion, and hold on to Christ *in private*, so as really to be at *liberty* to *yield* to *temptation* and enjoy *forbidden indulgences* without being called to account publicly and charged with inconsistency. What is this but parleying with the tempter, and giving him an advantage in the fact of their feeling a lessened responsibility, by not making a public confession of Christ? And, besides, such a disposition makes it evident that they are not sincere; else they would know that none of us have sufficiency in *ourselves* to withstand the tempter, and that our sufficiency is in *Christ*, who is always ready to help and strengthen those who look to and lean trustingly on him. There are and can be no silent partners in Christ's firm.

It is stated that a minister in Brooklyn, New York, was once called on by a business man, who said: "I come, sir, to inquire if Jesus Christ will take me into the

14

concern as a *silent partner*." "Why do you ask?" replied the minister. "Because," said he, "I wish to be a member; and do not wish anybody to know it." The minister's reply was : "Christ takes no silent partners. The firm must be Jesus Christ & Co.; and the names of the *company*, though they may occupy a subordinate place, must all be written out on the sign-board." Now all these, and such as these, are "halting between two opinions"; and to them is addressed, by way of rebuke, the sharp and cutting inquiry of the text. It is all the more pungent and awakening, because, in the face of accumulative, convincing evidence of the superior claims of the Christian religion as regards its nature and origin, its influence and advantages both for time and eternity, they are without *excuse* and all the more *guilty*, if they do not with positive conviction and resolute determination accept it as their life religion, and by faith and practice hold fast to it under all circumstances and until they reach and wear the promised crown.

3. This leads me to remark that God has wonderfully condescended to establish by the most undoubted proofs those truths which concern himself; and which, in their practical application, will secure our present and eternal happiness. Elijah, although alone and single-handed, nevertheless challenged the four hundred and fifty prophets of Baal to make trial with him as to which was the true God. His proposal was so reasonable that the people at once agreed to it; and, therefore, Baal's prophets were left to the alternative of either complying with it, or of admitting that their God was a dumb and impotent idol. They agreed to the proposal; and consented that he who should answer by fire, in consuming the sacrifice offered him, should be regarded as the true God, and worthy of supreme and exclusive worship and adoration. In this

trial Elijah conceded the preference, in every external circumstance, to the false prophets. He gave them every outward advantage, in order that his victory might be the more noticeable and complete, and that Jehovah, the true God, might receive greater honor. He therefore dug a trench about the altar, and filled it with water. He also poured a great quantity of water upon the altar, upon the sacrifice and upon the wood, with the view, doubtless, of avoiding all possible suspicion that any fire had been concealed. This would make the divine interposition more illustrious and convincing. When everything was ready, and the prophet had invoked the divine presence so as to make good the claim that he was God alone, and to turn back again to himself the hearts of his astrayed people, *then* the fire of the Lord fell and consumed the burnt sacrifice, the wood, the stones, the dust, and licked up the water that was in the trench. Nothing could have been more convincing; and the people, therefore, prostrated themselves before God with mingled feelings of terror and reverence.

Thus did God condescend to prove to his ancient and misguided people his claims as the true and self-existent Jehovah, who alone is entitled to the exclusive worship of all his creatures. To have hesitated after that, and still to have withheld from him their exclusive service, would have been indeed a most wicked and obstinate rebellion.

Now the same condescension is still shown in furnishing proofs that ought to be equally convincing, not only of his existence, but also of the revelation he has made in the sacred Scriptures to man as a spiritual and immortal being, and of the divine origin of those doctrines of grace and salvation which are suited to his condition as a sinner.

But I address myself particularly to those who are not skeptical, and would scorn to be classed among infidels, atheists, and blasphemers of sacred things. I take it for granted that you are convinced that there is an all-wise, intelligent, self-existent being called God, who created, governs and controls all things, both animate and inanimate.

You instinctively feel that there is such a being; and, therefore, you involuntarily cry to him for help when in great straits. You know that everywhere and among all tribes and nations this feeling or opinion prevails; and that, therefore, they appeal to and worship what they call God, whether true or false. This must be either from the fact that the idea of God is innate, born in us; or that this truth is so very obvious that it is discovered by the very first exertion of reason in persons of the most ordinary capacities; or that it has been handed down from the first man by tradition through all the ages. You know that as the beautiful landscape could not be put on canvas by pencil or brush without the guiding hand of a skilful artist; that as the machine, which is intelligently constructed for the accomplishment of a particular purpose, could not have come into existence without a designer and artificer; that as no building of any sort, great or small, and exactly suited to its aim, could have come together in all its wise arrangements by chance, but must have been the work of an intelligent, independent thinker and designer; so the universe with its wonders, our world with its adaptations to our use, its order, variety, and beauty, could not have merely happened thus, or come into existence without the agency of an all-wise Creator, who could think, and plan, and execute. You know all this; and are, therefore, convinced that there must be a self-existent and eternal being, with infinite wisdom and capabilities, whom we call God.

You admit the fact that as God's creatures, the work of his hands, we belong to him for his service and honor; that the ability he has given, the powers with which he has endowed us, are to be exercised and used as he originally intended; and that he holds us, as intelligent beings who are capable of choice, accountable for what we do in the matter. He is our Creator, and we his creatures, who owe him all the service we are made to give, just as man's inventions and productions are intended for his service. He is our Ruler, our Sovereign, and we his subjects, whose duty it is to obey; just as in civil government the citizen is expected to be in subjection to those in authority. If we fail in rendering due service to God as our Creator, or proper obedience to him as our Sovereign, then we incur his displeasure, and are exposed to the penalty.

You are ready to acknowledge, at least theoretically, if not practically, that all mankind, and you yourselves included, have come sadly short of such justly-expected and rightly-required service and obedience. You have come short in thought, word and act; and you know it well, and would feel it most keenly if you would only thoughtfully and prayerfully consider the matter in all its bearings; in the light of Scripture, reason, observation, and history. In the sight of God you are transgressors of his law, rebels against his authority, and acting contrary to his holy and righteous will, and against your own truest and best interests, both for time and eternity. The Scriptures plainly declare this; and your own conscience confirms it. You are then guilty before God, exposed to the penalty, and already condemned.

You know that you have not the ability and cannot, through your own sufficiency, escape from under this sentence of condemnation. Your kindly, honest, and upright dealings with your fellow-men will not be a sufficient covering of your guilt from God's judicial eye. Such righteousness may be good currency among men, and helpful in social life, but God will not accept it in exchange for his pardoning favor and the gift of eternal life. By the deeds of the law shall no flesh be justified before God; and, in his sight, all our righteousnesses are as filthy rags. The laws of men are not our rule in the matter of salvation. Simply to obey them and nothing more is too narrow and short to commend us to God. Men make laws, just as tailors make garments to fit the crooked bodies of those they serve. In making laws, men try to suit the humors or whims of the people who are to be thus governed; but surely such laws are not sufficient to convince us of sin and to lead us in the way of true happiness. It is God's own prerogative to give a law to the conscience, and to the renewed motions of the heart. Human laws are good to establish proper converse with man, but they are too short and insufficient to establish proper converse with God; and, therefore, we must consult that rule which is the law of the Lord, that we may not come short of true blessedness. But God's law enjoins more than man in his morally weak and depraved state can accomplish; and when he seriously attempts to conform his life in thought, speech, and act to all its precepts, so as to be perfect in every respect, and satisfy God as well as his own conscience, he cannot but feel that he has made an utter failure, and come far short of what is required. He then turns longingly to God for light and for the help he needs, in his ignorance and helplessness. "Oh, that I knew where I might find him " is his earnest, impassioned cry. And this suggests another very important fact, which you know, and that is, that God, who is love itself, and whose loving nature reaches out mercifully, wisely, and justly to all his creatures, especially to those created in his own image, responded to that earnest cry for help which only he can give. He has responded by giving them his only begotten Son, Jesus Christ, who is able to save to the uttermost all who come unto God by him; who has done all that was needed to be done to remove every hindrance and open up for them completely the way of salvation; and who, as their surety and substitute, met every legal demand and paid all their debts. In his twofold person as God-man he was abundantly qualified for such a work, and triumphantly finished it to the glory of God and the redemption and salvation of all true believers. He is, therefore, what man, in the consciousness of his guilt and helplessness, longs for—the mighty Saviour.

You know and acknowledge all this, because in the Bible you have God's own inspired word, a special revelation from him, which comes to you in language and form so thoroughly human as to be suited to every capacity. It gives in a way that all who are accountable can readily understand all that they need to know for their salvation. It is all there, not mathematics, nor scientific lore, but what is able, through God's blessing, to make us wise unto salvation. The Bible was not intended to be a teacher of secular knowledge, or an expositor of the laws which govern the material universe. These things it refers to only incidentally and by way of illustration; and then it is usually according to commonly received and prevailing opinions on these subjects, so as to adapt its religious teachings the better to the people. Thus while it is thoroughly inspired and divine, it is, at the same time, an intensely human book. Now since man needed just such a revelation, is it not at least probable that God would give it, and give it, too, in this very shape? It was love and mercy that prompted him to give us a special revelation, and to adapt it thus wisely to our condition, so as to be within our ready comprehension. Moreover, that the Bible is really God's word, his revelation to men of how they are to be saved from guilt and sin, is made evident from its own claim, its own testimony. I need not particularize here, because if you are a reader of it you cannot but see that such is its claim. But aside from its own testimony, the evidence both *internal* and *external* is *cumulative*. Its fulfilled prophecies and its recorded miracles are credentials to show that it is God who speaks. The frank and candid way in which its inspired writers speak of their own faults, and those of God's people, shows that it is a book which aims at the truth. The fact that it is composed of so many books, written by so many persons varying in culture, style, and surroundings, and stretching through many centuries; and that yet with it all there is such a remarkable oneness of spirit and aim, shows that they must have been under the guidance and control of a divine agency, such as the book itself claims. The loftiness of its teachings, the grandeur of the characters it has helped to fashion, and the comforts and even joy it imparts to the sorrowing and suffering, show that it is more than a mere human production, and must be from him who is the source of all true consolation. The testimony of experience, from those who have received its teachings and acted upon them, who have tasted of this good word of God, and seen that it is all it claims; and who, like the blind man with sight restored by Jesus, can say, "Whereas I was blind, now I see," is a proof of its lofty claim, and shows that it can be relied on to do what it promises. Now these, and more which might be given, are powerful proofs that the Bible is God's word; his revelation to man, as a spiritual and immortal being, of what can be learned nowhere else; how he may be saved and eternally blessed; how God can be just, and the justifier of the ungodly.

All this you know and acknowledge; for it is not the skeptical I am addressing. You believe in God; in the immortality of our souls; in our personal accountability as God's creatures and subjects; in the fact that we have sinned and incurred his displeasure, and are, therefore, under condemnation; in our own insufficiency and helplessness to effect a deliverance; in the Bible as God's special revelation of what we need, and how we can be delivered and saved; in the fact that Jesus Christ is there made known and offered to us freely as the divinely-appointed and infinitely-sufficient Saviour; the way, the truth, and the life; the only way through which we can come into the reconciled presence of God the Father, and finally reach heaven; you have an intellectual belief in all this, for you accept and are convinced by the evidence that it is all true.

But now, what are you going to do about it? What do you propose to do about it to-day? What do you really think is your present duty to God in Christ, and to yourselves in view of all that has been done in divine love for your spiritual welfare? Will you still, and for an indefinite period, be contented with this mere intellectual believing; with merely believing these facts, and go no further? Will you halt right there, and while leaning with the intellect toward God, and Jesus Christ his loving, unspeakable gift, and the great salvation thus pro-

vided, be at the same time leaning toward the world
with the heart, and actually preferring it to what you
cannot but know is your greatest good? Will it be for
your honor and safety to be thus two-faced, double-
minded, reaching out in opposite directions; wavering
between God and the world? Do you not know that to
waver thus between duty and the world contrary to your
own convictions of God, and to refuse all persuasion to
resolve and be decided one way or the other, is exposing
you to the risk of an eternal loss, and may allure you to
a point beyond which there will be no help for you?
Unresolvedness and half-purposes are an absolute hindrance to a sound conversion. If you would be converted and saved, as no doubt it is your intention some
day, do not stand wavering, but resolve at once, and
turn to God through Christ with a believing, trusting
heart as well as *intellect;* and let it be seen and known
that you are acting up to your real convictions of duty
to yourself and your God.

If this were a doubtful business, I would not persuade
you to do it rashly; or if there were any danger to your
souls in thus resolving, I would say no more. But when
it is a business that should be beyond all dispute with
men and women of reason, why should you still waver
and stagger, as if it *were* a *doubtful* business? What a
shame it must be to be unresolved as to whether God or
the world is to have our hearts, and command chiefly our
affections and services. If it be a disgrace and an exhibition of folly for a man to be unresolved as to whether
a bed of thorns or of feathers were the easier, or as to
whether the great sun or a mere clod of earth was the
more luminous and glorious, it must be a far greater
shame and folly for a man to be unresolved as to whether
it be God or the world that must make him happy, and

that should have the chief place in his heart; and whether
a life of sin or a life of holiness is the better life. Those
who halt and waver between two opinions, in the matter
of religion, are "like travellers who halt in indecision at
cross-roads, with a furious storm and a dark night rapidly
approaching; or like a pilot who doubts what to do with
the helm when the ship is driving before the wind
through a dangerous channel." To hesitate or waver
at such a time about what to do involves a most fearful
risk; but not nearly so fearful as that which accompanies
halting, wavering delay in the matter of religion; in
deciding the question of salvation by a prompt and immediate compliance with the provision made for it and
with the terms on which it is offered. Nothing should
be allowed to stand in the way and hinder such a decision. The dissuasions of the best and dearest friends
should be rejected firmly and persistently for the sake of
the soul; its present and eternal welfare. A young man
thus made up his mind and devoted himself to a religious life. His ungodly parents sent him many letters
to dissuade him from it. But being fully decided to go
on in his chosen course, when any such letters came to
him he paid no attention to their contents, and threw
them into the fire; and so when friends, kindred, or
associates stand between us and Christ, and try to turn
us away from him, and to keep us from becoming his
believing and devoted followers, they must be disre-
garded; for it is a question of eternal life or eternal
death, and should be decided at once; because the
future is still uncertain, and we know not when the
curtain will fall.

"Choose ye this day whom ye will serve;" and may
God help you to make a right choice and to make it
now.

CONSECRATION.

BY REV. G. B. STRICKLER, D. D.,
Pastor of the Central Presbyterian Church, Atlanta, Ga.

"I beseech you, therefore, brethren, by the mercies of God,
that ye present your bodies a living sacrifice, holy, acceptable
unto God, which is your reasonable service."—ROMANS xii. 1.

IN many minds there is considerable prejudice against
doctrinal preaching. It is said that many of the doctrines are very obscure; that some of them, indeed,
are incomprehensible; that there is too much difference
of opinion about them for them to be profitable subjects
of discussion; that the only result of such discussion is
to confuse and bewilder the understanding, and to lead
the attention away from the practical duties of life into
a region of barren speculation. Besides, it is sometimes
added, it does not make much difference what any one
believes in regard to the doctrines of religion, provided
only he keeps close to the duties laid down in God's
word; and that, therefore, the kind of preaching that is
to be preferred is that which clearly points out those
duties and earnestly insists on their discharge.

Those, however, who hold these views have entirely
failed to apprehend the connection that subsists between
doctrines and duties. What are the doctrines of religion? They relate to such subjects as the nature and
attributes of God; the relations in which he stands to
men; the relations in which they stand to him; and
man's past history, present condition, and eternal destiny. These are some of the subjects to which the doc-

trines relate. And now every true doctrine is only the assertion of a fact in regard to one or more of these subjects. It is a doctrine of religion that there is a "God, infinite, eternal, and unchangeable in his being, wisdom, power, holiness, justice, goodness, and truth"; but that is also a fact. It is a doctrine of religion that man has fallen from the high estate in which he was created by sinning against God, and has become spiritually totally depraved; but that is also a fact. It is a doctrine of religion that "there is none other name under heaven given among men whereby we must be saved" except the name of the Lord Jesus Christ; but that is also a fact; and the same is true of all the doctrines. They are all facts; so that the doctrines of religion are nothing more, nothing less, than the facts of religion. Thus they lie at its foundation. They make it possible, since they furnish the basis on which it rests. What sort of a religion would that be that was not grounded in, and built upon, well ascertained facts? But, since the doctrines of religion are its facts, how is it possible intelligently to preach it except by making its doctrines known and their meaning understood?

But what is the relation that subsists between doctrines and duties? Plainly this : the doctrines make the duties. Why is it my duty to love God? To find an answer to that question, must I not go back to certain doctrines of religion ; and do I not say it is my duty to love him because he is infinitely excellent and glorious in himself; because he is my Creator, Preserver, and Redeemer; because he has bestowed great blessings on me in the past, and offers to bestow on me still greater blessings in the future? And do not these doctrines thus make the duty of loving him ; and if these doctrines were not facts, would there rest on my heart the slightest obligation to fix its supreme affections on him? Why is it my duty to believe on the Lord Jesus Christ? To answer that question, must I not again go back to certain doctrines of religion; and do I not say that it is my duty to believe on him because I am a lost and helpless sinner; because he is the only Saviour; because he commands me to believe on him; because he is worthy of all my confidence; because only by believing on him can I be brought into that spiritual condition in which I shall be able to render to him the worship and service of which he is infinitely worthy? And do not these doctrines thus make the duty of believing on him; and if these doctrines were not also facts, would there be any reason whatever why I should give him the supreme confidence of my soul?

Thus the doctrines of religion make its duties. There is not a single duty imposed upon us in God's word that is not created by one or more of the doctrines there inculcated. This being true, we can now see why doctrines are to be preached. They are to be preached that duties may be known. Since doctrines create duties, it is impossible in the nature of things that any one can know anything more about his duties—their nature; their number; their importance; their obligatory force—than he knows about the doctrines out of which they spring. Doctrines and duties, therefore, ought always to be preached in closest connection; the doctrines as giving rise to the duties; the duties as flowing out of the doctrines.

I make these remarks in introducing this discourse because I have observed that it is in this way that the apostle presents doctrines and duties in this epistle, and in all his other epistles. In the previous part of this epistle he establishes a number of doctrines; and amongst them the doctrine that God is infinitely merciful and has bestowed infinite mercies on the human race through the Lord Jesus Christ; and now at the beginning of this twelfth chapter he beseeches those to whom he was writing by those mercies to perform the great duty to which they give rise: "present your bodies a living sacrifice, holy, acceptable unto God, which is your reasonable service."

In considering the text, I shall follow the apostle's method. I shall point out the duty to which he summons us, and, then, the doctrines out of which it springs:

I. A careful analysis of his words will show that he here teaches that it is our duty to make a voluntary and entire consecration of ourselves and all we have to the Lord as an act of religious worship. He expressly says that we are to present our bodies to him. "Present your bodies a living sacrifice." That means, of course, that every power of the body is to be his. The eyes are to be his to survey his glory in his word and in his works. The ears are to be his to listen to his commands. The mouth is to be his to proclaim his name, and celebrate his praise. The hands are to be his to labor for the promotion of the interests of his kingdom. The feet are to be his to run in the way of his commandments. The whole body is to be his to serve him in every way that he shall require. Clearly so much as that is meant when he says, "present your bodies a living sacrifice."

But is that all that is meant? Can it be possible, that after eleven chapters of solid argument, the design of which in great part is to make known the extent of our obligations to God, he could draw no broader, nor grander conclusion, than that our bodies only are to be presented to him? Surely not. That under the word "bodies" he necessarily includes our souls is evident from the fact that our bodies can be consecrated only by our souls ; and they can make the consecration only when they see it to be due to God, and are honestly willing to make it because it is due. But when they see that, it is impossible that they should not also consecrate themselves to him, for they will then see that that is due to him even more, if possible, than the consecration of the body is. It is further evident, that under the word bodies he necessarily includes our souls, from the fact that our bodies are controlled by our souls, and, therefore, can be of no service to God unless our souls are consecrated with them. Of what service would a ship be to us unless we had control of that which guides the ship? And so, of what service can our bodies be to God unless he has control of that which guides our bodies? The soul, then, as well as the body, is to be consecrated to him. All its faculties are to be devoted to his service. The understanding is to be his to know him. The will is to be his to choose him. The heart is to be his to love him. The conscience is to be his to represent his authority in the soul, and to enforce obedience to all his commandments. The whole soul is to be his to glorify him in every way he shall make possible.

But can we stop here? Does the apostle mean that we are to stop here, and conclude that only our bodies and souls are to be consecrated to God? Every writer must be understood to mean, not only what he directly asserts, but everything else that his language necessarily implies; and this rule of interpretation is specially valid in application to the Scriptures, because they were written under the inspiration of the Spirit of God. But he distinctly foresaw every necessary inference from every statement there made ; and, therefore, every such necessary inference is just as true as every explicit statement is. Does not the apostle, then, necessarily imply that more is to be consecrated than simply our bodies and souls? Does he not imply that all that is ours—our time, our possessions, our influence—is also to be consecrated to him, and as entirely as our bodies and souls? Nothing can be more evident. When we consecrate our bodies and souls to him, that is, when we consecrate ourselves to him, the very idea of the consecration is that we are thereafter to live for him. But how can we live for him except as our time is spent for him, and our possessions are employed in promoting the interests of his cause and our influence is exerted in behalf of his kingdom? The very idea of consecration, then, carries in it, not only our bodies and souls, but everything else that is in any sense ours.

So far as we have examined the text, then, it teaches that we and all that is ours are to be presented a living sacrifice unto the Lord. But we have not yet exhausted its meaning. It needs to be emphasized that all that is ours is to be actually devoted to the Lord. It will not do to present it in theory whilst we keep it in reality. It will not do to present it in profession whilst we keep it in fact. It will not do so to present it that a kind of joint proprietorship in it is established between ourselves and him by which we permit him to share with us in its use. It will not do so to present it to him that we shall graciously allow him to have for his purposes what we think we do not need for our own purposes. That is not the consecration here inculcated. We are to present it a sacrifice. We are to lay it all on his altar to be consumed in his service. This is a very different view of the great duty from that generally entertained by Christians. The prevalent view amongst them seems to be that they are

15

first to set apart for their own use so much as they think
they need for that purpose, and then give to God the
remainder.   Unfortunately, their selfish conceptions of
their own wants are usually so great that there is no
remainder, or it is very small ; and that is the reason why
the treasuries of the churches are almost always empty,
and why the great causes in which the church is engaged
have to go around amongst the churches, and at almost
every door beg and beg, like poor mendicants, to get
enough to keep them from perishing; and even then
generally get only the trimmings and parings of liberal
incomes.   It is no such consecration as that the apostle
here enjoins.   The consecration he insists on is first to
present to the Lord all that is ours, and then receive
back from him for our own purposes so much as we see
in his word he permits us thus to employ.   And if that
were the consecration characterizing his people, his treasuries would overflow, and his work would be prosecuted
with something like that vigor of which it is worthy.

But there is still more in the text on this important
subject.   Not only must all that is ours be presented to
the Lord a sacrifice, but it must be presented a living
sacrifice.   Under the old dispensation the time necessary
for a sacrifice was very brief; perhaps an hour was
abundantly sufficient for the purpose; and the sacrifice
was consummated by the death of the victim.   But it is
to no such sacrifice as that that we are here summoned.
The time necessary for our sacrifice is the whole time
from this moment forward to the end of our earthly
history; and the sacrifice is to be consummated, not by
our being slain for the Lord, but by our living for him ;
and, therefore, it is called a living sacrifice, a sacrifice
that is to be repeated, continued, protracted to the last
moment of our earthly existence.

And not only must it be a living sacrifice, but it must be a holy sacrifice. Under the old dispensation it was necessary that the sacrifice offered should be without essential physical defect. The lamb must be without spot or blemish. It is necessary that this sacrifice to which we are here summoned shall be without essential, spiritual defect. That is, it is necessary that the motives prompting us to make it shall, at least prevalently, be such as are acceptable to God. It will not do to make this sacrifice simply because it is expedient, or because it is seemly, or because it secures the applause of men, or some other merely secular end, or because only by making it we can escape the righteous retributions of eternity. These may come in as subordinate motives prompting us to make it; but if we would so make it that it shall be ''holy'' in his sight we must make it because he requires it, and because we love him, and because we wish to do his will, and to glorify his great and holy name.

But the apostle has more yet to say on this important theme. Not only must we present all that is ours a living and a holy sacrifice unto the Lord, but we must do it voluntarily and cheerfully. He does not ask us to do it simply as a duty, or under the constraints of conscience, or that we may escape the divine displeasure; but he beseeches us to do it by the mercies of God—the infinitely great and precious mercies that he had just been pointing out, and we are to make it gladly and gratefully in response to those mercies. And, then, once more, it is to be of the nature of religious worship. Such was the nature of all the sacrifices under the old dispensation; and much more, if possible, must it be the nature of the more purely spiritual sacrifice here enjoined.

Such is the apostle's teaching as to this great duty; and if we now sum up all that has been educed from the text, I think we shall find that the statement made at the beginning is true, that he teaches that it is our duty to make a voluntary and entire consecration of ourselves and all that is ours to God as an act of religious worship.

II. And now let us consider some of the doctrines that give rise to this duty; or, what is the same thing, let us consider some of the reasons by which it is enforced. "I beseech you," says the apostle, "by the mercies of God, to present your bodies a living sacrifice." I suppose he appeals both to the mercies that are in God and to the mercies that are from him. I may say, then, in the first place, that he here appeals to the mercies that are in God; or, in other words, to the fact that God is a merciful being, to induce us to consecrate ourselves to him; and there is good reason for this form of appeal. Men are by nature afraid to consecrate themselves to him. They are afraid their enjoyments will be abridged, their happiness diminished, their liberty infringed upon, and their secular prosperity interfered with. They are afraid that they will lose something desirable and valuable that they might else enjoy in this world. So far as the future is concerned they are convinced that it would be better to be the Lord's; but so far as this life is concerned they can hardly help believing that much more that is desirable and enjoyable may be secured by standing somewhat aloof from God and his service, than by entire consecration to it, and, therefore, they refuse to perform this duty. Now the apostle would remove that erroneous impression by assuring them that God is a merciful, an infinitely merciful being; and that, therefore, he cannot mean by the consecration here asked to do them harm;

but must mean to do them good. He cannot mean to make their condition worse; but must mean to make it better; must mean to bestow on them richer enjoyments, and a higher happiness, and a truer liberty, and better qualifications for the discharge of all the secular duties of life. Certainly his people have always so found it. There never has been a man who truly consecrated himself to God who did not find it a change for the better in every important respect, and that all his highest interests for time and for eternity were promoted by it. He has found his "ways ways of pleasantness, and his paths paths of peace"; his yoke easy and his burden light. He has found him "a very present help in time of trouble"; "a friend that sticketh closer than a brother;" a guide in perplexity; a comforter in sorrow; a defender in danger; and that the longer he continued in his service the richer became its rewards; and those who have finished their course in his service have found that he went with them down into the dark valley of the shadow of death, and that he permitted them even there to fear no evil; and that on the farther side he took them up and presented them faultless before the presence of his glory with exceeding great joy. Such has been the experience of all those who consecrated themselves to him and spent their lives in his service. Here, then, is the apostle's appeal: "I beseech you by the mercies of God"—these mercies that he has bestowed on all his people in the past—I beseech you by these mercies to consecrate yourselves to him, that he may bestow these mercies on you. Ought not such an appeal to prevail with us? Unconverted friends, why should you hesitate to respond to it? What is the character of the master whom you are now serving? How does he treat his servants? Perhaps you may find an illustration of his character and of the manner in which he treats his servants in a fable that you may remember to have read. A tyrant once called one of his subjects into his presence and asked him what was his employment. He answered that he was a blacksmith. "Go," said he, "and make me a chain of such a length." He went and did as he was commanded, expecting to be suitably rewarded when he presented the chain completed in his master's presence. But his master only bade him go and make it twice as long; and this he did again and again, until the poor man's life had been worn out by his unrequited toil. Finally he presented himself in his master's presence for the last time, hoping that then at least he would have compassion on him and minister to his long neglected wants. But, to his amazement, he only bade his servants come and take the chain he had made and bind him hand and foot and cast him into a furnace of fire! Such is the character of the master you now serve. You are engaged in the service of sin. You have not yet received any very satisfactory reward; but you are expecting it here often; and so you continue in that service. Alas! you know not that all this promise of reward is mere delusion. You know not that you, too, are engaged in making a chain that is at last to fetter your own limbs. Every day you are making it longer. Every sinful thought; every sinful feeling; every sinful word; every sinful act adds an additional link to it; and soon it will be sufficiently long to enwrap your whole being in the folds of an endless bondage, and then will come the dreadful command, "bind him hand and foot, and cast him into the furnace of fire." It is absolutely certain that this is to be the result of your service of sin; "for the wages of sin is death." Why, then, should you hesitate to give up the service of such a master as that, and engage in the service of such a master as this, who never practises cruelties on his servants, and who never keeps back any promised rewards; but who multiplies unto them grace and mercy and peace in this life, and in the life to come bestows on them glory and honor and immortality?

But the apostle appeals not only to the mercies that are in God. He appeals also to the mercies that are from God. He appeals to the mercies that are from God in providence to induce us to consecrate ourselves to his service. No thoughtful person can deny that he is kept in being every moment by the providential mercies of God. I know that many have the notion that they are their own preservers in life; that they provide for themselves that on which they subsist, and so do not realize their dependence on God. But the groundlessness of the notion is easily revealed. Whose is the air we are now breathing, and who pours it around the world in such abundance and keeps it so fresh and pure? Whose is the light that every day shines down upon us from above, shedding around us its genial warmth and illuminating our pathway? Whose are the clouds that traverse the heavens, bringing us the early and latter rains and fruitful seasons, so that there is enough for man and for beast? Whose are the springs that rise among the hills and flow among valleys, quenching the thirst of every living thing? How does it come to pass that these natural agencies are constantly ministering to our ever-recurring wants? Are they the provisions of man's skill? He has no more to do with their existence and activites than he has to do with the remotest star that shines in the depths of space. God is their author, and all their movements are regulated by his will. But, now, without their ministrations we could not continue in existence for an hour. Let him take away the air we are now breathing; let him extinguish the lights that shine in the heavens; let him stop the kind ministrations of the clouds; let him bid the springs hide themselves in the caverns of the earth, and what then would become of man's vain notion that he is his own supporter in life? As quickly as he sprang up out of the dust would he return to it and be no more. Thus we are kept in being every moment by the mercies of God. But do these mercies deserve no recognition at our hands? Do they call for no love and for no service? Can anything be plainer than this: that if we are kept in being every moment by the mercies of God that being ought to be consecrated to him? This is the appeal the apostle here makes from the providential mercies of God. Ought we not to respond to it also? I confess I know not how to characterize the conduct of the man who sees that he is thus kept in being by the mercies of God, and yet deliberately goes on in sin against him. It may be illustrated by an historical incident. It is said that in the battle of Alma, in 1854, a wounded Russian soldier fell into the hands of the English and was piteously crying for water. An English captain stepped aside from the ranks of a passing regiment and ministered to his wants, and then hastened on to join his command. The wounded man was much refreshed, and struggling up in the use of the strength that captain's kindness had ministered to him, picked up his gun, deliberately took aim, and shot him as he passed away in the distance. Now we are amazed; we are indignant at such ingratitude as that. But what does the poor sinner do who is kept in being every hour by the mercies of God? He does not, indeed, in the use of the strength that God every hour confers upon him, inflict on him a mortal mound; for he is beyond his reach, and, besides, is invulnerable to his assaults. But he does inflict on him the only wrong in his power. The very breath he gives him he breathes out before him, perhaps, in words offensive to his purity and insulting to his majesty. The very powers of body and mind he bestows on him he employs in violating his law, and the very being he preserves for him he moves up and down on the earth right before his face in the constant attitude of rebellion against his authority! Dear unconverted friends, abhor such ingratitude as that, and since you are kept in being every hour by the mercies of God, do what is here insisted on : consecrate that being to him.

But as the apostle appeals to the mercies that are from God in providence, so he appeals to the mercies that are from him in redemption. In this epistle he proves that all have sinned ; that all have gone astray ; that all are exposed to the penalty of the law ; that all are so unde-serving and so ill-deserving that they are justly exposed to the doom threatened against the finally impenitent ; but that, nevertheless, God has given for their redemp-tion the very most and the very best even he could give : the blood and life of his own Son ; and it is specially in view of this mercy—so wonderful ; so immeasurable— that he entreats us to devote ourselves to his service ; and if we appreciate his appeal as we should, we will gladly say :

> " Lord, I am thine, entirely thine,
>   Purchased and saved by blood divine;
>   With full consent thine I would be,
>   And own thy sovereign right in me.
>
> " Thine would I live; thine would I die;
>   Be thine through all eternity."

The last appeal the apostle makes to secure this conse-

cration is that it is our reasonable service. And who can
say anything against it? Who can present anything
that will have even the appearance of a reason why we
ought not to do what is here enjoined? Shall we not,
then, do it? Shall we follow reason everywhere except
where it is most important to follow it? If so, let us
not be surprised if the disastrous consequences shall
hereafter be in proportion to the magnitude of our folly.

I make one remark in conclusion. If Christians would
perform the duty here enjoined, many of them would be
much happier than they now are. They are in doubt as
to the relation in which they stand to the Saviour. They
walk in darkness; and most probably the reason is that
they are not performing this duty as they ought. They
are not wholly consecrating themselves to God. If we
keep back anything from him, he will keep back something from us. If we keep back this consecration from
him, he will keep back the evidence that we are his.
But if we give ourselves to him, he will give himself to
us. If we give ourselves wholly to him, he will give
himself wholly to us; and he will so dwell in us that we
shall have the consciousness that we are his, and so have
the ''peace that passeth all understanding,'' and the
''joy that is unspeakable and full of glory.''

PERSONAL WORK FOR THE MASTER.

BY REV. WILLIAM N. SCOTT, D. D.

Pastor of the First Presbyterian Church, Galveston, Texas.

"And let him that heareth say, Come."—REV. xxii. 17.

[Read in connection John i. 40–51; Mark v. 18–20, and Rev. xxii. 17–21.]

THE subject before us is one which cannot be presented amiss to any assembly or congregation of worshippers. It is a duty to which we are all called by the Master, and by every prompting of a gracious and regenerate nature. To take part in this great work of calling men to repentance and to life; to "*say*" to men about us, "*come*." No Christian, young or old, is excepted and exempted. His word to all of us is, son! daughter! "*Go, work to-day in my vineyard.*"

Let me say in the outset that there is a great deal of work—work that is necessary and important—done in the church and in connection with the church, which, while bearing on this work, is not precisely that to which he calls us when he says: "And let him that heareth say, Come." Many of us, perhaps, do other work, do it well and faithfully, who do but little, if any, of this work.

What, then, do we mean by "*Personal work for the Master*"? We have several striking illustrations of it in the Scriptures read for our lesson to-day—*e. g.* (1), We read that when *Andrew* had found the Messiah, and had become convinced that he was the Christ of God, he

went after his own brother, Simon''; went after him
earnestly and persistently, and ''found him'' and
''*brought him to Jesus*.'' He could not convert him—
save him! but he could *invite* him and ''bring him to
Jesus,'' who could save him! Here, then, we have a
''brother'' going after his own brother according to the
flesh; and, saved himself, seeking to save his brother.
(2), Next, we have the case of Philip, who, when
he had ''found *him* of whom Moses in the law and the
prophets did write,'' immediately sought out and found
his *friend*, Nathaniel, and called and invited him to
Christ. And when Nathaniel, like many of our friends,
would have objected and argued the matter with him, he
gave the wise and sufficient answer: ''*Come and see*.''
The Christ to whom he called him would be the sufficient answer to all his difficulties. Here we have the
case of a man converted to God, possessed of a religious
hope, in turn going after his *friend*—his *bosom companion;* and, in the language of this text, ''*saying* to
him, Come''—inviting him to Christ, the Saviour of
men. (3), Again, take the case of that *poor sufferer*
whom Jesus healed in Gadara, who was possessed of
many devils and driven by them into the mountains
and the tombs. You remember that when he was
healed and given back his reason, the first cry and
prayer of his heart was that he might *abide* with the
Master! that he might still sit at his feet and listen to
his gracious words! It was a desire that we can all understand and sympathize with. But the Master said to
him, ''Not so; I have work for you to do, the time of
rest is not yet. *Go home* to thy friends and tell them
there what great things the Lord hath done for thee,
and hath had compassion on thee.'' Here, then, we
have the *head of a family*, father or mother, commanded

and commissioned to go first to *their own* and tell the story of God's love and grace, and seek the salvation of those whom God has given them. (4), And, in fine, in the language of the text, the "last message" of Jesus ascended, we have the solemn and tender charge, given to *all*, without regard to human ties and relationships, to say to *men about them*—to *all men*, to every sinning, suffering soul—"God bids you come!" God sets before you "an open door!" "We pray you, in Christ's stead, be ye *reconciled to God*." What, then, is the *meaning* of our subject? It is God's call to all of us, to every one who loves him and obeys his voice, to take part in this great work of saving men—to " SAY " to men about us, " Come! " to *invite* others to Christ!

Our duty is personal; our opportunites are personal; our responsibility is personal; our reward will be personal. *"Let him that heareth say, Come."*

In urging this subject upon my brethren—

Remark I.: That this duty would seem, in advance of all statement and argument, to be both *reasonable* and *natural.* Saved ourselves that we should seek to save others. Plucked from the "miry clay and the horrible pit," our "feet placed upon the rock" and a "new song put into our mouths," we should as instinctively " tell to sinners round what a dear *Saviour* we have found," as one rescued from the gates of death by the skill of his physician hastens to commend him to others about him who are suffering with the like affliction. Surely there is nothing unreasonable or fanatical in this! He who should sit down at ease and indifference to the sufferings of others about him, and yet profess that he himself has been healed by the Great Physician of souls, would be a monster of ingratitude and inhumanity !

God has in mercy and in wisdom ordained this as our

duty, and called us to this work. In *mercy*, because it
is thus that we are enriched and blessed ourselves. "He
that watereth others shall be watered himself." There
is no joy like this joy! The joy that filled a Saviour's
heart. The joy of those who "turn many to righteousness." And, then, in *wisdom*, too. For after all, though
it be but an earthen vessel," yet none other can so tell,
so effectively and so sympathetically tell, the joys of deliverance and salvation as those who have themselves
been rescued by his wondrous power and grace! Dr.
Thomas Guthrie, in his "*Gospel in Ezekiel*," tells of
a *sun-burnt stranger* from some far-off eastern clime
who one day stood on the streets of a great city, beside a
spot where birds were offered for sale. As he saw them
ruffling their gay plumage against their prison bars, the
tears were in his eyes. Great was the wonder of those
who stood by, when he bought first one and then another
and another of the birds, and opened the doors and set
them free, till they were all soaring and singing in the
bright sunshine! And when they asked him what it all
meant, he answered, with deep emotion, " I was myself
once a prisoner and I know the joys of liberty."

No angel of God, or messenger from a sinless heaven,
could ever so paint the pangs of sin or the joys of salvation
as a redeemed and ransomed sinner! Yes; it should be
a most natural thing to a gracious soul.

Remark II. : Yet it is to be feared that it is a *sadly-
neglected work*. There are many fair and reputable
church members who take but small, if any, part in it.
There are many who teach Sunday-school and Bible
classes, and who prepare well for these duties, who do
but little of this direct personal work. Nay, there are
many who stand in the sacred desk and fill the responsible place of ministers of the word who are sadly derelict

here, who find it easier to preach to the great congregation than to "carry the gospel from house to house," and from heart to heart.   Our own heart and pastoral experiences differ much from those of others, if these testimonies are not sadly true.   How often have we met with those who found it easier to talk to others on the subject of personal religion than to their own—the members of their own family circle!   *Parents* who could talk to a neighbor's child with more readiness than to their own flesh and blood!   Husbands and wives who have kept silence so long towards each as to the inner life that it seems impossible to break it.   We are called here to "utter forth"—to "say"—to others—to *our own*— "COME."   I am not urging a noisy obtrusiveness—a testifying which is of the lip, and not of the heart! God forbid!!   And yet a silence that is unbroken on such themes and with such motives, urging us to *speak out*, must be a "*guilty silence.*"

Remark III.: It is evident that this work *greatly needs to be done.*   The opportunities of Christian ministers and of those Christian workers who give their whole life up to God's service are necessarily limited, however great they may be relatively.   They can only reach a certain limited number; and then, too, there are often those who, for one cause or another, are not accessible to them.

But what if all the Lord's people were in this matter "prophets indeed"?   What if the hundreds and thousands of Christians all about us were obeying this call and command: "Let him that heareth say, Come." Who can measure the results which would follow? What if our noble Christian physicians in the exercise of their high vocation did this work as they had opportunity?   What if our business men, with the scores and

hundreds employed under them, used their great influence to this holy end? What if the humblest Christian
man or woman were faithful here, who can measure the
glory to God in the salvation of men which would be the
blessed result? Why, we should have Pentecost all the
year round! And this is the divine order and plan for
securing it: "Let him that heareth say, Come." Let
there be this warm, tender, universal call given! and in
answer to it the "rivers of salvation" will flow all
about us!!

It is greatly-needed work. Men expect it of you if
they have confidence in your piety and Christian character. It is the consistent thing they expect you to do.
Your silence may be a great stumbling-block in their
way, leading them to doubt the truth of all that which
you profess. For, say they, "if you believe these things
how can you keep silent"!

Said a young lady to her Bible-class teacher, when at
length the teacher had broken silence and spoken to her
warmly of her soul, "I have been praying for months
that you would speak to me." That teacher, perhaps,
was not more remiss than most of us are! All around
us in life there are those who are waiting for the word
at our mouth, and God is saying to us: "Keep not
silence, but say to them from me, '*Come.*'" It is
greatly needed.

Remark IV.: Such work is *greatly* FRUITFUL. There
is none like it for fruitfulness. This work of going and
carrying the invitation personally to men; consecrating
our personal affection, sympathy, and influence to the
work of wooing and winning men to Christ. It is undoubtedly true that in all times of true and heaven-given
revival the best and largest results are reached mainly
thus: Christians are stirred up and go to work; those

who have been silent take up the gospel invitation and extend it with warmth and love; and the quickening Spirit thus brings into the kingdom those who would otherwise never have been reached. It was so at the beginning, at Pentecost, when "they were all assembled with one accord, in one place," that the Spirit came in mighty power! It was God's answer to the earnest cry and awakening of his people. It is ever so. It ever shall be so. God never lays a command like this in our heart and conscience without pledging his divine power for our help. When those who were "scattered abroad" by the persecutions raised at Jerusalem, "went everywhere preaching the word," they made converts and planted churches wherever they went. In answer to universal efforts there were universal results. Can we doubt that if such a spirit took possession of the church of Christ to-day, if every Andrew should bring his brother Simon, if every Philip should bring his friend Nathaniel, if every Christian now alive upon the earth should by God's help bring another to Christ, that ere the new century had advanced far into its decades the world would have been ransomed for God; the hallelujah chorus of redeemed millions would be heard from isle to isle, from continent to continent, yea, "from the river to the ends of the earth!"

Remark V.: I cannot now speak of the *glory* and *blessedness* of *this work;* of the richness, the joy of that soul who, "laboring with Christ," has turned many to righteousness," and in whose crown of rejoicing in heaven "stars" shall shine for ever. Such an one needs no monument of brass or marble to tell the story of his or her life. His monument is builded where there are "neither griefs nor graves." It will be unveiled when the King himself shall rise up and say, "Well done, thou

16

good and faithful servant." "Come in, thou blessed of my Father, inherit the kingdom."

In closing let me add *three thoughts* as to *how* this work is to be done. We are agreed that it should be done. We have been remiss; we confess it with sorrow. Now *how* shall it be done. I answer:

(1), *Prayerfully*. It should only be done, it *can* only be done, *thus*. Prayer is the only preparation which can avail; not our eloquence, or learning, or skill in urging, but only that "power with God and men" which comes through much prayer can give success here. One of the old Puritan fathers has well expressed this truth in the words: "First, go plead with God for men, and then go plead with men for God." Prayer, prayer alone unlocks the door and opens the way.

(2), It must be done *earnestly*. It is no matter for idle conversation. If you would impress others you must be deeply impressed yourself; if you would move them you must be moved. Nothing is so quickly recognized as a deep and sincere interest in one's welfare, temporal or eternal. Let this be seen; under God it will win its way.

(3), It should be *done at once*. While we neglect and put off our duty to friends about us, they are passing away out of our sight one by one; there are few of us, I suppose, who have not felt the sting of reproach for such neglect. "Let him that heareth *say, Come!*" Let him say it *at once*, ere it is too late. When John Wesley was asked by Sophia Cooke "*how she should live*," he is said to have replied, "*live to-day*." Yes, "redeem the time." "Whatsoever thy hand findeth to do, do it with thy might for there is no work, nor device, nor knowledge, nor wisdom, in the grave, whither thou goest."

Joseph of Arimathea.*

THE CHRISTIAN OUTSIDE OF THE CHURCH.

BY REV. JOHN A. PRESTON, D. D.

Pastor of the First Presbyterian Church, Charlotte, N. C.

"And after these things Joseph of Arimathea, being a disciple of Jesus, but secretly for fear of the Jews, asked of Pilate that he might take away the body of Jesus."—JOHN xix. 38. "And went in boldly unto Pilate, and craved the body of Jesus."—MARK xv. 43.

RESPECTABLE burial has ever been the dictate of enlightened friendship, and the records of the race are not older than the account of the efforts of friends to lay their dead lovingly to rest. Abraham would not receive the cave of Machpelah as a gift, but preferred the inalienable title by purchase. From Egypt to Machpelah was not too long or expensive a funeral journey at the death of Jacob; while the bones of Joseph, preserved through centuries, were carried through the entire exode to be laid in the ancestral tomb.

Nor was this instinct confined to God's people. The ancients, in some cases, even went so far as to condition immortal blessedness upon burial on earth; and one of the most stirring of the Greek tragedies has as its pivotal

---

* A word as to the suggestion of this topic may not be out of place: I was riding, some years ago, through one of the grand old country congregations of the Synod of Virginia. The devoted pastor pointed to an attractive farm-home, shaded by ancient trees, and said, "There lives one of our best Christians, but he is a Joseph of Arimathea." I have since seen and plead with many such.—J. A. P.

SOUTHERN PRESBYTERIAN PULPIT.

point the heroic determination of a sister to brave the king and his death-threat, and to throw the needed handful of earth upon the body of her brother. That this sentiment has lost not one whit of its power in modern times, the tears shed and the money expended at the graves of our loved ones abundantly prove.

And we are peculiarly impressed by any attention paid to our dead. Many a stranger, in our own land, has made a lasting friend of the old father by taking the boy, slain in battle, and giving him decent burial. Possibly the exigencies of the times forbade more than an undressed pine coffin, still the old man remembers, upon his death-bed, to charge his children if ever they shall meet the stranger to be kind to him who had been kind to them and theirs.

This debt every Christian owes to the man whose life we are considering, Joseph of Arimathea. He kept Christ's body from being thrown unburied into the valley of Hinnom, or if even lightly buried, yet from being unearthed and devoured by starveling dogs. The very thought makes the lover of the Lord shudder, to say nothing of the destruction of prophecy. This man saved our adorable Lord's body from the felon's fate and gave it the burial of friendship. We can linger but a moment over this solemn scene. What a contradiction in terms! That he should die who was himself the author of life, yea, life itself! It is the best illustration possible of the indestructibility of faith, that these Christians could handle the dead hands, and touch the dead person, and yet say, my Lord. Not having the key to this mystery, Christ's death to them seemed the utter overthrow both of their hopes and of the truth of the Lord's words, and yet then, as often since, faith refused to surrender to perplexity.

The scene was probably not as we have pictured it, a taking down from the cross, for Rubens' famous picture probably halts in this respect; but it was rather with the cross prone upon the ground, while trembling hands first draw the nails, then wash the wounds, then wrap the body and the precious head in fine linen inlaid with spices; and then these ministering men and women disappear with the precious burden, for time presses. Of the burial of Moses it has been said, ''That was the grandest funeral that ever passed on earth,'' but this one must be excepted. Alone and unique in the history of all time was this burial of the Lord of glory. As he had come into the world unheralded, so was he buried, with no requiem save the sob of the weeping women. As those highly-privileged ones carry their precious burden to lay it in a new rock-hewn tomb, we allow them to disappear, and turn our attention to the instigator and chief actor in the scene, Joseph of Arimathea.

The notices of him are scant. Nothing is known of his previous history. Probably he had yielded to the impulse so potent in our own day, and had left his obscure village for the larger business opportunities of the city. But few as are the lines devoted to the history of this man, there are several exceedingly significant statements. Joseph was probably a member of the Sanhedrin, the great court of the Jews, deprived at that time, indeed, of its power, but not of its august authority in the eyes of the Jews. Then Joseph was rich ; from the emphasis given, he was probably very rich; relatively speaking, he was a Jerusalem millionaire. But he had not been seduced by his money, for he was righteous. Nor did his goodness stop here, for he was religious, and not only did he fear Jehovah, but he had first waited for, and then accepted the Messiah. Thus this man possessed money, position, and character, that enviable trio of gifts, and, best of all, faith in Christ. Brief as the record is, we already see that Joseph is a marked man. But we have yet to mention that which should give him a place among the world's heroes, his *splendid courage*. The danger was so intense that even the bold Peter shrank from the cross ; indeed, no one of the followers of Christ, save only John, whose love could not be daunted, dared mingle with that blood-thirsty crowd, and even John was wisely quiet. But this man went boldly to Pilate and asked to be permitted to honor the man whom the crowd had just murdered, thereby accusing every one who had taken part in the crucifixion of being a murderer. Especially would this act on the part of a member of the Sanhedrin be an insult to those Pharisees and rulers who had led the murderous mob.

Joseph imperilled his all by this act. His place as a ruler he absolutely forfeited; he could never again meet with the Sanhedrin. Should he ever presume to attend its meeting, it would happen to him as to Cataline in the Roman Senate, that all men would shrink from him and leave him alone. Thus Joseph threw away the highest position within reach of his ambition. And then his great wealth was also exposed to robbers. In *Ben Hur* we have probably an accurate picture of the peril in which property stood when the owner had fallen under suspicion. The greedy Roman officials were all too eager and able to combine with local enemies and filch away the wealth they so lusted for. There was thus every reason for Joseph to fear that his act would impoverish him. More than this, his very life was endangered. How easy for those Pharisees who had maddened the mob by the cry, "crucify him," to point to the home of Joseph and say, "crucify *him*." Especially does this splendid act of courage move us when we remember that it was not under the impulse of passion, or moved by the hope of renown, but for *pure principle's sake*. The deeds which have called out the world's shout of admiration have usually looked to this applause and have been inspired by it. In one of the famous naval battles of old, spectators lined the shore as far as the eye could reach, so that even the coward felt himself a hero, for the eyes of the world were upon him. We are made to believe that old Horatius standing at the bridge's mouth in the early dawn of history, though he dared not look around, yet felt that all Rome was looking on, and that his wife stood upon the porch of their home a spectator of the deeds of her husband; and that his was his country's cause, for was he not ready to die for "the ashes of his fathers and the temple of his gods"? But this man, Joseph, had none of these incentives. No martial music stirred his blood, no tattered banner fired his imagination, no praise for which to hope, but only contempt. As this man sat in his home awaiting the hour, he could see that disgrace would fall upon his family; men would curse his very memory, as they had done that of Jereboam, son of Nebat. There was nothing to inspire, but everything to discourage, and yet he went forward, sacrificing wealth, position, and very life if need be, for *pure principle's sake*. As we erect statues to the great men of the past, might not a modest statue point to the memory of the man who held duty above the opinion of friends or considerations of safety?

But as much as we admire Joseph of Arimathea, yet when we remember what he *left undone* we are tempted to forget what he did. *He refused to confess Christ during his life;* he buried the Lord when dead, but took no part in his work. And the Saviour needed *just such a friend as Joseph;* when the contemptuous question was asked, "have any of the rulers believed on him?" this man should have been the answer. What strength he would have been to the disciples, and what comfort to the Lord. To think of his shutting his door against the weary Christ on those evenings when the Son of man had not where in Jerusalem to lay his head, but must needs go to Bethany for sympathy and shelter. He may have been a great man, but it is hard, indeed, to forgive him for his neglect of our Saviour. As we exercise the sweet privilege of hospitality, how often we wish we could have had the Master under our humble roof. To think of a believer, who could have done so, and yet would not entertain the Lord, and that in the hour of the Master's need! To think of this man standing by and hearing the rude Jews jeering the Lord without taking the Master's part! Shame upon such a man and shame upon his memory! He did much, but he left more undone!

From the violent contrasts of this striking history, three pointed truths claim attention—

I. The first is a sweet and most consoling lesson : *That there is salvation outside of the visible church.* Joseph was a true Christian, and had he died before his great act he would have been saved. We believe many do thus die. An earnest Christian once asked the speaker not again to make this statement, lest it confirm souls in the sin of neglecting church membership, but the preacher is not responsible for the influence of truth ; and this is truth, and consoling truth. For are there not many whose memories make it impossible for them to enjoy the thought of heaven, lest they should be lonely there? Now if the loved ones, already gone before, were not

Christians, then a merciful God help you to bear this heaviest earthly sorrow, and he will! But if these loved ones were Christians, only not professing Christians, does it not lift a crushing weight from the heart to hear that in the olden times there was a true disciple, but one secretly, for fear of the Jews?

II. The second lesson is almost in the teeth of the first. It is: *That however God may forgive, nothing can excuse the neglect of church membership;* with double emphasis upon the negative—*Nothing* can excuse! And by church membership we do not mean simply enrolment in the church, nor a passing expression of faith—Joseph once voted for Christ—but whole-souled consecration to the work. In these days of easy profession the outer circle of the church is naturally large; many unconverted, and many converted but unconsecrated; while the true church is the inner circle, who are making an honest effort to give Christ their all. Now we repeat our proposition, that nothing can excuse a true believer from *at once* taking a stand within this inner circle. The battle has been joined, and we must stand upon one side or the other. It is for Christ or against Christ. If we will not take one stand, the devil claims us for his own and gains all the credit. A solemn statement upon this point fell from our Saviour's lips, "He that is not with me is against me, and he that gathereth not with me scattereth abroad"; where not simply the act of being on Christ's side is made necessary, but we must belong to the *harvesting-force*, otherwise we undo his work. It is admitted that it is not fair for Satan to claim the influence of a secret Christian, but what cares *he* for fair means or foul? The fact is undeniable; a father may go from his knees to the sanctuary, but if he does not take his seat with the communicants how can he expect

his son to consider him a Christian? Is it not entirely
possible that the sons of Joseph of Arimathea took part
in the crucifixion and dyed their hands in the blood of
the father's Christ? What had their father ever done to
show his allegiance to the Nazarene? No parents need
expect the conversion of their children if they neglect
church membership; and even if one parent is a devoted
Christian, yet the children are naturally inclined to follow
the one whose life is such as their unrenewed hearts
love. We believe that fathers who either neglect the
duty of church membership, or who live formal church
lives, are responsible for unsaved children! The same
is true of every relationship which gives influence. The
head of a mercantile or manufacturing establishment, or
one holding any part of trust in these great enterprises,
is directly responsible for this influence. The church is
the great means of witness-bearing, and work in the
church, for instance, the Sabbath-school work, devotion
to the sick, liberality and regularity, all have a far wider
influence than the visible results; for whenever the unsaved think of religion, the life of their business superior enters as a helping factor. It makes it easier to
love Christ and lead a pure life : the influence is on the
right side. On the other hand, how natural for a factory
girl to dismiss religious convictions when she meets her
employer upon the street and recognizes in him one who
has taken no stand for Christ. The devil very gladly
suggests that this man has had the time and opportunity
for investigation, and that if he is not a Christian there
can be no reality in religion. This is a deadly influence,
and there is no mode of escape save a hearty profession
of Christ. This influence is probably more potent in the
case of teachers in our schools and colleges than in any
other work, and for obvious reasons; but we forbear;

suffice it to say that a student cannot learn sufficient mathematics to calculate, or language to state the harm a non-professing teacher will do in a life-time, by unsettling the convictions of students at the critical time of their lives. While blessed is the memory of those teachers, who, while worshipping in the temple of learning, acknowledge no king but Jesus!

It is, however, when we remember that this influence is not only certainly hostile, but that it destroys the immortal part of man, that we see the full strength of the case; and if additional argument were needed we have only to remember the insult to Christ, the unpardonable neglect of his precious love. We condemn Joseph of Arimathea for neglecting the Lord, but we know more fully and see far more clearly than he the merits of the great Christ. To accept his wonderous redemption and yet be afraid to acknowledge the giver is base ingratitude. Nor can there be any excuse or reason for delay; for we are not arguing with unbelievers, but with those who already believe. We return to the statement that it is unpardonable ingratitude to Christ, and cruel injustice to any within the circle of your influence, not to stand out at once and boldly. *Nothing can excuse this sin*. This whole truth may find fitting expression in a case which occurred in one of the quiet God-loving homes of our church. The gentleman was an earnest Christian, but a Joseph of Arimathea; in answer to his wife and pastor when they urged him to join the church, he plead the fact that he was not in exact doctrinal accord with the church he attended, and it was his wont to add, "after all the Christian life is an inward one, and I strive to live that life." But after this Christian had grown old outside of the church, a young man came to him and said that he had thought of *being a Christian*, but had concluded to follow his example. Imagine the shock to this godly man : follow his example, and reject Christ! The very next Sunday the man not simply asked to be received into the church, but demanded it. He could scarcely wait the week out! And thus he testified to this one young man that he was not against Christ; but could he go back over the past fifty years of his life and undo what those years had done, or speak to the many young men whom his example had influenced! We are convinced that many make the irretrievable mistake and that theirs is the experience of another Joseph of Arimathea. When dying he drew his pastor close to him, and, with almost his last breath, said, ''I go to heaven, for I have for years trusted Christ, but oh! that I had confessed him.'' *Nothing can excuse this sin*, nor can there be any valid reason for postponement.

III. There is yet another lesson enfolded in this history: *Joseph was hindered by fear, and it is still fear which prevents confession and destroys Christian testimony.* We seem to have here a decided inconsistency. We have just spoken of Joseph as a hero of splendid courage, while now we charge him with cowardice. But is not this the paradox of the human heart? There are many men among us who have proven their courage on the field of battle. Their bravery has gone upon record, and even if they should have the good sense to decline a score of foolish duels, no one could dare call them cowards; and yet these dauntless heroes are *afraid* to attempt family worship ; and that, too, when there would be no hostile audience, as the overjoyed wife gathered the children around their fireside. And yet the hero of half a hundred battles is afraid !

This paradox of the human heart is all too apparent.

We believe Christians would still die for their faith; that if the enginery of hell was again set in motion, those inventions of Satan to crush the foot, torture the hand, draw apart the limbs in slowness of exquisite torture, or burn the body; that if the hell-inspired Inquisition was upon us, if the air was shattered by the shrieks of our own family; that yet, rather than curse Christ, we would die! Rather than take any of the Inquisition's hideous forms of blasphemous recantation upon our lips, we would submit even to these hell-devised tortures. And yet we are afraid to speak for Christ. We are afraid to testify in our daily lives. This sad failure was aptly expressed by a Christian woman. I asked her to try and reach a poor old woman, whom I had failed to interest. This Christian woman said, "I cannot speak to her; I do love Jesus, but I am such a *coward in the little things.*" This was precisely the failure with Joseph; rather than see his Lord's body thrown to the dogs, he would die—would face a mob of devils, but he shrank from the gaze of the Sanhedrin or the smile upon the streets. Brave at a crisis, but a coward in little things; and in this we all fail; men who would die for Christ are even afraid of the church session as it meets to welcome Christ's children to his fold. We hold our finger just here upon the weakness of the church; our testimony is deadened through our cowardice in little things. We need to learn the lesson of a blind girl during the days of later Rome: several drunken ruffians are said to have stopped her before a statue of the emperor and commanded her to kneel and worship. The child's simple answer was, "we kneel to no one but Jesus"; nor would she yield, although those fiends crushed her poor body with brutal stones. It is an immortal lesson, to have courage in small things and great; to kneel to no one but Jesus.

We leave this striking life-story with this pleasing thought: its great mistake was made good before it was too late. While Joseph could not recall the priceless opportunity of ministering to the Son of God during the days of his earthly humiliation and need, yet he did come out boldly at the last; and when he was again ushered into that august presence, he came not as a lean, barren soul, but was welcomed by the angels as one of the privileged few who had been permitted to take part on the Lord's side in the great tragedy which culminated at Calvary.

The aim of this discourse has been to plead with you to follow the same course; to come out before it is too late. It is a plain step. Many truths which are pressed by the preacher are beset with perplexity in their application. Not so this; the need is a simple, straightforward step of duty. Take your stand decidedly within the inner circle of the church; undertake her work; bear her burdens; share her disappointments; and you shall enjoy her rewards.

THE STRIVING SPIRIT.

BY REV. ROBERT P. KERR, D. D.,
Pastor of the First Presbyterian Church, Richmond, Va.

" My Spirit shall not always strive with men."—GENESIS vi. 3.

IN the sixth chapter of Genesis we have set before us the imposing spectacle of God the Holy Spirit striving with a wicked world and race of men. Sin had reached its hideous culmination. Crime of every kind was almost universal, and earth seemed to have become a province allied to the dominion of Satan. The cup of iniquity being nearly full, God was going soon to press it to the guilty lips of men, that they might drain to its dregs the bitter draught; and the cloud of divine wrath was soon to break with the crash of world-wide destruction upon the human race.

But though the progress of iniquity had been steady and rapid, it had not reached its culmination without divine interference. In all their wretched criminality there had been present and active among men the august personality of the Holy Spirit. The text lifts the veil which hides the unseen, and we behold, from the divine standpoint, a progress which had not gone on unresisted from above.. God the Holy Ghost placed himself in the way of this terrible defection of the world from truth and righteousness. The men of that day and their fathers had travelled far from all that is good, but at every step they had been confronted and opposed by a divine barrier. Over God's most gracious influences they had trod, and in spite of a resisting omnipotence of love they had progressed until they reached a height of crime that lifted its face into the very presence of the majesty of heaven.

It may be asked, How could man surpass resisting omnipotence? How could man overcome God? The answer is easy. Man is not a puppet, without power of choice; he is not a beast, without intellect, soul, conscience. He is a free moral agent originally imaged after God; and his Maker has never forced him against his will to do anything good. This would be to unmake man, to degrade him to a brute. God respects man in his freedom, nor does he seek a slavish service of the soul. In later times Christ, at the threshold of man's volition, declares, "Behold I stand *at the door* and *knock*." So in the days before the flood the Holy Ghost strove with man, but did not force his will.

How great the rebelliousness of mankind was may be estimated from what it was able to overcome. For in the gigantic struggle with divine grace they came off winners, gaining for themselves by this overmastery the victory of black and awful success.

This could not continue forever. The Spirit would not be insulted with perpetual impunity. God's wrath is aroused, and over the heads of men fall those pregnant words, "My Spirit shall not always strive with man." The world had lived out its probation, and the hour was set on the dial-plate of time for the destruction of the human race by a catastrophe the most stupendous that history records. The Spirit departed; grieved, he turned away, and the blow fell in swift retributive justice upon mankind, in the flood by which all perished except the family of one righteous man.

How did the Spirit strive then, and how does he strive with men to-day?

It was, and is, by the use of the whole apparatus of the universe; in other words, by the use of everything that is. The powers of nature show in turn the goodness and the wrath of God. Does calm sunshine mean nothing? Is there no lesson in the sunset; no invitation in the yellow harvest-fields? Have all the joys of life no heavenly undertone of love and mercy?

Yea, and tempest, disease, fire, famine, death ; is there no warning in them to listening minds? Nature tells us in unmistakable utterance that whatsoever a man soweth that shall he also reap. Surely, she says, sin against law means misery, sorrow, and death. God has put a voice in everything that he has made, from glittering star to lily, rose, or wheat-sheaf; in disease, lightning flash, death, and even hell, to tell men that sin must have its awful fruition and punishment. All this prodigious universe, thrilled with the living presence of the eternal Spirit, throws its barrier across the path that leads away from God and truth. It was so before the flood; it is so to-day.

Then, also, God had living witnesses. He has never been without some to rebuke a wicked and perverse world. By example and by preached word the Spirit strove to recall the prodigal race of man. A line of preachers extends back in unbroken procession from this day to the gates of Paradise. Men have not been left to the mute testimony of nature alone, nor the foreign interference of angels, but they have had witnesses for God of their own flesh, and blood, and kindred. There have always been, under the guidance of the Holy Ghost, men to preach to men; men to strive, and pray, and weep over the iniquity of their fellows. Noah and his predecessors preached righteousness to their contemporaries, and Noah's successors have never ceased thus to

17

preach, from the time of the flood to this hour, when by the Spirit's appointment souls are warned, by human voices, to fly from the wrath to come.

In our time the magnificent institution of a gospel church, that touches every shore and nation, preaches from ten thousand pulpits, and from house to house, the truths of responsibility, judgment to come, and mercy through the cross. These are preached, and prayed, and sung in the hearing of millions. On the myriad pages of journal and bound volume Christ is set forth, and civilization is but the rostrum for the preaching of the gospel.

Is not all this a striving of God's Spirit? Never since the gospel promise blazed over Eden's wreck has he put forth such energies for the resistance of evil, and the salvation of sinners.

But what of words and example in the sphere of private life? Take we no account of a devout father's life and admonitions; of the teachings of a gentle, believing mother, at whose knees we learned our earliest prayer? Are not these and all the gracious influences by which loved ones have sought to win us for God and heaven the very doing of the Holy Spirit? They are, and his power is present in all of them. His influence touches us at every point of life's varied story.

Leave now all consideration of these external means. Shut out the world, and in thy inmost soul sit down, where only the heart beats, and conscience whispers. Is not this the Holy Spirit's agent also? Yes, and above, behind, and under conscience there is his voice itself. God the Holy Ghost breathes upon the soul. You know this, you have felt it; yes, and alas! you have resisted it. Unconverted man, you have resisted it as many days as you have lived since the dawn of moral consciousness; and, it must be added, you have resisted successfully.

Shall this resistance and this striving of the Holy Ghost go on forever? No. It shall not go on perpetually with the world, with any nation, or any single soul. The striving of the Spirit has an end. A day comes when it is all over, and the soul is forsaken forever to its own chosen lot and fate.

This always occurs at the death of the unbelieving and impenitent. Death ends the conflict. Probation is only in time. The Holy Spirit has no work in hell to save the lost. Of time, it may undoubtedly be said: IT IS NOW OR NEVER. The funeral of the body is sad enough, but what shall we say of the funeral of a lost soul? No angels to bear it singing to eternal rest, but only the fellowship of the doomed and hopeless. He does not always wait for the end of life. The striving Spirit sometimes leaves the resisting soul long before death. There is a sin against the Holy Ghost, for which no prayer is commanded to be offered, which no penitential tears can follow, and upon which no pardoning grace can ever fall.

Though the sin against the Holy Ghost is a matter shrouded in mystery, we have reason to believe that the Pharisees committed it when they said of Jesus, "This fellow doth not cast out devils but by Beelzebub, the prince of devils." The gracious miracles of healing done by our Lord in driving demons from the breasts of men, the Pharisees ascribed to a partnership with Satan. This was a sin against that Holy Spirit by whom these works of mercy were performed.

Just how this sin may be committed it is impossible definitely to say. In general terms we may venture to state that it is blasphemy against the Holy Ghost, and also a deliberate and persistent rejection of his presence and influences, though we cannot point out the definite acts of the soul by which this is done.

The most dreadful thing we know in this world is the desertion of a soul by the Spirit. The fittest symbol of such a case is a human body forsaken by the soul. The most mournful of all sights is that of a corpse. The tabernacle of the mind is empty. No flash of thought lightens the eyes. No gleam of intelligence illumines the countenance. The silver cord is loosed and the golden bowl is broken. The wheel is broken at the cistern. The mansion is desolate, untenanted, and doom, death, decay, are written all over it. The most melancholy of all buildings is a crumbling, deserted house; and as we gaze upon it, the mind vibrates between the present desolation and the past, when living forms moved and happy voices sounded within its walls.

So with a body deserted by the soul. A marble statue, a precise counterfeit of the body, is not mournful, because we know it never was the dwelling-place of mind; but the body dead stands for desertion, and we grieve to look upon it because it has lost the life it had.

Thus the state of a soul bereft of the Holy Ghost is mournful because of its awful loss. Within it once the Holy Spirit dwelt. Along its halls of thought and feeling passed his gracious life and breath. But now he is gone, and gone forever. No more shall holy influence wrap it in gentle warmth. No more shall tender thoughts of God, and penitence for sin be felt within it. Nothing now is left but a deserted moral tenement, a soul doomed to decay forevermore.

In view of sorrowful meditations like these, many an anxious heart has asked itself the question: Have I committed the sin against the Holy Ghost which is never forgiven in this world or the next?

Well, let us see: To ask the question sorrowfully, tenderly, hoping you have not committed this sin, this itself furnishes an answer. You have not, or you would not ask, in this spirit, the question. Have you any sorrow for sin that is more than mere regret occasioned by wounded pride or fear of punishment? any longing for salvation and peace with God? Then you have not sinned away the Spirit. The reason is plain: These tender yearnings are the Spirit's own work. He has not left you, for he has made you anxious and concerned about your soul.

Let us see what ground you have for hope. This anxiety you feel about your soul is proof that you may yet be saved. Your holy guest has not departed. These tender drawings are your hope of salvation and blessed peace. As a practical question, in view of this, what shall you do to be saved?

Give way to the Spirit's drawings. Cultivate and cherish his influence on your soul. Strive not to banish your rising sense of sinfulness. Do not turn off your thoughts on other things, and try to quench that which is bringing you to repentance. A very slender silken line is fastened to your heart, and by it he is drawing you towards life and light. Do not break this gentle fetter.

Pray for your own soul. Have you ever really asked God for eternal life? Have you truly and sincerely sought pardon at the cross? You have uttered words, but has your heart prayed? have you wrestled with God for his unspeakable gift? Certainly you have not, if you are yet away from God. We look with utmost sorrow on a prayerless person, and are dismayed to think of knees that never bend before the throne of grace, and of lips that never open to utter the name of him who is the giver of all good. Little better is the soulless prayer, the petition made up of words, without feeling, and without faith.

Do the things he suggests. What are they? Put that besetting sin beneath your feet. Is there some darling thing that stands in your heart and keeps the Holy Spirit from the sway he seeks? Turn his hateful rival out. It is more than folly to risk eternal life for a mere pleasure, and that one which is unworthy of a place within your breast.

Seek in God's holy word to know the way of life. Here are the teachings to point you to pardon and peace. Read it to know the truth, not from habit, nor necessity, but with a motive to learn the way to God. Seek the guidance of the Spirit as you read. He will make the word a living power in your soul, and the very light of everlasting life.

The soul not deserted by the Holy Ghost has great reason to *hope*, and this hope may be turned at once into fact and sweet fruition. Your soul is yet his abiding-place. He is not very welcome; you allow rather than invite his presence; you do not make your breast his home. He is but a visitor whom you do not admit to intimacy. There are some parts of your soul you do not allow him to enter. If you have guests in any room which you could not present to him, bid them depart at once.

Let him dominate your beliefs, your affections, and your will. Say: I will believe the things he teaches, will love the things he loves, will do the things that please God, and my will shall follow the promptings of the Holy Spirit. He will assume control if you submit, and will undertake a work of renewing, sanctifying power, by which you shall be cleansed from sin and made comformable to the image and character of Christ. The work is grace and the end will be glory.

APPLIED CHRISTIANITY.

WHO IS MY NEIGHBOR?

BY REV. R. K. SMOOT, D. D.

Pastor of the Free Presbyterian Church, Austin, Texas.

'And, behold, a certain lawyer stood up, and tempted him, saying, Master, what shall I do to inherit eternal life? He said unto him, What is written in the law? how readest thou? And he answering said, Thou shalt love the Lord thy God with all thy heart, and with all thy soul, and with all thy strength, and with all thy mind; and thy neighbor as thyself. . . But he, willing to justify himself, said unto Jesus, And who is my neighbor?"—LUKE x. 25–29.

THE one who introduced this conversation claimed to be seeking the way of eternal life. He was on the right track. Had he pursued it he might have been saved. He had gone to the right person. For Jesus Christ is the only source and fountain-head of all the knowledge the world has of the thing which this man sought. Through him alone comes the fact of redemption and the truth of salvation. The way to that unknown God, in search of whom the whole world was groping, was all dark and trackless till Jesus Christ brought life and immortality to light through his gospel. To him we must go, whether we would have that knowledge or the wisdom whose function it is to guide all knowledge. It was in the image of God that man was created "in knowledge, righteousness, and holiness," but the wisdom to adjust and keep these in their proper play was the one thing that man had not. And seeking to find that wisdom in forbidden ground, his hopes, for time and eternity, were wrecked. And man was broken to pieces on the adverse wheel of fortune in· this rash experiment upon the veracity of the Almighty. From that day to this, in all ages, among every people and kindred of the earth, there has been a longing of man to get back to God.

And why? Because in all the vast range and wide sweep of creation man alone is the only creature endowed with a moral nature; a nature in which there could be planted a moral standard of action—the proper and only field for the existence and exercise of conscience. It is this moral nature which separates man—by the whole diameter of his conscious being—from all the other animal creation. The wild beast of the field devours his victim; the bird of the air consumes his prey; the fish of the deep live on their kind. But with them there is no regret, no remorse, no conception of crime, no idea of murder, simply because they are not rational, they have no moral nature, no conscience. Nowhere in all animate nature, outside of human nature, is there such a thing as social life, or fellowship, or binding reciprocal obligation, or sense of duty. Where there is no moral nature there can be no moral law, and consequently no moral accountability, no duty to God, no duty to man, no final judgment, no eternal life. It is in man alone that both duty and accountability to God and his fellow-man is vested. And every time that a question of conscience arises it involves both of these, either directly or remotely.

I. "What shall I do to inherit eternal life?" is a moral question. "Who is my neighbor?" is equally a question of conscience. This lawyer, eminent, distinguished and learned in his profession—"a certain lawyer"—was dealing with a question of conscience. He came to the proper person, the only one who could lead him as an unerring guide and instruct him as an infallible teacher.

"What shall I do to inherit eternal life?" A question which each one of us must ask at some time. A question the solution of which each one of us must find if we would escape eternal death.

But the context says, he "tempted him." Yes, that is the way it reads—"a certain lawyer stood up, and tempted him." After such investigation as I have been able to give this passage, governed, as I have been, by the accepted rules of interpretation of Scripture, I have reached the conclusion that this lawyer was not "in contempt." I do not believe the question was asked in any spirit of hostility, even though there may have been no great and overpowering desire for a clear and unequivocal answer. Habits, of thought, and investigation, and utterance, fasten themselves on men like a "second nature" and characterize the individuality of each. This man's habits were those of a lawyer. He wanted to find out, by questions, what this great Teacher from Galilee knew of this the chiefest of all issues. He was testing the Saviour. He was moving along the lines of investigation for information. In proof of this we must not forget that the word here translated "tempted" is a broad word in its meaning. It may indicate, as I think it does in this case, no bad purpose, but a test merely to bring out fully facts before unknown. For we must remember that it is the intent of the one putting the test, the motive in the heart, which makes it either good or bad. Many illustrations of this might be given. In Luke xxiv. 28 our Saviour tempted his disciples when "he made as though he would have gone further." Also in Mark vi. 48, when he came unto his disciples and "would have passed by them." I do not mean that the language in each one of these passages is the same; but I do mean, that in each case the disciples were put to a test by their Saviour. And I do further claim that the meaning of the word here used does, in the original language, justify fully the interpretation I have given it. Then, again, the question itself involves an issue too grave and too grand to allow any malignant intent to attach, and the final answer of the lawyer himself is offered in proof. We find all through these Scriptures that the "Son of man" never failed to give a respectful hearing and a suitable answer to any and all who came to him with honest doubts and serious questions. This lawyer was evidently feeling for the truth. He would test the power of God's greatest witness by putting the greatest of all questions, one involving the issues of eternal life. The Saviour turns him back upon his own profession, asking him to state the laws of the case. He was its professed teacher, now let him become its practical expounder. "What is written in the law? how readest thou?" A double question, involving a double answer. What is the text of the law? How do you interpret it? To the law he went. His perfect knowledge of that law enabled him to refer at once to the very passage in question. (Deut. vi. 5, and Lev. xix. 18.) He quotes correctly and gives the meaning, "Thou shalt love the Lord thy God with all thy heart, and with all thy soul, and with all thy strength, and with all thy mind; and thy neighbor as thyself." A true and correct answer, a fair and consistent interpretation, a manly, frank, and open confession. Then said the Saviour, "This do, and thou shalt live."

II. How near many a man comes to the kingdom of God and then stops in a dead halt, a stubborn, selfish resistance, a refusal to yield any further; but moving off at right angles, springs with amazing alacrity, a side issue, a different and subordinate question. And so here a difficulty comes up, a new obstacle arises. "But he, willing to justify himself, said unto Jesus, Who is my neighbor?" Self-justification. It is the old Adam. It first made its appearance in the garden of Eden. This man, ''willing to justify himself,'' willed exactly as the first man willed, to justify himself, as ''he heard the voice of the Lord God walking in the garden in the cool of the day. (Gen. iii. 8.) It is one of the wayside arguments for the unity of race. It tells of the origin of man, and the nature of sin. We feel it in our own sinful nature and wicked hearts. We see it all around us and on every hand. Every man ''willing to justify himself.'' It is the outworking of man's depraved nature. It is the wild growth of original sin.

The question is raised by this lawyer as to what constitutes neighborhood. The question itself implies much. It indicates a troubled condition of mind, an anxious solicitude of heart. It is a partial confession of a consciousness that something is wrong, that somehow some duty is left undone ; while at the same time it intimates a readiness to do if he only knew when and where and how to do. ''Who is my neighbor?'' As though he would say I am ready to show mercy, but, to whom? I must know before I do lest my doing should be wrong. Difficulties lay in the way of this lawyer which need never lay in our way. Perplexities arose in his mind which need never arise in ours. The training of ages had taught him, and his people, that he and they owed no duty to man, woman, or child, outside of the Hebrew commonwealth. The very law which he knew so well had been used to teach him that no Gentile was his neighbor. The Hebrew statutory, criminal law would not put an Israelite to death for killing a Gentile, for he was not his neighbor. If a Hebrew saw a Gentile in danger of death he was under no obligation to save his life. Such statutes had been enacted from that covenant constitution given them by the Almighty. This rubbish Jesus had to clear away in laying the deep foundations for the gospel to the Gentiles. Jesus swept by these criminal statutes, trampled them under as he went along, and opened up the wonderful law of love as it lay in the heart of God and the covenant promises.

But with us no less, or hardly less, than with this learned jurist there is a hazy indistinctness as to who is our neighbor. Our compound derivative from two Anglo-Saxon •words, *neah* and *gebur*, signifying near and to dwell, or one dwelling near, has led the masses of the people to feel that a neighbor is merely a contiguous settler whose farm or home joins ours, separated only by a division fence, the children of both families making common playgrounds of the woods and the meadows lying between, and belonging to each. We thus limit "neighborhood" to hamlet, village, or district, and the busy lives of our narrow surrounding constitutes our neighborhood. The word which our Saviour here chooses to define his meaning is one of a broader and deeper import and a wider and more comprehensive range. The Greek word is *plasion*, signifying the same in kind, having no reference to proximity of location except in a secondary sense. He makes it generic and applies it to the race. Humanity is the field of operation; distress, want, poverty, misfortune, pestilence, famine, and crime are the conditions calling for action. He who understands the deep and wide import of the word will bound the limit of his charity only by his ability to do. Village and city, state and country, and suffering humanity everywhere lay claim to our beneficence, and it is only God's providential dealing with us, as emergencies may arise, that can determine how great shall be our ability to do or where our liberality shall end. This is God's law of love to our neighbor. It demands that all the powers of our nature shall be brought into requisition in the fulfilment of our duty to him who made us and to those whom we call our fellows.

III. Humane nature is one,—one in its origin, essence, aims, and purposes. There is a base line of humanity from which all the wonderful surveys of its relative bearings and final courses must be taken. And the lesson when cast up will be that every part is like the whole, and every human heart is human. There is a similarity, a kinship, a brotherhood running through the race from its origin to its close. For God "hath made of one blood all nations of men for to dwell on all the face of the earth, and hath determined the times before appointed, and the bounds of their habitation." (Acts xvii. 26.) Here is the revelation of the origin of man, and the argument for the unity of the human race. It is not in the similarity of skeletons and bones, nor the peculiar build of the spinal column. It is not to be sought in the vertebræ or tibia. The argument lies not in the curves of the back-bone, or the fluting of the shin-bone. But it does lie and is to be found in the "one blood." For the stream of life in the whole human race is one and flows from one fountain. It was this human nature, with its life and the unity of that life in the "one blood," that Jesus Christ assumed when he became man. His human nature consisted of "a true body and a reasonable soul." And so the human nature of the Son of God having its life in this "one blood" made it possible for that blood, when it flowed on the cross, to atone for the sins of the chosen people of God out of every kindred, and tongue, and nation in all times and through all ages. The base line of salvation lies in the "one blood." Without the shedding of blood there could be no remission of sin. (Hebrews ix. 22.) It was the blood of the nations which flowed on the cross, that some of all nations might be saved by the cross. It is that "one blood" which saves to the uttermost them that come unto God by Jesus Christ (Hebrews vii. 25), who poured out his

life in that "one blood" when on the cross he bowed his
head and gave up the ghost. (John xix. 30.) For, "God
set him forth as his Son to be a propitiation through faith in
his blood" for the remission of sins. (Romans iii. 25.)

But in this unity there is a marked and wonderful diversity, physical, social, intellectual and moral,
as marked as that of the various trees which make
up the forest with its "deep contiguity of shade," or the
flowers which adorn the earth with their rich fragrance,
their delicious perfume, and diversified beauty. For
God, who made man and appointed the earth as the
habitation of the children of men, deals with man through
his providence in time and space. The appointments of
the divine mind are determined in his ordering of providence. Nothing comes by chance. God has appointed
the time of our coming into the world, the part we are
to play, the little or much we are to do, the circumstances by which we are surrounded, and the time of
our departure. (Eccl. iii. 1, 2.) Our times are in his
hands, to be lengthened or shortened, to be embittered
or sweetened, as it may please him. His deter-
minations are not rash, sudden, or equivocal. They
correspond to an eternal purpose. They counterpart the
divine decrees. God has harnessed man for the whole
draft. Some are in the lead and some are at the wheel,
for the mighty pull, that the secrets of eternity may be
drawn to the light. Of the chosen ones there are some
who stretch out their hands to God; they stir themselves
up to lay hold upon him; they agonize for the dawn of
that light. These are they who gather the graces of the
Spirit for the joy of church, as the lofty peaks of the
great mountains gather the snows and send down rivers
of waters to refresh the earth. There are others of the
"many called" who, as the parable tell us, are "compelled to come in." But, alas! for them that are the

cast out. Still,—it all works together! The lilies which grow, the young lions which are fed, the hairs which are numbered, and the sparrows which fall, are but the fractions in one vast and mighty sum to be worked out in time. There is no place in the everlasting covenant of God " which is both ordered and sure," (2 Sam. xxiii. 5.) for the wild disorder of the anarchist or the commune of the socialist. No place for the Utopian dreamer or the spiritual somnambulist. He who said, "in the sweat of thy face shalt thou eat bread, till thou return unto the ground" (Gen. iii. 19), meant that word " face " to represent the whole person, soul and body. It is intended to include all labor, manual, intellectual, and moral. "It means a sweat of the brow, and a sweat of the brain, and a sweat of the heart." The hewer of wood, and the drawer of water, is no less in his place than the man who measures the stars, or codifies the laws, or guides and trains the conscience. That sweat of the "face" mitigated the primeval curse, and stands as the seal of the covenant promise that our bread and our water are sure if there be sweat on the face, but not otherwise. Just as that other sweat in the garden of agony was to mitigate the curse on the soul, and stands as the seal of the other covenant promise that the soul shall have the bread and water of eternal life if it be found believing in Christ, but not otherwise. (Luke xxii. 44.) For the same God who said, "He that believeth not the son shall not see life," (John iii. 36.) said also, "that if any would not work neither should he eat." (2 Thess. iii. 10.)

As far back as the confusion of tongues, at the building of Babel in the plains of Shinar, God outlined this physical, social, moral and intellectual distinction, existing then, existing now, and to continue as long as there shall be a race of men on the face of the earth. Yet we find it is equally true touching the one great

issue of redemption, salvation and eternal life; there is
no difference, "for all have sinned and come short of
the glory of God." (Romans iii. 9.)   It is just here that
God applies the unit rule.   The Gentiles, who had not
the law by revelation, had "the work of the law written
in their hearts, their consciences bearing witness, and
their thoughts the meanwhile accusing or else excusing
one another." (Romans ii. 15.)   Not because they were
Gentiles, but because they were of that "one blood,"
and therefore belonged to that humanity, the secrets of
which God shall judge by Jesus Christ according to the
gospel. (Romans ii. 16.)

IV. We must believe, then, that God's law of love is
the inculcation, and the practical application, so far as
our fellow-man is concerned, of universal equity.   It
has nothing to do with vocation, or grade, or rank in
organized society.   It draws no line between peasant
and king, or monarch and vassal.   The rich may sometimes need it, and the pauper may stand at our gate
begging for bread.   It has nothing to do with the adjust-
ing, or readjusting of the inequalities of life—social, civil,
or political.   It is not lodged in that sentimental philosophy which would level all men to the same social
plane; neither does it lift itself up into a frigid condition
of normal justice merely.   In obeying this law of love
we must not be expected to conform our actions to the
arbitrary demands of humanitarian schools of philanthropy, or associations of men.   But it does require us to
render precisely the same equity to others, in given conditions, which it would be reasonable and equitable for
us to expect from them if we should be placed in their
circumstances and surrounded by similar conditions.
We may very reasonably infer that it was to bring out
these facts, touching the duties of the second table of
the law, which induced our Saviour in predicating the

condition of this parable to select a Samaritan, whose
social, civil, and political condition could never be so re-
adjusted, under the Hebrew law, as to make him the
neighbor of a Jew. And the man who was the recipient
of that equitable charity, who had been sorely beaten
and bruised by these merciless robbers, stripped of his
raiment and left half dead, may or may not have been a
man of rank and a Jew. Nothing is said of his social
standing, his civil position, or his political predilections.
The Samaritan made no inquiry about these, nor did he
propose to change them or in any way interfere with
them. It was suffering humanity that lay before him; it
was a fellow-man suffering, and it stirred his compassion;
it was one of the sons of humanity, and he ministered to
his wants. He met the conditions in personally adminis-
tering to the relief of the sufferer with his wine and oil, and
used his pennies to foot the hotel bill. There is no proof
and no argument to prove that this "good Samaritan"
did anything more than comply, as opportunity offered,
with the requirements of the second table of the moral
law. For the argument all along this line was to develop and establish the unity of the race in the "one
blood," and the consequent necessity for the exercise of
the kindlier offices and the heart's compassion in times of
suffering and distress; and to show that this obligation
was enforced by the authority of God and conduced to
the relief of human need, and thereby promoted individual happiness. Along this line much has been done,
and much will yet be done by unregenerate men for
relieving the distress of the world. Hospitals, homes of
charity, reforms of every kind, works of philanthropy,
and compassion of pity and mercy, all go to establish
the truth of the proposition. And so whatever may
come from the kindlier feelings of unregenerate nature,

18

is better than no response to the call for sympathy and
help. Light is better than darkness, but all nature would
lose her beauty, the earth would grow sick, and the
world would die, if no other light fell upon the face of
creation than the light which rules by night—the moon's
pale light. It is the light of the morning, the splendid
beams of the rising sun, which lights the world in glorious day. The one illustrates the charity of unconverted
men, the other illustrates that charity which is done in
the name of Christ by the believing child of God.

It was precisely along this line of the second table of
the law which pertains to our fellow-man that the rich
young man had lived and acted, who, responding to our
Saviour, said: "All these things have I kept from my
youth up: what lack I yet?" A model specimen of a
cultivated gentleman of the best and most refined society
in the world. His great wealth, open heart, and sunny
life had made him an object of personal admiration with
all. His frankness, sincerity, and very nearness to the
kingdom of God, drew out the love of Jesus Christ
toward him. But there was one thing lacking, and because he would not pass up to the requirements of the
first table of that divine law of love he turned from the
loving look of that compassionate Saviour and went away
sorrowful. (Matt. xix. 20–22.) Could we but get a
glance into the hearts of the very best of these unregenerate benefactors of the race, and hear these hearts speak
out in the frankness of their own conscious wants, there
would no doubt come from each of them the inquiry,
"What lack I yet?"

V. The whole duty of man can be performed only when
the life and power of that law which underlies both tables
shall enter into the heart and dwell there with complete
control over all its thoughts and actions. When this
takes place, and the graces of Christianity are planted

and rooted in the human heart by the Spirit of God, its capacity for doing good is enlarged in every direction, whether in human charity, personal benevolence, general philanthropy, or Christian privilege and duty. Man cannot be a lover of his race, as God would have him love that race, without first having the love of God shed abroad in his own heart. It is only when human charity proceeds from the heart in which Christ dwells that it becomes Christian charity. In that matchless delineation of gifts as arranged by Paul (1 Cor. xiii., *passim*) of understanding, and knowledge, and charity, this one grace of God's love underlies and overlaps them all. Though one should give all his "goods to feed the poor," and hath not this divine love (*agape*) planted in his heart, "it profiteth nothing." It is deemed necessary just here to speak with emphasis of this fact, because of the very strong disposition and tendency on the part of many to make the outworkings of the kindlier feelings of unregenerate nature answer both conditions of the law of love—duty to God and duty to man. Christian charity can no more exist in the human heart without first coming from God than the love of God can exist in the heart without producing that charity. Christ was never in prison; neither did you ever visit him, or feed, or clothe him; yet when done to his people in need of them, the full conditions are met, and you have done these things to him. Herein lies the germinal idea of preaching the gospel at home and sending it to the uttermost parts of the earth. It is the love expanding, but not dividing; widening, but not breaking. This law lies at the foundation of that comprehensive teaching of Paul (Romans xiv. 7) that "no man liveth to himself, and no man dieth to himself." The man who loves the Lord Jesus Christ obeys his commandments willingly and cheerfully. There is no such thing as physical compulsion in all the vast round and range of Christian life. The will is free to fall in with the eternal purpose of God, and the heart is responsive to every call. Applied Christianity may consist in giving vast or small sums of money, according as God has prospered us (1 Cor. xvi. 2), for the support of the gospel at home and for the conversion of the world, or a cup of cold water to a thirsty beggar, or a crumb of bread to a hungry outcast, or the bread of life to the perishing soul. Christianity enlarges the heart so that it does not serve God with a spirit of resistance, or even of reluctance, for God makes his people willing in the day of his power. (Psalm cx. 3.) It makes a man seek out opportunities to do good, and run with alacrity to do it. At every turn of the road, in this "valley of tears," we can find some one who has fallen by the way, with many passing by on the other side, leaving the Samaritan's work for us to do; or when, weary in our journey, we sit on the curbstone at the brink of the well, we may see many a poor outcast seeking to draw from the deep waters of earth, whom we might lead to fountains the streams whereof would bring gladness and joy.

Some of the grand masters, who are worthy to be read and studied, have so systematized their great works that certain personages appear at given points, and many times in rapid succession, and then pass out and are seen no more. Their parts are performed, their work is done ; and yet they have given all the tone and character to the play. But God, in the grander unfolding of his eternal purposes through human instrumentality, has made this truth even more impressive. His mysterious hand guides the footsteps of his people in ways they know not of; and by bringing the incidents of one man's life into the necessities of many others, is perfecting that splendid fabric of glory which he is weaving for himself out of the lives of us all.

THE THREE CAUSES OF SALVATION.

BY REV. W. W. MOORE, D. D.,

Professor of Hebrew and Literature in Union Theological Seminary, Virginia.

"Of his own will begat he us with the word of truth, that we should be a kind of first-fruits of his creatures."—JAMES i. 18.

THIS is one of the most comprehensive statements in the Bible. It outlines the whole scheme of redemption. As the acorn contains the oak in embyro, so this text in its small compass contains the whole substance of divine revelation concerning the divine activity, method and purpose in the work of human redemption, not in full development, of course, but in germ. It tells us at once the source, and the means, and the purpose of our salvation from sin. It tells us the *source* of our salvation: "Of his own will begat he us." It tells us the *means* of our salvation: "With the word of truth." And it tells us the *object* of our salvation: "That we should be a kind of first-fruits of his creatures."

Philosophical writers are accustomed to distinguish three kinds of cause. They make a distinction between what they call the efficient cause, the instrumental cause, and the final cause of any effect. The distinction is a good one, and will be of value to us in the interpretation of this text. The efficient cause is the power that produces the result, and without which the result cannot be produced. The instrumental cause is the means by which the power is applied. And the final cause is the object contemplated in producing the effect.

For instance, in the locomotion of a train of cars, the efficient cause of the motion is steam, the instrumental cause is the engine with its appliances of cylinder, piston, driver, and other machinery for bringing the power to bear, and the final cause is the transportation of passengers or produce. In writing a letter the efficient cause of the letter is the person who writes it, the instrumental cause is the pen with which it is written, and the final cause is the object for which it is written, such as communication with a friend, or the transaction of business. In felling a tree the efficient cause of its fall is the woodman who chops it, the instrumental cause is the axe which cuts it, and the final cause is the purpose for which it is cut, fuel, or lumber, or what not.

These three kinds of cause enter into the work of human redemption, and in the text before us we have a statement of what John Calvin has well called the efficient cause, the instrumental cause, and the final cause of our salvation.

I. *The efficient cause:* "Of his own will begat he us." The person referred to is God. The power that regenerates a human soul is nothing less than divine power. And this power is exercised according to his sovereign pleasure, unmoved by any external cause. There are some who teach that man is the efficient cause of his own salvation. These misunderstand the Scriptures. The only efficient cause of salvation is God. This is shown conclusively by the terms used in the Bible to describe the condition of man before regeneration, as well as by the terms which are used to describe the process of regeneration itself. Hear this statement of the Apostle Paul in his epistle to the Ephesians: "You hath he quickened, who were dead in trespasses and sin; wherein in time past ye walked according to the course of this world, accord-

ing to the prince of the power of the air, the spirit that
now worketh in the children of disobedience; among
whom also we all had our conversation in time past in
the lusts of our flesh, fulfilling the desires of the flesh and
of the mind; and were by nature the children of wrath
even as others.   But God, who is rich in mercy, for his
great love wherewith he loved us, even *when we were
dead in sins, hath quickened us together with Christ (by
grace ye are saved)*: and hath raised us up together, and
made us sit together in heavenly places in Jesus Christ:
that in the ages to come he might shew the exceeding
riches of his grace in his kindness toward us through
Christ Jesus.   *For by grace are ye saved through faith:
and that not of yourselves; it is the gift of God; not of
works, lest any man should boast.   For we are his workmanship, created in Christ Jesus unto good works, which
God hath before ordained that we should walk in them.*''

Observe the force of these terms.   "*Dead* in trespasses
and sins.''   Can the dead work?   Can a man effect his
own salvation?   It were as reasonable to suppose that
one of these quiet sleepers in our silent city of the dead
could, by his own inherent power, rise from the grave
and resume his wonted activities among us as to suppose
that a being who is dead in trespasses and sins can work
out his own deliverance therefrom.   And so the apostle
writes to Titus: ''Not by works of righteousness which
we have done, but according to his mercy he saved us,
by the washing of regeneration and renewing of the
Holy Ghost, which he shed on us abundantly through
Jesus Christ our Saviour, that being justified by his
grace we should be made heirs according to the hope of
eternal life.''   Further, this great change is described by
the apostle in the passage quoted from Ephesians as a
creation; we are said to be ''God's workmanship created

anew in Christ Jesus unto good works." The good
works follow, they do not percede, regeneration. It were
as reasonable to suppose that a mere man could, by the
word of his power, speak a universe into existence with
its suns and systems and living creatures as to suppose
that a sinner could be the efficient cause of his own salvation.   The same truth is taught by our Saviour in his
conversation with Nicodemus, where he says, "Except a
man be born again he cannot see the kingdom of God."
It is taught there even more emphatically than appears
in the English Version, for, as the marginal reading
shows, the original says, "Except a man be born *from
above* he cannot see the kingdom of God." (John iii. 3.)
And so the Apostle John, "As many as received him to
them gave he power to become the sons of God, even to
them that believe on his name, who were born not of
blood, nor of the will of the flesh, nor of the will of man,
but of God."   The argument of the Apostle James in
the passage before us proves the same thing.   He is
showing his readers that all the evil which afflicts us
comes from our own depraved hearts, but all the good
which we enjoy comes from God.   "Let no man say
when he is tempted, I am tempted of God: for God
cannot be tempted with evil, neither tempteth he any
man; but every man is tempted when he is drawn
away of his own lust and enticed.   Then when lust
hath conceived, it bringeth forth sin: and sin, when it is
full grown, bringeth forth death.   Do not err, my beloved brethren.   Every good gift and every perfect gift
is from above, and cometh down from the Father of
lights, with whom is no variableness, neither shadow of
turning."   The crowning proof of it is that "of his own
will begat he us," unmoved by anything meritorious in
man's character or conduct. (James i. 13-18.)   This is

a specially important statement as coming from the
Apostle James, for he has been supposed by some to
teach the doctrine of salvation by works, in contradiction of the Apostle Paul, who teaches everywhere that
a man is "justified by faith alone, without the deeds of
the law." Even Martin Luther seems to have been
under this impression at one time, and he spoke of the
epistle of James as an epistle of straw. But there is no
contradiction. It is simply the old story of the two
knights who were approaching each other, and saw a
shield suspended over the road. "What a beautiful
golden shield," said one. "It is not golden," said the
other, "it is silver." The first knight insisted upon his
view, the second continued to deny, and as they were
about to pass from the clash of words to the clash of
swords, a white-robed figure, whose name was Truth,
rushed between them and required them to change
places, and lo! the shield was golden on the one side and
silver on the other. So in regard to Paul and James.
There is no real contradiction between them. The difficulty is solved by understanding the point of view of
each. Paul is right; we are justified by faith alone.
James is right; we are justified only by a working faith.
But without pausing to dwell upon the manner of re-
conciling the apparent difference, let us note that there is
nowhere in Scripture, not even in the writings of Paul,
a stronger statement of the absolute sovereignty and
sole efficiency of God in salvation than is here made by
the apostle who has been supposed by some to teach
that a man is justified by his own good works. The
efficient cause of salvation is God: "Of his own will
begat he us."

II. *The instrumental cause:* "With the word of truth."
It is not denied that God sometimes regenerates a soul

without the intervention of means. But his rule, well-nigh universal, excepting, for instance, such cases as infants and idiots, is to use means. And the means that he uses is the word of truth. The Apostle Peter speaks of believers as "born again, not of corruptible seed, but of incorruptible, by the word of God, which liveth and abideth forever." The Apostle Paul reminds Timothy that "from a child thou hast known the holy Scriptures, which are able to make thee wise unto salvation through faith which is in Christ Jesus." And in the twenty-first verse of the chapter before us the Apostle James exhorts his readers to "receive with meekness the engrafted word, which is able to save your souls." Some of the truths of this word which God uses as means of salvation are these: That the original condition of man as God created him was one of knowledge, righteousness, and holiness; that man fell from the estate in which he was created by sinning against God; that all men are sinners, guilty, polluted, and helpless; "that God so loved the world that he gave his only begotten Son, that whosoever believeth in him should not perish, but have everlasting life"—facts, warnings, invitations, promises.

But let us now note the relation between these two causes, the efficient and the instrumental. There is no intrinsic efficiency in the word for regeneration without the spirit. As a pen is powerless to write a letter, as an axe is powerless to fell a tree, unless there be an agent to wield it, as an engine cannot move cars without steam, so the word is powerless without the creative spirit of God. "There are two conditions necessary for the production of a given effect. The one is that the cause should have the requisite efficiency; and the other, that the object on which it acts should have the requisite susceptibility." The sun and rain shed their genial in-

THE THREE CAUSES OF SALVATION.   283

fluences on a desert, and it remains a desert; when these
influences fall on a fertile plain it is clothed with all the
wonders of vegetable fertility and beauty.   The mid-day
brightness of the sun has no more effect on the eyes of
the blind than a taper; and if the eye be bleared the
clearest light only enables it to see men as trees walking.   It is so with moral truth : no matter what may be
its inherent power, it fails of any salutary effect unless
the mind to which it is presented be in a fit state to receive it.   The minds of men since the fall are not in a
condition to receive the transforming and saving power
of the truths of the Bible; and therefore it is necessary,
in order to render the word of God an effectual means of
salvation, that it should be attended by the supernatural
power of the Holy Spirit.   The apostle says, expressly,
"The natural man receiveth not the things of the Spirit
of God; for they are foolishness unto him : neither can
he know them, because they are spiritually discerned."
An eminent Presbyterian minister of New York city
says that when he was a youth he attended a certain
religious service and heard a sermon on the subject of
regeneration, in which the preacher stated that conversion consisted of two things : first, a recognition of himself as a sinner, and secondly, a recognition of Christ as
a Saviour.   The gentleman says he left the church with
an unsatisfied feeling in his mind, and as he walked
homeward, those words, learned in early boyhood, came
back to him with great clearness and force of meaning :
"Effectual calling is the work of God's Spirit, whereby,
convincing us of our sin and misery, enlightening our
minds in the knowledge of Christ, *and renewing our wills,*
he doth persuade and enable us to embrace Jesus Christ,
freely offered to us in the gospel."   The preacher to
whom he had been listening had omitted from his defini-

tion the most vital point. Let us not refuse to accept the whole truth of the Bible concerning our helplessness as sinners and God's sole efficiency in our salvation, even though it expose us for a time to the underserved charge of teaching fatalism.

Having now defined the efficient cause of our salvation, and the instrumental cause, let us look, lastly, at III. *The final cause:* ''That we should be a kind of firstfruits of his creatures.'' Under the old dispensation, the firstfruits of the harvest and of the vintage, of the flocks and of the herds, and even the firstborn of their own families, were by the Hebrews given to God. On the day after the Passover Sabbath every year, a sheaf of the first ripe barley of that season's crop was waved by the priest before the Lord as an offering, and as an expression of gratitude, dependence and devotion, and by this consecration of the firstfruits the entire produce was consecrated. In like manner they did with the first loaves made from the new grain fifty days later at the feast of Pentecost, and so of the best wine and the best oil. The firstlings of their flocks and herds also were given to God as victims for sacrifice. In accordance with the same principle, and in special commemoration of the mercy of God in sparing their households when he inflicted the tenth plague upon the Egyptians, the firstborn son of every Israelitish family was devoted to God as a minister of the sanctuary. The Lord afterwards substituted the Levites for the firstborn in the service of the tabernacle, in order, no doubt, to the more orderly conduct of public worship; and the overplus of firstborn sons for whom there were no Levites to substitute had to be redeemed from the service of the sanctuary by the payment of five shekels apiece into the tabernacle treasury. The great idea, then, connected with the firstfruits was that of consecration, absolute devotion to the service of God, and when James says that "of his own will begat he us with the word of truth, *that we should be a kind of firstfruits of his creatures*," he meant the same thing, to-wit, that the object of our salvation is consecration to the service of God, and that our regeneration is a pledge of the ultimate regeneration of the world at large.

For what purpose, then, are sinners saved? That they may finally escape the punishment due them for their sins? Yes, but that is secondary. That they may finally attain to the happiness of heaven? Yes, but that is secondary. The primary object of our salvation is consecration to God's service. I once heard the late Bishop Kavanaugh, of the Methodist Church, say that he had always greatly admired the first question and answer of *The Shorter Catechism* of the Westminster Assembly: "What is the chief end of man?" "Man's chief end is to glorify God, and to enjoy him for ever." And truly they are among the noblest uninspired words ever written. Some forty years ago there was an infidel editor in this country, who used to make shallow sport of this great statement; but it is the worthiest answer ever yet given to that momentous question. What, then, is the chief end of a sinner's salvation? To glorify God by a life of whole-hearted consecration to his service.

It is said that when Oliver Cromwell visited York-minster, in England, he saw in one of the apartments statues of the twelve apostles in silver. "Who are those fellows there?" he inquired, in his brusque way, as he approached them. On being informed, he replied: "Take them down, and let them go about doing good." They were taken down, and melted, and coined into money, and went about the commonwealth doing good

as money. It has been well asked, "Are there not some
Christians who occupy places in God's house more for
show than for service? Stately, formal, disinclined to
work for God, though doubtless his own children, sinners go unsaved, and believers go uncomforted and un-
helped, for all the effort they make to aid them. They
need to be melted down and sent about doing good.
Statuary Christians, however burnished and elegant
they may be, are of little real service in the cause of
Christ." They have misapprehended the final cause of
their salvation. They seem to have forgotten the second
part of that great statement in the second chapter of
Titus, where we are told that Jesus Christ "gave himself for us, that he might redeem us from all iniquity,
and purify unto himself a peculiar people, zealous of
good works."

My brethren, let us bear these things in mind. It is
well for us to remember by whom we are saved, and by
what we are saved, and for what we are saved. It is
well for us to recognize in our salvation the power of
God as the source, and the word of God as the means,
and the glory of God as the end; for "of his own will
begat he us with the word of truth, that we should be a
kind of firstfruits of his creatures."

THE NECESSITY OF CHRIST'S RESURRECTION.

BY REV. J. F. CANNON, D. D.,

Pastor of the Grand Avenue Presbyterian Church, St. Louis, Mo.

"Whom God hath raised up, having loosed the pains of death; because it was not possible that he should be holden of it."— ACTS ii. 24.

THE disciples of Jesus Christ had no expectation that he would rise from the dead. The sepulchre in which his dead body was entombed had closed upon their hopes. Those loving women who visited the sepulchre on the morning of the first day of the week went with their spices to embalm a dead body, not to meet a living one. The two who journeyed together to Emmaus said, "We trusted that it had been he which should have redeemed Israel." (Luke xxiv. 21.) Such *had* been their hope, but it had been turned into despair. Without exception they were incredulous when the glad news of the resurrection was first announced to them. The words of the messengers "seemed to them as idle tales, and they believed them not." (Luke xxiv. 11.) The idea of the resurrection was strange to them, and even alarming. Slowly, jealously, almost reluctantly, they yielded to the evidence. But when the fact was accepted it became the chief inspiration of their lives. It was the corner-stone of their faith. Their supreme business, henceforth, was to proclaim, and bear witness to it.

Peter was here preaching on the day of Pentecost to

an excited and astonished multitude in Jerusalem. The subject of his sermon was a crucified and risen Messiah. He reminded his hearers of the spotless character of Jesus of Nazareth, and of the pure, benevolent life which he had lived among them. He boldly charged them with the crime of having, wantonly and with wicked hands, taken his life. Then he affirmed that this Jesus had been raised from the dead: "This Jesus hath God raised up, whereof we all are witnesses." (Vs. 32.) He, and more than five hundred others whom he could summon, were ready to testify to the fact, and seal their testimony with their blood. It is significant that none who heard him ventured to impugn the testimony. The Sanhedrin were doing their utmost to crush this new movement in its inception, yet they did not undertake to refute the assertion that Christ had risen. The fact of his resurrection was proclaimed loudly and persistently in the very midst of Jerusalem itself; yet there is absolutely no cotemporary denial of it, except the clumsy story which the sentinels at the tomb were bribed to tell, that while they slept the disciples came and stole away the body. Had there been any more valid rebutting evidence within their reach, we may be sure these busy enemies of the gospel would have gathered and made use of it. But so far as history shows there was not a man of them who dared to take issue with the apostles as to the great fact which they alleged.

But Peter was not content to rest the resurrection of Christ upon the testimony of human witnesses, conclusive and overwhelming as that was. He had learned something from the example of the Master himself. When Christ showed himself alive to his disciples after his passion he was not content to show them his wounded hands and side; to speak to them by name in his old familiar tones, and, by such means, to relieve their doubts and establish their faith. He wished to have their faith founded, not simply on the testimony of their bodily senses, but on that which is the only proper foundation of religious faith, *the word of God*. Hence, "beginning at Moses and all the prophets he expounded unto them in all the Scriptures the things concerning himself." (Luke xxiv. 27.) He showed them how, in order that the Scriptures might be fulfilled, it behooved the Christ to suffer, and to rise from the dead on the third day. Peter followed this example. Choosing a passage from the Old Testament Scriptures, he showed his hearers that its only possible fulfilment was in the resurrection of the Messiah. David had prophesied in one of his psalms, "Thou wilt not leave my soul in hades, neither wilt thou suffer thine holy one to see corruption." This word, in its full meaning, could not have been spoken of the psalmist himself, for it was not fulfilled in his experience. His body did see corruption. The sepulchre containing his dust was still among them. But it was fulfilled, literally and completely, in the experience of Jesus of Nazareth, who was the son of David according to the flesh, and his promised successor on the throne. His body was not allowed to see corruption, as his empty sepulchre conclusively proved.

In like manner, as the same apostle teaches in one of his epistles, the Holy Spirit, through all the prophets, had "testified beforehand the sufferings of Christ *and the glory that should follow*." (1 Peter i. 11.) Through a multitude of prophecies and types the great event was foreshadowed. Deny the resurrection of Christ, and the Old Testament is a sealed book. Admit it, and every page becomes luminous with meaning. What the head is to the body, what the flower is to the plant, or the

19

fruit to the tree, such is the fact of the resurrection to the
body of revealed truth.   It is the crown and consummation of all God's revelations to men.   He who "died for
our sins according to the Scriptures," as Paul says,
"rose again the third day *according to the Scriptures*."
(1 Cor. xv. 4.)   It was not possible, then, that he should
be holden of death, because "the Scripture cannot be
broken."

But in the words of our text the apostle seems to
take a bolder position still, viz., *that, from the very nature of the case, the resurrection of Christ was inevitable
and necessary*.   Not only was there abundant historical
proof that he had risen, and numerous scriptural predictions that he would rise, but, in view of the circumstances of the case, and on account of the principles involved, there was an absolute necessity that he should
rise.   "It was not possible that he should be holden of
it."   That such an one as he was should be held under
the power of death was a simple impossibility.

First, there was a *moral* impossibility in the case.   To
appreciate this, consider what manner of man he was.
Peter here speaks of him as "a man approved of God";
that is, he was divinely attested and sealed as one commissioned of God.   Not only so, he was one upon whom
the eye of God rested with unqualified approval.   "He
knew no sin."   He distinctly claimed that he had no
consciousness of sin.   He said, "I do always those
things that please the Father"; "the prince of this
world cometh, and hath nothing in me." (John xiv. 30.)
To his enemies he said, "Which of you convinceth me
of sin?"   (John viii. 46.)   And his whole life was consistent with this high claim.   No wrong was ever discovered in him, either by the intimacy of his friends or
the malignity of his foes.   The judge who condemned

him said, "I find no fault in him." The apostate who
betrayed him confessed, "I have betrayed the innocent
blood." The centurion who superintended his execution said, "Certainly this was a righteous man." (Luke
xxiii. 47.) Nor has the searching scrutiny of later
times discovered aught to change this verdict. So far as
I know, the man has yet to be found who, after a careful
study of the facts of his life, has dared to stand up before
an intelligent public and charge Jesus Christ with any
moral obliquity. By common consent he is acknowledged to have been a man without sin. He was "holy,
harmless, undefiled, and separate from sinners." Yet,
upon the testimony of suborned witnesses, he was condemned and crucified as a malefactor. For the first time
since the world began was an innocent, sinless man
brought under the power of death. Never before had
death taken such prey in his toils. Abraham, Isaac,
and Jacob, David, and Daniel died, and their bodies saw
corruption. But they were sinners, all of them, and
hence the legitimate prey of death; for "the wages of
sin is death." Here, however, was one who had done
no sin; in whom nothing worthy of death was found by
God or men. Was it possible for death to hold such an
one? Not if righteousness reigns. If death may reign
where sin has not reigned; if death may invade the
realm of innocence and claim as his own one who belongs
to that realm, then the cause of God and righteousness is
a losing cause. If there be a just and almighty God
upon the throne of the universe, and if Jesus Christ were
such an one as he is here represented, and as he is generally acknowledged to have been, then there was a divine
necessity that he should rise. We do not forget the uni-
formity and inviolability of natural law, but we remember likewise the awful supremacy of *moral* law. We

admit that the forces of nature are mighty; but we insist that the forces of righteousness are mightier. These are the forces which were appealed to, and which fought for his deliverance. What boots it to say that the alleged event was exceptional, a revolt from the established order of things, and therefore incredible? Our answer is, the man was exceptional. Never was there another like him among the sons of men. Find another man who is "without sin"; let him be "crucified, dead, and buried," and we promise you another resurrection; for, if might be on the side of right in God's universe, it is not possible for a righteous man to be holden of death.

Again, there was not only a moral necessity that Christ should rise, there was also a *natural* necessity in the case, a necessity "planted in the nature of things." To appreciate this we must remember that he claimed to be something more than a sinless man. He claimed to be, and was proven to be, in a sense peculiar to himself, the Son of God, "his only begotten Son," possessed of a divine nature and a divine life. Simon Peter had been led to know and acknowledge him in this character. In response to the question, "Whom say ye that I am?" he had made the noble and accepted answer, "Thou art the Christ, the Son of the living God." (Matt. xvi. 16.)

The charge preferred against him before the Jewish high priest was that he called himself the Son of God, thus making himself God. And when the high priest adjured him to tell them if he was the Christ, the Son of God, he gave an affirmative answer. Upon that they adjudged him worthy of death, because he had spoken blasphemy. (Matt. xxvi. 63-66.) It was a stupendous claim for one in the form of man, but every part of his life was in harmony with the claim. It was a divine

life.   He showed a wisdom which was more than human.   "Never man spake like this man," was the
testimony of his cotemporaries, and is the confession of
the thinking world to-day.   He exercised a compassion
and love which were divine.   His purity was divinely
stainless.   He wielded a power which was the power
of God.   The winds and the waves obeyed him; devils,
and death itself, were subject to his word.   If he was
not divine, pray tell us wherein he lacked of being
divine?   What attribute of God did he fail to exhibit?

Such being his nature, and his relation to God the
Father, his life was not the created, dependent life of a
creature.   He says, "As the Father hath life in himself,
so hath he given to the Son to have life in himself."
(John v. 26.)   "In him was life; and the life was the
light of men."   (John i. 4.)   Again, he says, "I am
the resurrection, and the life."   (John xi. 25.)   "I am
the way, the truth, and the life."   (John xiv. 6.)   He
is the Prince of life; the author, the source of life; as
Schaff says, the "life of every life."

Now, remembering all this, let us go to the tomb of
Joseph of Arimathea, and what do we see?   The eternal
Son of God, the Prince of life, held in the embrace of
death!   That he should have condescended to that condition is the marvelous mystery of grace; that he should
be kept in it is an impossible thought.   Death must
yield his mighty prey.   A grain of sand may be held,
passive and submissive in the bosom of the earth; but
not so a living grain of wheat.   It must and will spring
up in a new and higher life.   In the city of Hanover,
Germany, there is said to be an old graveyard in which
is the tomb of a woman who belonged to an ancient
and noble family.   It is covered with massive blocks
of stone, which are fastened together with heavy iron

clamps.   On one of the stones these words are carved:
"This grave, bought for all time, must never be opened."
But years ago a little seed found lodgment in the crevice
between the stones.   It took root and grew, until now
a splendid tree waves its branches over the tomb.   And
as the roots have grown, and the trunk enlarged, heed-
less of the carved admonition, the great stones have
been lifted, and the iron clamps broken asunder.   Such
is the power of life, even of the created life that is
wrapped up in a little seed.   What wonder, then, that
he who had "life in himself," who was "the resurrection, and the life," should burst the bands of death, and
triumph over the grave?   Men rolled a stone to the door
of the sepulchre, and sealed it, and set armed sentinels
to guard it.   But how vain their efforts were!   As well
might they have tried to seal up the morning in the
womb of night, and prevent its dawn; or to lock up the
spring in the embrace of winter, and forbid the flowers
to bloom and the trees to bud.   It was not possible for
him to be holden of death.

Then, my brethren, "we have not followed cun-
ningly-devised fables" when we have built our hopes
on him "who was delivered for our offences, and was
raised again for our justification."   "The Lord is risen
indeed."   His resurrection is not a myth, but a fact.
A fact attested as no other fact in ancient history has
been attested.   A fact foreshadowed by numerous prophecies and types in the Old Testament Scriptures.   A
fact to be expected as the inevitable and necessary outcome of the eternal principles which were involved.   Let
us be glad and rejoice in it.   It tells us of an accepted
sacrifice, a completed redemption, a purchased inheritance of life and glory.   It is the pledge of our own
resurrection.   The risen Christ is the firstfruits of them

that sleep. "If the Spirit of him that raised up Jesus from the dead dwell in you, he that raised up Christ from the dead shall also quicken your mortal bodies by his Spirit that dwelleth in you." (Romans viii. 11.)

Yes, if his Spirit dwell in us, the text becomes true of us, as of him. It is not possible for death to hold us. We must rise. "Blessed be the God and Father of our Lord Jesus Christ, which according to his abundant mercy hath begotten us again unto a lively hope by the resurrection of Jesus Christ from the dead, to an inheritance incorruptible, and undefiled, and that fadeth not away." (1 Peter i. 3, 4.)

Natural Law and Divine Providence.

BY REV. PEYTON H. HOGE, D. D.,
Pastor of the First Presbyterian Church, Wilmington, N. C.

"Are not two sparrows sold for a farthing? and one of them shall not fall on the ground without your Father."—MATTHEW x. 29.

TWO theories of the universe contend for the mastery in the world to-day, the mechanical and the paternal.

Modern science has demonstrated by an ever-widening induction the universal reign of law. The silent movements of the heavenly host; the revolutions of the earth as it turns on its axis or swings in its orbit round the sun, causing the alternations of day and night and the ever-changing panorama of the seasons; the rise and fall of the tides, the shifting of the fickle wind, the circulation of moisture as it ascends in vapor, condenses in cloud, descends in rain, and flows in rill and torrent and river back to ocean again; the springing of the germ in the earth, the growth of blade and flower and fruit, till the earth is clothed with beauty, and waving harvests and ripening fruit provide food for man and beast; all have been shown to come under the operation and dominion of regular and unchanging laws, inexorably working out fixed results. Every element has its fixed laws of combination with every other element; every force its regular play of action upon every other force;

every form of life its changeless conditions for development, retrogression or destruction; even sentient beings have their prescribed modes of action; the flight of the lark, the song of the nightingale, the roar of the lion, the spring of the tiger, are as much in obedience to law as the fall of an apple or the flash of a thunderbolt. Man himself is born, grows, labors and dies, the subject of natural law. The very configuration of the earth we inhabit is the result of the operation of law. Law-abiding waters sifted its elements and built up its rock-ribbed frame. Law-abiding earthquakes heaved up the solid mass of the mountains; and waters descending in obedience to law carved them into hills and valleys.

From these known facts of science, men have leaped to the conclusion that this mighty mechanism of nature is *only* a machine; that whether originally caused by some being who has left it to work out its own results, or whether itself uncaused, and evolving all its laws out of its own inherent forces, it is now a mere machine, blind to results and regardless of consequences.

Such a universe must be *purposeless*. If there is no intelligence there can be no will. The sun shines because it must, and not to clothe a world with beauty or to ripen the harvests for the food of man. The rains descend from necessity, and not to water the earth that it may give seed to the sower and bread to the eater. The rivers flow because water runs downhill, and not to fill the valleys with corn, and to girdle the hills with joy.

Such a universe must be *heartless*. It is nothing to the mill whether it grinds the corn to feed the hungry, or whether it mangles the limbs of a helpless child. So nature is as indifferent to the sorrows of her children as to their joys. The wind cares not whether it sinks the laden ships or wafts them to their desired haven. The sea will sport with a child upon the beach, and then engulf it in its treacherous embrace.

Such a universe must be *conscienceless*. It has no concern for the righteous or the wicked. It may pour its plenty into the lap of the wicked, and heap its sorrows upon the head of the righteous; and there is no court of appeals where wrongs can be righted, sin punished and virtue rewarded.

In such a universe worship is an absurdity, prayer a mockery and religion a delusion. Let us eat and drink, for to-morrow we die.

Over against this mechanical, soulless theory of the universe we place the paternal theory as it is found in the words of the text and in all the teachings of our Lord. Not that he announced it as a *theory*. Nothing was theory in his teachings. A theory is a supposition that gives a reasonable explanation of known facts; but with him the explanation is announced as known as clearly as the facts. He taught as one having authority. ''We speak that we do know, and testify that we have seen.'' But to the world, before it accepts the teachings and authority of Christ, his revelation of the Father, and the Father's care for his children must be considered as one of the theories on which we seek to account for the facts of the universe.

According, then, to the teachings of Jesus Christ, God, the Creator of heaven and earth, exercises a fatherly care over all his creatures. He singles out one of the least by way of example. Their little bodies could be seen any day hanging in the market in long strings. A trifling copper coin could purchase two of them for a meagre meal. Yet, says our Lord, no winter's blast is keen enough, no bird of prey is swift enough, no archer's aim is sure enough, no fowler's snare is cunning enough to bring to the ground one of the least of these creatures until God's time has come to still the beatings of the little fluttering heart, and fold forever the wings that bore it in happy flight. They have neither store-house nor barn, they sow not, neither do they reap; yet the Father feedeth them. It is he who clothes the very grass of the field with fabrics of richer lustre than the royal robes of Solomon, in all their glory of Tyrian dye and gold of Ophir. All of beauty, all of sustenance, all of protecting care our heavenly Father gives to the earth and its creatures. Then what of his children? "Are ye not much better than they?" "Fear not," says the Master to them, "ye are of more value than many sparrows." So tender is the Father's care of them that the very hairs of their head are all numbered.

This theory of a divine providence, universal and special, wide as creation and particular as the hairs of our heads, governing the stars in their courses, and the sparrows in their flight and fall, is what we all as Christians profess to believe. And yet there are few of us, perhaps, who have not sometimes been troubled as to just how to reconcile such a providence with the known facts of natural law. What place is there for providence, faith, and prayer, in a universe governed by unchanging and inexorable law?

In answer to this question, I would suggest, first, that if this universe is a machine, it is a machine of God's planning. Science has nothing to say against that. When men make a machine they make it to do a certain work, but it may do other things for which it was never intended. We make a locomotive to pull our trains; it may crush the life out of its own maker. But God's planning is complete and perfect. "Known unto God are all his works, from the beginning of the world." In planning his universe, the least as well as the greatest events enter into his plan, and often the greatest events turn upon those that seem the most trivial. God is too great for anything to appear insignificant in his eyes, and if the sparrow cannot fall to the ground without your Father, it is because the sparrow, with all the forces and circumstances that govern its life, is a part of God's great plan.

Some of you have seen at the World's Fair, or other recent expositions, those beautiful machines for weaving pictures in silk. If you examined them closely you must have noticed that folds of stiff paper, perforated with many holes, were regularly fed to the machine from above. That was the pattern. The position of those holes governed the shifting threads of the warp and directed the motions of the many-colored shuttles as they flew in and out. A defect in the pattern, or a failure in any part of the machine to respond to the pattern, would have marred the perfect picture. So God has ordained all causes as well as all effects, and we need not fear even to pray to our Father according to his word, for if he has made this universe to run by prayer, the prayer is as essential to the working out of his plan as the force of gravitation to the movements of the spheres.

But if we look only at this aspect of the subject, we may fall into a fatalistic conception of God and his universe. Our prayers, if we pray, may become perfunctory and formal, and we will not pray and trust as those who are coming to the sympathetic heart of a living Father. Let us remember, then, that God's universe is not a machine which he has planned and wound up, and then withdrawn himself from all interest in its working. We must picture him as rejoicing in the work of his hands; as watching with sympathetic interest and pleasure the development of all his plans. If, in the working out of his gracious purposes, his creatures, or, yet more, his children, suffer, his heart is responsive to their cry, even while he is too wise and too really tender to turn aside from the beneficent ends that he has in view; and when he sends deliverance, it is just as truly he that sends it, and it comes as fresh from his fatherly heart, as if both the sorrow and the respite had not been a part of his purpose from before the foundation of the world. Thus tenderly he loves the sparrows, thus tenderly he marks their fall. Are ye not much better than they?

But God's present relation to his universe is not confined to his loving and sympathetic interest in the development of his purposes. I do not believe that science has reached the ultimate source of power when it has discovered a law of nature. There is no inherent power in a natural law. It is only an observed order of action. In itself it explains nothing. Take, for instance, one of the most universal of all these laws, the law of gravitation. We know that if we let go an object from our hands it will fall to the earth. We know that the same force swings the earth in its orbit round the sun, and binds together all systems by invisible chains. But why has matter this attraction for other matter? Who can tell? One of the most brilliant of American astronomers has said that the more he has studied it the more has he come to the conclusion that the only explanation which can be given is just that God wills it so. To this source at last we must trace all energy. Natural laws are but the modes in which God's power expresses itself. Hence, all energy and life in the universe are but manifestations

of the life and power of the living God.   He upholds all
things by the word of his power.   In him we live, and
move, and have our being.   He is the God in whose
hand our breath is, and whose are all our ways.   If for
one moment he withdrew the sustaining power of his
will, all things would return to chaos, or vanish into
nothingness.   But he is faithful to his creatures.   Seed-
time and harvest, and cold and heat, and summer and
winter, shall not fail.   Thus, it is God that feeds the
ravens and clothes the lilies.   And we, too, may come
with trusting hearts and pray, ''Give us this day our
daily bread.''

And is this all?   Is God's providence confined to the
sustaining of natural laws and his sympathetic interest
in the working out of his eternal purpose?   Those who
argue thus strangely forget the domain of the action of
the human will.   All things in the world are not the unaided and unmodified result of natural law.   Whatever
is true of other beings, men are endowed with the power
of *interference*.   Man can play law against law, so as to
bring out results just the opposite of unaided natural law.
It is the nature of water to run downhill.   Man confines
it, and makes that very law force it upward into his
dwellings.   Gravity draws objects to the earth.   But
by that very law man lifts himself to the clouds by at-
taching himself to a bag inflated with some gas lighter
than the surrounding air.   Whether or not Elisha by a
miracle made the iron to swim in ancient days, men,
without any miracle, are in these days sailing the seas
in iron ships, and fighting each other with massive cannon from floating fortresses.   Every product of art and
manufacture, every achievement of invention and discovery, is the interference of human will with the natural working of nature's laws.   Even the harvests that

spring from earth's bosom are the cultivation of man, and the breeds of cattle that walk the earth are improved by art and man's device. Even where the naked savage roams the forest, we can trace him by his handiwork. Life, the supreme gift of nature, may be destroyed by his wrath, or prolonged by his skill and care. He may strike down the sparrow on his nest, or his fellow-man in his bed; or he may drive away the destroyer from his victim; or his own heart may relent when his hand is raised for the blow.

This wide sphere of freedom is left to man, as our own observation and experience teach us. And has the creature a power the exercise of which is denied to the Creator? Let us see.

Of the action of the divine will upon the human will science is silent. Whatever takes place in that realm is back of human consciousness, and so does not offer itself to investigation. But for that very reason science opposes no objection to the revelations of Scripture. "The king's heart is in the hand of the Lord; as the rivers of water, he turneth it whithersoever he will." "It is God that worketh in you both to will and to do of his good pleasure." We cannot open the door to the action of the human soul upon the material universe without at the same time opening the door to the action of the divine Spirit through its influence upon the human soul. And when we consider the almost infinite possibilities for our weal or woe that are lodged in the hands of our fellow-men, and how at every turn our life may be blessed or blasted by their actions, it is no small part of the comfort of our faith in divine Providence that he holds the hearts of men in the hollow of his hand, and guides, directs, suggests, controls their thoughts and words and actions, to bring about his purposes of grace to the meanest of his creatures and to the least of his children. If he stays the hand or mars the aim that seeks the sparrow's life; if he sends the hand that scatters seed or crumbs when winter's snows have covered the ground, need we fear for protection and sustenance? We are of more value than many sparrows.

But if man, without violating nature's laws, can interfere with and modify their actions, what shall we say of those more highly-endowed beings whose existence is revealed to us in the Scriptures? "Are they not all ministering spirits, sent forth to minister for them who shall be heirs of salvation?" So the Scriptures teach, but what has science to say? Nothing, except this, that it finds no trace of their action. Is that conclusive against their agency and ministry? Not at all. The beast that treads the earth leaves his footprints behind by which we can trace his path. But who can follow the track of the fish that parts the mobile waters, or the bird that cleaves the yielding air? We see the marks of the tool upon the stone rough-hewn from the quarry, but not upon the polished slab or the finished statue. It is the perfection of the work that obliterates the traces of the workman. So this angel ministry may be all about us, guiding and controlling the forces of nature, and yet their footfalls make no sound and leave no trace, and the marks of their handiwork remain, like themselves, unseen. However that may be, it is surely preposterous to say that God may not thus work through nature's laws, albeit with an unseen hand. We watch the musician as his fingers pass over the keys of the organ, and we understand why the key goes down and the note sounds, because we see the touch of his finger. But couple the lower to the upper bank of keys, and when he plays on the lower the corresponding keys of the upper bank go down as though touched by unseen fingers. And it would be easy to connect both key-boards with another key-board out of sight, played by an unseen musician, while the visible keys responded to the touch of an invisible hand. Such a mechanism would seem to the uninitiated to be automatic. So with God's interference in nature. Nature's laws are but the keys and levers that connect his will with the results achieved. We hear the sound, we even see the movements of the keys and levers, but we see not the hand; yet God's controlling hand is on every key, and at his touch the great organ sings and throbs with the eternal harmonies of his will.

It is idle to say that the facts of nature are *sufficiently* accounted for without supposing the immediate action of God. The sphere of our ignorance is still too vast for us to say there is no need for God's intervention. When the Son of God was on earth the winds and the waves obeyed him, and at his word or touch disease fled away. In the wide demain of the elements in their ceaseless play, in the recondite laws of life and health and their constant warfare against disease and danger, we never know when the modifying touch of the divine hand produces results that nature unaided could never have achieved. God is still the Lord of nature. He is still the great Physician. And not a sparrow falleth to the ground without your Father.

This world, then, is still our Father's house. The universe is still subject to our Father's will. It is a universe, then, with a *heart* in it, and it is no idle thing for us to draw near to God in spirit, and say, "Our Father which art in heaven." Prayer is not a mere spiritual exercise. It reaches the heart of God, and sways the hand that rules the universe.

This is, likewise, a place for *righteousness*. "Say ye to

20

the righteous, It shall be well with him,'' is a living voice
to-day.   ''Seek ye first the kingdom of God and his righteousness'' is no obsolete command, and it is no meaning-
less promise that ''all these things ''—food, clothing, protection—''shall be added unto you.''   A life of trust is
still the true and only life for happiness and peace, since
it is our Father that is making ''all things work together for good to them that love him.''

And in this, our Father's house, there is a place for
pardon, for redemption, for salvation.   The birds, which
know only his providential care, may sing in unconscious innocence a Father's praise.   But we, his children, may sing a new and nobler song, a song of pardoning, redeeming love: ''For God so loved the world, that
he gave his only begotten Son, that whosoever believeth
in him should not perish, but have everlasting life.''

TAKE HOLD OF GOD.

BY REV. JAMES I. VANCE, D. D.,
Pastor of the First Presbyterian Church, Nashville, Tenn.

"Let him take hold of my strength, that he may make peace with me."—ISAIAH xxvii. 5.

GOD is the speaker, and he sends us a call through this verse of Scripture. He wants us to come up to his side and touch him. We have been standing off, standing aloof, with a great stretch of territory between us and God. We have been finding fault with the Almighty. He fails to manage the universe to suit us. As a coterie of self-elected critics we have been standing away off there, harping ceaselessly the dismal clamor of our complaints. God says: "Come up closer, and you can see better. Stand beside me, and you will get a new perspective. Touch me, and your querulous complaints will change into peace." "Let him take hold of my strength, that he may make peace with me."

We spend so much of our time on trifles. Suppose you work out a little sum in arithmetic. Take the past week and tell us how you spent it. One-third of it went into sleep. Of the remainder, how much was spent in idle conversation that left no more behind it than the wind that whistles past you on the street? How much was spent in amusement, in the arduous effort to make leisure that would otherwise be insufferably tame pass with some degree of delight? How much was spent in that which is purely material? How much was spent in

eating and drinking and reading? How much of the
past week did you devote to that which will live on after
your seventy years are out and bring something at the
bar of eternity? After all we are like children blowing
soap-bubbles out of a clay pipe, forgetting that the bubbles burst fast and the clay is soon broken. But the
process is entertaining, time passes, and the bubbles are
beautiful, as a sunbeam falls upon the shining disk and
paints it over with rainbows. Still the air moves and
the bubbles burst; but we can blow another, and so we
keep on blowing, blowing !

God says there is bigger work for us. The text calls
us to spend our life on that which is not a trifle—God!
Take hold of him. God is not a trifle, heaven is not a
bubble, religion is not a form of amusement. Take hold
of these. They dignify and ennoble life here. They
invest the insignificances of time with importance, and
have a durable value which eternity will not destroy,
but enhance.

There is a downward drift in everything that belongs
to this world. The law of the world is degeneration.
You have only to let anything alone and it will go to the
devil of itself. Let a ship alone and it will wreck itself.
Let a house alone and it will by-and-by tumble down of
its own depravity. Let a man alone and he will degen-
erate. God would counteract this downward drift. His
whole effort is to make something out of us—the best.
For degeneration he substitutes regeneration. He would
put an end to our trifling and set us afire with great ambitions to amount to something in his glorious kingdom
of redeemed and enthroned manhood and womanhood.
He says to every one of us: ''Take hold of my strength,
that you may have peace.'' There are three thoughts
in the text: First, the human element in religion;

second, the divine element in religion; and third, the product of their union.

I. *There is a human side to religion.* Man has something to do with getting himself saved. "Let him take hold." People do not drift into heaven any more than a ship drifts up to its landing at the pier. If you want to possess yourself of God you must take him. You cannot buy salvation, to be sure ; you cannot earn it, you cannot deserve it, but if it is ever yours you must take it.

There are those who believe altogether too much in divine sovereignty, or rather who frame into their creed a monstrous distortion of the doctrine of divine sovereignty. They make it synonymous with fatalism. They reason this way: "The Almighty made the universe and he is responsible for it. I shall not attempt to interfere with his prearranged plans. If he wants me redeemed, he must see to it. If he wants to send me to hell, he must bear the responsibility of it. I am here without my choice, the creature of environment and accident. If I were to fail to perform the specific part assigned to me in the economy of God's plan, I might throw the machinery of the whole universe out of gear. So I shall merely remain passive and allow whoever is at the head of this world to manipulate me to the greatest advantage."

That is the caricature of the truth of divine sovereignty, in the baldest, most repulsive, coarsest, Ingersolian form.

The same spirit comes to the front also with more subtle speech, pretending to be most humble in its submission "to the Lord's will," and prating in pious cant about its longing for "divine guidance." "God knows what I ought to do, and what I ought not to do," it says. "I am in the Lord's hands to be used as he may see fit. If he wants me to do this, he will make me do it. If he wants me to avoid that, he will make me hate it. I have just handed over my entire personality to him, and he is responsible. I am merely a bit of drift-wood floating on the great sea of divine providence, subject to the winds and tides which the Lord may send. How delicious it is not to bother about steam and chart and compass, but just to float, float, float.''

Yes, and you will wake up in hell on that schedule. When God saves us he does not take from us conscience, senses, mind, or Bible. That is an awful travesty on religion. We have our part to do, we must ''take hold,'' and if we fail to do that, all the cant and pious profession of submerging our identity in the divine purpose will not get us into heaven.

Sometimes it is charged that the Presbyterian Church, through its system of theology known as ''Calvinism,'' teaches this doctrine of fatalism. It is said that we believe that God has foreordained one section of the human race to heaven, regardless of what they may do in the matter, and another section to hell, regardless of what they may do. ''If you are going to be saved, you will be saved; lost, you will be lost, and all your efforts to the contrary cannot thwart the divine decree.'' It is said that we believe so mightily in the divine sovereignty of God that we have left no place for the free agency of man. Some one burrows away in his study until he un-earths the spectral figure of fatalism, and calling that ''Calvinism,'' walks out into the world and proclaims ''Calvinism the disgrace of theology.'' Yes, it would be if the cap fit, but it does not; and I may be allowed to say in passing that Presbyterians do believe that the human element is vital. We do not believe in the decrees of God in such a way as to reduce to zero the freedom and responsibility of the human agent. The statement of our *Confession of Faith* on this subject ought to be sufficient for all those who will take the trouble to examine it. There it says: "God hath endued the will of man with that natural liberty, that is neither forced, nor by any absolute necessity of nature determined to good or evil."*

If that is not enough to settle any doubt on this subject, a brief examination of the practical evangelism of our dear old church will amply refute the statement that her creed is fatalistic. She is in the forefront of the effort to carry the gospel to all mankind, believing that when her Lord said: "Whosoever will may come," he meant it. The Presbyterian Church has sent out and supports one-fourth of the entire missionary force of the world. She leads the world in the grace of Christian giving; and Mr. Moody was speaking from past experience when he said that if he wanted to raise $100,000, he expected to get $80,000 of it from Presbyterians.

We are not fatalists. There is a human element in religion, and I may say in the name of my church, no less than in the name of the Bible from which the church gets her creed, that if you are living as your fancy dictates, fast and loose, trying to shelve the responsibility for your moral inaccuracies on your Maker, and expecting some day to wake up in glory and hear him say: "Well done, good and faithful servant!" you are only preparing yourself for an awful disappointment. A man who here on earth crushes the poor, takes advantage of his neighbor's necessities, lays hold of the world and the flesh, believing that after a while he will hear the Master say: "Forasmuch as ye have done it unto one of the

---

*Chapter IX., Part 1.

least of these my brethren, ye have done it unto me; enter into the joy of your Lord,'' that man is hugging an empty delusion.

The Lord says, if we want all of this, we must "lay hold of him." Isn't that a rich phrase with which to express our part in the soul's salvation. " Let him take hold." We are not required to be theologians. It is not demanded of us that we exhaust the metaphysical subtleties of theosophy. We are merely to "take hold." God has prepared salvation. He offers it as a gift. We are not required to do God's part over again. We are not told to die on the cross, to make atonement, but to *take*. That is faith, and faith is our part. Faith is the open, empty hand that reaches up to lay hold of what God has provided. Faith is:

> " Just to follow, hour by hour, where he leadeth,
> Just to draw the moment's power as it needeth—
> Just to trust him: that is all."

If you are thirsty, the rivers of the world might be flowing at your feet, but unless you dip a goblet and drink you will never slake your thirst. Salvation is the bounty of God's free grace, but before it will ever do you any good, you must take the cup of salvation and call upon the name of the Lord.

Nor is it difficult to understand why this must be the case. You can send your boy to school, as some one has suggested, and pay all the expenses of his tuition, but you cannot give him an education regardless of the hard work which the boy must do himself. A general may promise victory to his soldiers, but they do not expect to obtain it without fighting. God may offer us salvation as a free gift, and does, but it can never become ours until we take it and experience it. Salvation is not a change of surroundings, but a new life.

Heaven is no more a harp and crown and shining robe
and saintly face than education is an armful of books
and a wise expression of countenance.   If one wants to
be saved, let him take hold of God.   Have you done
this?   No?   And yet you wonder that you are not
saved.   You expect God to take you by the throat and
force you into his kingdom.   You are drifting along,
living as you please; and the meanwhile you are blam-
ing the Almighty, and saying, ''the Bible is false, the
church is full of frauds, prayer is not answered, providence is all topsy-turvy.''   Man, quit trifling!   Do your
part.   Lay hold of God.   Then, if God fails you, you
will have some just ground of complaint.   And will
you notice that it is not enough for you to stand away
off and barely touch God with the finger-tips of a decrepit faith.   ''*Let him take hold.*''   That means a good,
strong, honest clasp.   Your soul is to cleave to God as
Eleazer's hand did to his sword,* until you cannot let
him go.   Then your God will become a great reality
in all you think and do.

II. This brings us to the next part of our text—*the
divine element in religion.*   While there is a human element in religion, it is not all human.   Indeed, that is
the smallest part of it.   Let him take hold—of what?
Of education, and civilization, and art, and scientific re-
search, and moral culture?   It does not say that, for all
that, after all, would be but the man's laying hold of
some part of himself.   Higher is the call.   Richer is the
promise.   ''Let him take hold of my strength.''   That
brings God upon the scene, and introduces the divine
element in religion.

There are people who call this superstition.   Just as

* 2 Samuel xxiii. 10.

there are those who believe altogether too much in the
doctrine of divine sovereignty, or in a monstrous perversion of that doctrine, so there are those who believe
entirely too much in the doctrine of human agency, or in
a monstrous perversion of that doctrine. The rationalist
is at the extreme swing of the pendulum from the fatalist.
He says: ''Man is a god unto himself. Religion is
only a cult. Worship is spiritual gymnastics. The
only good prayer does is the moral disciplinary effect on
him who prays. What one believes about the various
dogmas at issue in religion is a matter of small consequence. Believe what you please, if you are sincere.
One church is as good as another. One god is as good
as another. One heaven is as good as another. The
only god and church and heaven you will ever know
anything about are within you. You are the great
reality. All else is pious fiction.''

Is that all there is of religion? Is it simply a colossal
temple of unmixed egoism, where God, church, heaven,
priest, worship, eternity, are all but varying moods of
the one and self-same ''his majesty myself,'' who makes
''self'' the centre of the universe and transmutes a lie
into the truth, by believing it sincerely? If that is all
there is in worship, let us pitch all religion overboard,
and cease chasing shadows. Religion is intended to
make man happier, stronger, purer than he is naturally.
It proposes, not to save him to himself, but to save him
from himself; to save him to something larger and
grander than he could ever otherwise attain. If it fails
of this, if there is nothing above our heads, worship is
only a pious pantomime; and we ourselves are but
shadows playing solemn antics in holy moods.

But there is something above our heads. We are not
more certain of our own existence than of that. God is

there. God! He is stronger, happier, purer than we. He is all of these in infinite perfection, and now his word to us, struggling and striving to be lifted from our low estate is, "Take hold of my strength." Take hold of God. How life mounts up when that is done. "My strength!" God's *strength!* That is a rich phrase with which to set forth the divine element in religion. Strength means certainty in the midst of doubt, wisdom in the hour of perplexity, stability when the strain comes, riches in poverty, light in darkness, serenity in storm. Christ is God's strength. Let us take hold of Christ. He will no more fail us than he did the woman in the gospel story who barely touched the hem of his garment.

God is a rock in the midst of life's great sea, standing whereon the raging flood cannot reach us. It howls and sweeps and surges at our feet, but it cannot overthrow our God, and we are safe. "Let him take hold of my strength." We do not have to understand it to measure it, to exhaust it, to follow it in all its works. We have only to take hold of it. You can do that. You cannot fathom God, but you can take hold of him. Maybe you cannot straighten out all of the theological intricacies to your satisfaction; maybe your daily shortcomings are a constant mortification to you; maybe you cannot even pray as you think you ought; but you can take hold of God's strength. You can accept Jesus. This it is to which the Saviour would have us devote life. Instead of spending time on trifles, catching at bubbles, fascinated by the glitter of empty nothings, let us drink in a deep breath of heaven's air and begin to live. Take hold of God and be saved.

III. And now we are beside the last part of our text. First the human element in religion, then the divine.

They meet, and then the product—*peace*. "Let him take hold of my strength, that he may make *peace* with me." A human life, in its frailty and need, lays hold of God, and God comes down and dwells in the human life, invests it with the power and majesty of his presence, communicates the calm of heaven to the perturbed spirit, and there is "peace." Brethren, that is religion in its effect. "That he may make peace with me." God is anxious for us to come to that. The only safety for anything or anybody in the wide world is to be on God's side. There is not room enough for two gods in the universe.

Peace! It is what we long most to possess. After all, it is the goal of life; and beyond our business tasks and social recreations, our toils and plans, beyond all that we strive to do here, we are looking for peace. We try to secure it in different ways.

Some attempt to obtain it by conforming to a low worldly standard and denying that anything better is possible. Others seek peace by surrendering themselves to the fullest gratification of all that is sensual and material. Still others strive to attain unto peace by stifling all anxiety with the stoic's dogma that "what cannot be cured must be endured." But any one who has tried it knows that all this is beggarly makeshift. Surroundings, external comforts, easy-going morals can no more bring peace to the soul than a soft couch can bring health to a fevered body.

A nation may secure peace, some one has observed, by two methods—either by conquering, or by being conquered. If it is willing to lay aside its national self-respect, to submit to insult and oppression, to submerge all prospects for national greatness and influence, it may have peace. There is a sort of peace possible to the individual on such degrading terms. If we are willing to submit to the incessant demands of the baser part of us, we may by-and-by reach a state of moral callousness, where conscience will be silenced, and we shall have peace. Who wants such peace? That is not what God offers. The Christian gets his peace, not by being conquered, but by conquering. He gets hold of omnipotence, and in the might of that defeats his adversaries and achieves peace. That is peace worth having. God lifts us above expediency. He dissipates anxiety about to-morrow, not by making to-morrow any the less a stern day, but by giving us strength to fight all of its battles successfully.

God's promises may not mature in sixty days, but they mature, and promptly at the hour of need they may be realized upon to their full face value, with compounded interest. "Wait on the Lord; be of good courage, and he shall strengthen thine heart: wait, I say, on the Lord." *

> "God holds the key of all unknown,
>   And I am glad;
>   If other hands should hold the key,
>   Or if he trusted it to me,
>   I might be sad."

Let us understand that to meet life successfully it is not necessary to understand all that is before us. Away with this diet of thin gruel on the table of those whose creed is a naked interrogation point. The life of faith is ever the strongest life. Believe in God and do your best and there is always certain victory.

> "The best men, doing their best,
>   Know, peradventure, least of what they do.
>   Men usefullest in the world are simply used."

---

* Psalm xxvii. 14.

God is responsible, to whoever trusts him, for all that life needs to make it great and good. How lines of care fade out and disappear for him who realizes that! "Let me take hold"—that is our part. "Of God's strength "— that is God's part; and the result is "peace."

You say all of this does well enough to preach about. It is a beautiful theory, but it breaks down in practice. Let us see. God has given us one perfect illustration of the text—Jesus Christ. In his earthly career the human and divine elements of religion met. In Christ human need took hold of divine strength, and the product was a life of absolutely undisturbed and unquenchable peace. Christ would reproduce his life in us. He would have us fight our battles as he fought his, and achieve the same glorious victory, for the same seraphic end. "My peace I give unto you." That is what Jesus has bequeathed to his followers from his cross. Peace! Let us take hold of God with the clasp of a fresh and living faith, and receiving into our souls something of the ineffable calm which always reigns wherever God is, let us enjoy Christ's blessed bequest of PEACE.

TO ME TO LIVE IS CHRIST.

BY REV. J. R. HOWERTON, D. D.,
Pastor of the First Presbyterian Church, Norfolk, Va.

———————

"For to me to live is Christ."—PHIL. i. 21.

THESE are the words of an earnest man and a ripe Christian. Even before his conversion Paul was a man of great earnestness, and of singular concentration of purpose. He was a Pharisee after the straitest sect. He excelled all other young men of his own age in his attainments in the Jewish learning. He was exceedingly zealous for the traditions of the elders. When that new sect arose which, as he thought, threatened to overthrow the religion of his fathers, he was among its most zealous persecutors. So exceedingly mad was he against them that he persecuted them even unto strange cities. While on a mission of this kind there came to him that voice out of heaven which changed his whole life. The tide which before had been striving to check the current of Christianity now turned and flowed with it in increased volume and force. Paul now became as earnest a Christian as he had before been a Pharisee. All that had been gain to him he now counted loss that he might win Christ. He devoted himself to the service of Christ until it became the absorbing purpose of his life. He now said, "This *one* thing I do."

This epistle was written near the close of his life. His labors and sufferings for his Master's cause, his life

319

of communion with him had ripened his character to that degree of consecration which marks this whole epistle. He was writing from prison at Rome. The news of his arrest must have spread consternation throughout Christendom. Especially must it have brought sorrow and dismay to this loving and beloved people. He wishes to cheer and encourage them. "I would that ye should understand, brethren, that the things which happened unto me, so far from proving to be a calamity to the cause of Christ, have turned out rather unto the furtherance of the gospel. For many of the brethren in the Lord, waxing confident by my bonds, are much more bold to speak the word without fear. It is true, some preach Christ from wrong motives, supposing to add affliction to my bonds. But whether in pretence or truth, Christ is preached, and therein I do rejoice and will continue to rejoice. It is my earnest expectation and my hope, that as always heretofore, so now also, Christ shall be magnified in my body, whether it be by life or by death. And it matters not to me which, for to me to live is Christ, and to die is gain."

"To me to live is Christ." Notice the singular wording of the text. It is a pregnant construction. Paul states an equation, of which "to live" is the first member, and "Christ" is the second. He affirms some sort of an identity between Christ and the Christian's life. What does he mean?

There are two very common senses in which we use the word "life." The first is in the sense of the vital principle, that mysterious force which animates dead matter, upon whose presence depends nourishment and growth. We use the word in this sense when we say, "Life is extinct." The second is in the sense of the sum of the activities of body and soul, the outworking of the inward principle. We use it in this sense when we say of a man that he lived a useful life, or when we say, "Life is real, life is earnest."

We use the word in both these senses when we refer to the spiritual as well as the natural life. When we speak of the spiritual life we may mean either its vital principle or the outworking of that principle in spiritual thoughts, desires, words and deeds. Paul affirms an identity between Christ and the Christian's life in both these senses. He affirms it in the first sense in Galatians ii. 20, when he says, "I am crucified with Christ, nevertheless I live; yet not I, but Christ liveth in me; and the life that I now live, I live by the faith of the Son of God, who loved me, and gave himself for me." That is, Christ is the author and sustainer of that inward principle of the new life.

But I think that in our text he is using it in the second sense. He refers to the outward development of the life that is within; the sum of its thoughts, purposes, activities, and sufferings; to his life as a whole. As Christ is the source of the inward spiritual life, so he is the end and object of its outward development. As the earth derives her life from the light and heat of the sun, develops that life into countless forms of use and beauty, then, circling within the orbit of his attraction, exhibits the infinite variety of her life, thus returning that which he gave; so the Christian derives his inner spiritual life from Christ, develops it into spiritual graces and activities, then, revolving about him as the great centre of attraction, consecrates to him the life which he has given.

"Christ liveth in me—to me to live is Christ!" What a philosophy of life we have in these two sentences! What a sublime explanation of its source and end! And

21

to think that it came from a prisoner, awaiting a felon's death ! Contrast it with the sad pessimism of the royal skeptic: "The living know that they shall die, but the dead know not anything."

I shrink from trying to analyze this text, lest I should seem to mar its force and beauty. But for the sake of confining our attention to it for a little while, let us look at it in this way: 1. Christ gives to life its purpose—his glory; 2. Christ gives to life its motive—his love; 3. Christ gives to life its character—nobility; 4. Christ gives to life its issue—success.

I. Christ gives to life its purpose—his glory. Life must have an end as well as an origin, a purpose as well as a cause. We are just as much compelled to believe that everything has a final cause as that it has an efficient cause. The one belief is just as intuitive as the other. To use the old illustration, if we saw a watch for the first time, we should not only believe that somebody made it, but that he made it for some purpose. If our first question were, Who made it? Our next would be, For what purpose did he make it? The second question is just as necessary as the first, and the mind will not rest until both are answered. The effort to find the answer to these two questions gives rise to all philosophy and science. This question rises to supreme importance when it concerns the human life. The question, How did we come into being? is of no more importance than the question, For what do we live? And as the efficient cause, so must the final cause of life be adequate to account for it. Life as a whole must have some sufficient purpose. It is not enough to find an object for the intellect, another for the faculty of taste, another for the affections. Man's life is not a mere sum of so many days, months, and years; it is not a mere bundle of thoughts, feelings, words, and actions. There must be unity in the purpose of life. This unity of purpose is necessary to the success of life as a whole. There must be some one object upon which all man's faculties may be centered, and which is worthy of their highest and noblest exercise. In any part of life singleness of purpose and concentration of effort are necessary to success. Some years ago I was passing down a river valley. One scene I remember, where the river spreads its whole volume of water into a broad and beautiful lake, surrounded by mountain walls. Beautiful, but useless. Just beside the river ran a canal, narrow, but deep. That canal perhaps did not contain one-tenth the volume of water which the river did, but it had once carried the commerce of a nation. So, if a man would attain success among the world's workers, he must choose his calling, and concentrate his powers upon it. Now, if this be true of the component parts of life, how much more of life itself? In an orchestra, not only must every instrument be in tune with itself, but every one must be attuned to all the others. So there must be some common chord to which all the faculties of the soul may be attuned, in order to make of life a perfect harmony. A man may seem to have been a success in his business or profession, to have been happy in his affections, to have had every taste gratified, and yet his life as a whole may have been one stupendous failure. When death comes, he will be like a tree whose fruit has been killed by an untimely frost, whose leaves have been scattered by the winds, and whose trunk, worm-eaten and decayed, has returned to the elements from whence it came.

Such a purpose was given man in his first creation— the glory of God. This alone is an end unto itself; this alone was worthy of man's life; this alone could call all

man's faculties into their highest and noblest exercise.
But when man fell he prostituted his powers to baser
ends.   He lost both the power and the will to live for
God's glory.   In redeeming man Christ has restored to
him this same purpose in a new form.   It is now the
glory of God in and through Christ.   Under the gospel
the glory of God as embodied in Christ, in whom
dwelleth all the fulness of the Godhead bodily, is man's
chief end.   Through him all approach to God must be
made, through him all work for God's glory must be
done.   ''Who gave himself for us that he might redeem
us from all iniquity, and purify unto himself a peculiar
people, zealous of good works.''   ''Whether we live or
whether we die, we are the Lord's; for to this end Christ
both died and revived and rose again that he might be
Lord both of the dead and the living.''

All that is worthy of human effort is embraced under
this purpose.   To seek the glory of Christ is to seek the
highest development of one's own soul, and the highest
good of one's fellow-men.   It includes all that humani-
tarianism offers as the end of human effort, and infinitely
more.   Christ is the chord to which all the faculties of
the soul must be attuned to make of human life a harmony which shall resound throughout eternity to the
glory of God.

II. Christ gives to life its motive—his love.   To make
a success of life as a whole there must not only be a
purpose worthy of all the powers of a human soul, but a
motive which will arouse them to their highest energy.
Motive is to the soul what steam is to an engine.   Without steam the most perfect machinery is useless; without
a life-motive the most highly-gifted soul is worse than
useless.

I once saw a painting in some art gallery of a beautiful vessel, under full sail, becalmed upon a glassy ocean. To me there was a sadness in the picture which was only enhanced by its beauty. I could not but think how many souls are like that vessel, endowed with the highest powers of mind and heart, yet becalmed upon the ocean of life—without a life-motive!

Said George Eliot, "What makes life dreary is the want of motive." How many wasted lives testify to the truth of that saying! "Is life worth living?" The answer depends upon the answer to the questions, "Has life an end? has life a motive?" There is a great deal of pessimism in the world to-day because men cannot answer these question for themselves, and will not accept God's answer.

> "Full many a gem of purest ray serene,
>   The dark unfathomed caves of ocean bear;
> Full many a flower is born to blush unseen,
>   And waste its sweetness on the desert air,'

is Gray's oft-quoted saying. So, hidden away in many a human soul precious gifts lie dormant, because no motive arouses them to exercise. How many Cincinnati or Putnams may be plowing in their fields to-day; how many Jacksons many be teaching in their little school-rooms, because their country's voice does not call them to arms! How many statesmen whose names might be written in their country's history are pursuing quiet avocations, leaving their places to be filled by demagogues, because patriotism does not call them to their country's service! Oh! how many talents are rusting in their napkins, because the love of Christ has not quickened the souls who possess them! How many are there in this congregation who are living selfish lives, prostituting precious gifts to the pursuit of filthy lucre or idle pleasure, because the love of Christ has no place in your hearts? How many young men are here to-day who might be preaching the gospel and saving the lost, because the love of Christ does not constrain you? How many missionaries are here to-day who have not heard the call of duty, because the love of Christ has not quickened your ears?

It was the love of Christ that made Paul what he was and enabled him to do the work he did. Without it his name would have been buried to-day in the annals of Jewish rabbis.

The love of Christ is the only motive that can arouse *all* the powers of a soul into their highest and noblest exercise. And that is the strongest motive in the world to-day. It is doing more for the human race than all other motives combined. Make all the allowances you please for apathy of Christians and coldness in the church, the love of Christ still inspires the noblest sacrifices and the most arduous labors. The love of Christ is the true altruism. And this is the motive which Paul commends to you when he says, "To me to live is Christ."

III. Christ gives to life its character—nobility. The life whose purpose is the glory of Christ, whose motive is the love of Christ, however narrow its sphere, however humble its condition, is a noble life.

Was not Paul's a noble life? We can all see it now, but in his day he was despised both by Jew and Gentile. The noblest lives in the world's history have been those of followers of Jesus, of men whose motto has been: "To me to live is Christ." Some of you may say: "But we cannot all live such lives. If I could preach like Paul; if I could win nations to Christ; if I could write books which would overthrow error, or edify and comfort God's people; if I could be a great reformer like Luther, or a great missionary; if I could write hymns which should voice the devotions of God's people, then I might feel that a noble life was for me. But I can do none of these things. I have neither the talents nor the opportunities.'' Who has not felt the wish that his talents were increased and his sphere of influence widened, that his name might be written in the catalogue of noble lives? But, it is not necessary to be a Paul, a Luther, a Bunyan, a Whitefield, a Carey or a Moffat, a Havergal or a Prentiss, to live a noble life. It needs only that the life-purpose be the glory of Christ, and that the life-motive be the love of Christ. Most of us must live what men would call commonplace lives. But however commonplace, however humble, it is a noble life if Christ be its centre.

Paul's was a noble life, but was not Hannah's life noble, too? That mother who first consecrated her son to the service of God, then brought to the temple from year to year the garments which her loving fingers had fashioned for him in quiet obscurity—did she not live a noble life? I know of a mother who, left early a widow with little children, had worked for years to support and educate them, looking forward to the time when her first-born son should take her burden from her shoulders. But just when he was emerging from boyhood he heard the call of God's Spirit to preach the gospel. Sore as the trial was, she gave him up to the service of her Master. Was not hers a noble life? And there are many such lives not recorded in man's history. Mary is only one of many thousands of women who have anointed their Saviour with the costly fragrance of their lives, yet she is one of very few whose names are spoken wherever the gospel is preached. All have heard of Augustine and Chrysostom, yet how many have never heard of

Monica and Anthusa, the Christian mothers to whom the church owes these men. The world resounds with Luther's fame, but how few outside of the students of church history have heard of John Staupitz, who led him to Christ. And there are thousands of lives just as noble which have not received even bare mention in church history. But when we come to study the history of the church which the recording angel is now writing we shall find their names in letters of gold.

In a life consecrated to Christ, the needle, the plow, the saw, the counter, the desk, are instruments in doing God's work. The humblest Christian life is nobler than that of warriors, kings, orators, and statesmen, whose names are immortalized in man's imperfect histories.

IV. Christ gives to life its issue—success. I have said that in order to the success of life as a whole there is need of unity of design. But we cannot plan our lives with any certainty for a single day, how much less for the months and the years to come! Still less can we make our lives work together with those of others. We work often in utter ignorance of the design of the work we are doing. But there is over all a Master-mind, overseeing, directing all in accordance with a foreordained plan of infinite wisdom. I was once invited to ride with an engineer along the line of a railroad in process of construction. In one place I saw some digging into a hill, others shovelling the earth into carts, others hauling it away and dumping it into a valley. Each was doing his own work without paying any attention to others. A mile or so further on I saw another gang of workmen without any apparent connection with the first. I saw some of these with drills in their hands patiently striking away at exactly the same spot in the rock for hours. I saw others putting dynamite into the holes thus drilled.

I saw others sharpening instruments, tempering drills, and forging tools. As we drove along the engineer showed me a line of stakes leading from one gang to another. The whole road had been surveyed. I saw then the connection between the different squads of workmen, and their different tasks. All were working together, each in his own place and task, under the superintendence of the engineer. Unity of plan pervaded the whole, so that not a blow of the pick or stroke of the drill was wasted.

So Christ, the great Engineer, overlooks and directs the work of all those in his employ, so that it effects his design. He thus unifies the life of the individual Christian, and of the whole church in all ages. It was by his direction that Paul became a missionary to the Gentiles, instead of preaching to the Jews as he thought he ought to do. It was by his call that Paul went to Europe. Even what seem to us to be disasters are parts of his plan, and work out the accomplishment of his purpose. Thus Paul's arrest, voyage, and imprisonment at Rome, which seemed to be a great calamity, was ordered by Christ, and turned out rather for the furtherance of the gospel.

Somewhere I have read a story of a monk who, in the century before the Reformation, had discovered the truth by reading the Bible. He was shut up for the rest of his life in a dungeon. There he contrived to write his views, and concealed them in the walls of his dungeon. Long after his death the manuscript was discovered, published, and became a means of advancing the Reformation. Even our failures are overruled for good. Indeed, in the Christian life there is no such thing as failure. We may not live to see it, but Christ will give it success. Even death, that black shadow of disaster, which lies across the path of every natural life, is to the

Christian the entering into the reward of his labors, the crown of success; for he can not only say, "To me to live is Christ," but "to die is gain."

Now, dear friends, will you not make this, " To me to live is Christ," the motto of your life? Oh! what a different world this would be, if it were only tried by men and women in every walk of life! If only the preacher, whenever he stands in his pulpit or visits the homes of his people, would forget himself, and remember, "To me to live is Christ"! Would that every physician, as he goes about with his ministry of healing; every lawyer, as he pleads in the courts of justice; every politician, as he accepts the office entrusted to him by his countrymen; every business-man, every laborer, made this the rule of conduct, "To me to live is Christ"! Oh! that every wife and mother would make this the spirit of the home, "To me to live is Christ"! Oh! that every woman to whom beauty, or wealth, or position, or talent, has given a commanding position in society, would consecrate that influence to Christ! What a different world it would be!

Young men! you who stand upon the threshold of life, who are seeking to determine aright your choice of a profession, who are making your plans for the future, will you not, before all these, make the choice of a life-purpose and a life-motive? Will you not determine, whatever your choice of a life-calling may be, that this shall be its aim and motive, "To me to live is Christ"! Then let other choices be what they may, your life will be a noble life, a successful life. Will you not all join me in the petition:

"Father, I lift my prayer to thee,
To grant me this, my earnest plea,
The motto of my life may be,
 'To me to live is Christ.'

"Thy strengthening grace, O, Lord, I pray
  That I, with each returning day,
  From loving heart may truly say,
    'To me to live is Christ.'

"My life, O, Christ, thou gavest me,
  A life from fear of death set free,
  That life I consecrate to thee,
    'To me to live is Christ.'

"One purpose o'er my powers shall reign
  One motive all my heart constrain,
  Through all my life run this refrain,
    'To me to live is Christ.'

"Thy glory be my life's sole end,
  To that let all my powers tend,
  To that all my ambitions bend,
    'To me to live is Christ.'

"The love of Christ constraineth me,
  That love my one incentive be
  Inflame my answering love to thee,
    'To me to live is Christ.'

"To loftier aim could soul aspire?
  What nobler life could heart desire,
  What motive such devotion fire?
    'To me to live is Christ.'

"Then when life's labors all are o'er,
  Its cares and sorrows are no more,
  And death stands knocking at the door
    'In Christ to die is gain.'"

THE VALLEY OF ACHOR.

BY REV. G. L. PETRIE, D. D.,

Pastor of the Presbyterian Church, Charlottesville, Va.

"I will give her the valley of Achor for a door of hope."—
HOSEA ii. 15.

TO appreciate this prophetic language we must, of
course, know something of the valley of Achor.
While it is a name not much used now, it marked
a spot once well known to the Israelite in the geography
of his land. Its precise location cannot now be traced.
It was near Jericho; it was closely connected with
Gilgal; it was in the deep gorge of the Jordan, nestling
somewhere amidst the spurs of the mountains that
formed the central feature of the promised land. The
name occurs only three times in the Bible. It has the
eminence of importance, if not of frequent mention. A
glance at its brief record may make it to us a door of
hope, as God, through Hosea, said he would make it to
Israel in the olden day.

I. THE VALLEY OF ENTRANCE.

Israel's first camp across the Jordan was in the valley
of Achor. ·It marked a great transition of the people.
For forty years they had been pilgrims on the march
or in the camp. They had camped on other people's
ground, and marched across alien lands. They had
never been at home. Their whole history is summed up
in two short chapters—slaves in Egypt, pilgrims in the
wilderness. But in the valley of Achor they had a new

experience—at home. Always it had been: to the land of which the Lord had said, "I will give it you." Now, this is the land. Here pilgrimage ceased, and permanent residence began; here was the throwing off of the old and the putting on of the new.

Some sudden changes took place in Achor's vale. Here was a camp in which Moses was sadly missed. The great leader had finished his work and gone to his reward. Joshua had now begun to be magnified in the sight of Israel. In the valley of Achor a new order of things began.

See! yonder cloudy pillar, guide of the host for forty years, rolls up and is borne away by unseen hands. The pillar, which was a cloud by day and a fire by night, is beheld no more. Its work accomplished, it retires from the scene. Israel has reached the land long sought, and there is no more need of guidance on the way. Another change. The morning comes. As the Israelite looks out from his tent door he sees no manna on the ground. The manna ceased, the bread from heaven by which a travelling host had been so long fed. A better food was now in reach, the old corn of the land and Canaan's luscious fruits. On these, with great delight, they fed. How great a change a day had made!

That change had been accomplished by the shortest march Israel had ever made. Many a long day's march Israel had made. Beginning in the morning fresh, in the evening worn and weary they had pitched their tents, yet seemed to accomplish naught. No progress, no gain, no betterment of their estate; or, if a change, only seeming worse for their long march. This last march, which brought them to Achor's vale, the shortest, yet accomplished most. At night they camp in sight of yonder eastern bank of Jordan, which in the morning

they had left; in sight of yonder heights of Moab, where
the tented host so recently had dwelt. Now let the
silver trumpet sound long and clear. Let its music ring.
Its prolonged note has reached the plain where the morning camp had been, and wakes the silence of its solitude.
Israel's shortest march of all in those forty years! How
great a change is by it wrought! Take down the old
signs; put up the new; Israel at home.

Why all this? Why can a little movement here and
now do more than great movements elsewhere and at
other times? That short journey led Israel across a
great dividing line. That made the difference. Some
places that are very far apart are very near—no line between them; no real difference, though there be a stretch
of miles on miles. Some places are very near, yet very
far apart. A line divides them. It makes a very great
difference on which side of the line we stand. By long
journeys we may only compass the mountain, or measure vast stretches of dreary desert sands or pathless
wilds, and after all be no better off, and at last die
wretched pilgrims. All the trouble goes for naught. A
step across the line may put us at home, may bring us
into the valley of Achor. To us it becomes a door of
hope, a gateway to the land.

Come over into the valley of entrance to-day. Some
of you have journeyed long, but have not reached the
Rest. You are clinging to the accompaniments of pilgrimage—cloud and manna, things that have brought
you to the border of the real blessing. You look over
into the valley of entrance, but cross not its dividing line.
Make this shortest march of all. In sight of the promised blessing, cross over and possess it. This final
act marks no great progress, but notes a mighty change.
God has put the door of hope across the line. He who

obeys God's call may enter, and entering cherish hope.
He may not know a great deal of the land. He may
not have seen what lies beyond the valley of entrance.
His progress may be measured by very short lines. He
may be just across the line, just within the boundary.
God bids him hope.

God puts the door of hope just across the line; not
up in the strongholds; not up in the high mountains,
approached by narrow, steep and difficult defiles, to be
besieged and stormed and scaled by heroic act; but in
the beautiful, lowly vale, into which the pilgrim cannot
help coming who will only cross the line. Hope is not
a matter of rich experience and great advance, but of
clear title and prompt obedience to God's call. It is not
a matter of profound feeling, but of camping on the
other side of the line God has drawn.

On Moab's heights; in Israel's camp. Come to the
brow of this mountain. Look over. See threadlike
Jordan in its deep gorge. Beyond it the beautiful valley
running up into the sides of the mountains, robed in
loveliness, arrayed in exquisite charms. It is a happy
place to be. But more: it is the gateway to the entire land.
When God calls, obey. Camp in the valley of Achor. You
will find, wreathed in its graceful vines, amidst its beautiful flowers and mellow fruits, a door of hope, a gateway
to the land. So God has put for us a beautiful door of
hope within reach, but across the line. If you will cross
this line, come. Come now to Jesus Christ. This first
stand will be to you a door of hope. Through it and
from it you may advance to all the treasures and delights
of grace and glory, too.

II. The Valley of Trouble.

It is a significant fact that Israel's first camp in Canaan, so beautiful and bright and full of hope, should be the place from which their army went forth to calamitous defeat, and to which the routed force rushed back in disorder and dismay. Strangely significant! Achor was a gateway to the entire land. Israel entertained no wish to lie always at the gate, but, having been happily ushered in, began to plan for pushing further on.

A city on the overhanging heights they conclude to take. They send a party up the mountain pass to reconnoitre and report. Their report: a few can take it. A little army climbs up, is completely routed, and hastily returns. Alarm seizes on the entire host. The secret of defeat God reveals. There is an accursed thing within the camp. Call the roll. Achan is singled out. Out of two million people God can discern the troubler, and single out the man. None can hide from him. A multitude is no defence from him with whom we have to do. God has no difficulties. He knows where sin lurks, and he can bring it forth into the light of day.

Achan stands helpless and exposed. What has he done? Is he a murderer? No. A blasphemer? No. Unclean? No. He is a young man; for Joshua says: "My son, what hast thou done?" He confesses all. In his tent is concealed a Babylonish garment and a wedge of gold, spoils of war. That does not seem so bad in itself. But it is fearful in this light: God forbade it. There can be no greater sin than to disobey God. "Achan, did you know it was wrong?" "Yes; I hid it." He weeps. But tears wash not away his sin. Make way. Stand around. Take now the stones, and hurl them at him, who brought the accursed thing into Israel's camp. Then, when he lay dead, they heaped the stones on him to mark the spot where Israel's troubler died. Whatever the beautiful valley before was named, henceforth they called it

Achor, Valley of Trouble. Then the army marched on to victory. So even by its gloomy name the valley of Achor was to Israel a door of hope. The trouble which they encountered there was after all a pledge of victory.

Certain hard lessons which we learn open to us the door of hope, and make way for further progress, and qualify us to advance. Religious life is not meant to cherish sin, nor to afford to sin a hiding-place, where unnoticed it may ply its deadly work. In the Christian God does not license sin. God is as sure to punish sin in his people as in any one else. God slew all the rebellious in the wilderness. They were not allowed to enter Canaan. On Moab's plains all who were led away into idolatry God slew. They were not allowed to cross the Jordan. But now the host has crossed the border stream, and is camped in the valley just beyond, none aged, none infirm. Will not God be indulgent to them now? See here a venture. Achan disobeys a known command. Will not God pass that by? Vain hope. Achan dies by God's command.

Sin is just as bad in a Christian as anywhere else. God will drive it out; by rough means it may be, by some means it will be, though by tears and sighs and groans. Your sin must leave. The process may be painful; but sin must leave. These hard places become monumental places in our lives, where by severe correction there is opened to us a door of hope. There is hope for one who has learned this lesson : no sin; no accursed thing.

The fruit of disobedience is defeat. All check to progress is in sin. There were two attacks on Ai. How different their results ! The same men, the same place, the same courage, the same zeal, the same expectation. One a disaster; the other a glorious success. Yonder

22

mound explains the difference. Sin was rooted out. The greatest obstacle in the way of the success of truth and of gospel triumph is not the number and prowess of the opposing host; not the strength of his towers and battlements and the bristling ramparts of his defence; but it is the disobedience that finds a lodgment in Jehovah's host. Defeat came to Israel, not when foes were mightiest, but when Israel in this was weakest, when Israel disobeyed the Lord.

An unwritten chapter in the history of the church: the causes of defeat. Not the might of foes, nor the number of them, nor their munitions of war; no more than it was Ai that by its might hurled back Israel's startled men. The cause is in the camp. The want is at home. It is in these tents where tabernacle the warriors of God. Search here. Find it; drive it out. Then there can be no successful resistance to the gospel work. When we find and kill the sin that causes harm, we, too, shall call the Valley of Trouble a door of hope.

All Israel did not sin in this; but all had trouble from it. The trouble, too, was to the entire host a blessing, because it became to all a door of hope. It is the hard lesson from which we get most good, and from which opens widest the door of hope. Israel little thought, as they camped in that beautiful valley, where all was so sweet and bright and lovely, where they had turned their backs on the dreadful desert and the howling wilderness, where there were no mournful desert winds, no rude storms, but musical brooks and gentle fountains and soft breezes, that they were going to have a terrible sorrow there. Yet it came, and through no fault of the entire host. They had to bear the burden, though they did not make it. But after it was all over they had learned a great lesson and received a great blessing.

Our rest in the valley of delight is often interrupted and disturbed. It may not be our fault. It may come like a mountain storm, quick, sharp, severe. The experience may give a new name to our abode, a name of sorrow. What shall we call our once happy vale, where our joys were many, and our hopes were bright, and our pleasures were as the sweet morning hours, where we were all together, and our songs were happy? What shall we call it now? Call it the valley of Achor. We know now what trouble is, and sorrow and tears. We dwell in the shadow now · valley of Achor.

Hark! From above a voice that speaks in accents of cheer, in contrast with our sad hearts and plaintive mood. Hear! The valley of Achor I will make to you a door of hope. A heavenly presence is felt. In the deep shadows the tumultuous soul is stilled. The cheering music of the heavenly voice gladdens the heart. The music of the heart is transposed from chord to chord, till all its plaintive notes are lost and only cheerful strains remain. The brightening light, breaking through the darkness, chases the shadows all away. It is the same scene, but the scene retouched and transformed. The valley of Achor still, but it has become a door of hope. Then we thank God, who brought us through the trouble into peace. Then, in the new light, we wonder that the valley ever seemed so dark.

III. The Valley of Renewal.

Many a long and weary year rolled by in Israel's checkered history in which Achor is not named. It seemed destined to oblivion. Many passing doubtless said, There Achan died. Judges ruled and kings reigned. Israel grew and prospered, then declined. The kingdom was rent in twain. Calamities befell. Disasters happened. Worse destinies seemed imminent. Apostate, wicked, abandoned, Israel became. Idolatries and crimes of all sorts prevailed. Oh, what a change! How sad and desperate! God calls Hosea, and says to him, Go, call Israel back. Invite them, allure them. Bid them recall the olden time of their zeal and piety. If anything will soften the human heart, it is calling up the happy past. Call to their mind the record of the good time when their fathers crossed the Jordan and camped in the valley of Achor, where they entered the land, and where they were delivered out of trouble. I will make it the door of hope to them again, and they shall sing just as they sang there long ago. So this long interval of sin and sorrow shall be cut out, and happiness and consecration be renewed.

We are all more or less familiar with the irreparable; the wrongs in life that we cannot right; the evils we have done that we now cannot undo; the sins that stay. A word you said, you would now like to recall, but cannot. An act your right hand did, you would give your right hand now to undo. You have lost your morning hours of life. Oh, if you could bring them back and use them better! You are suffering from early wrongs. A thousand sins perpetually haunt you, and mock your folly, by which so easily you were led astray. You have drifted into ways from which you cannot now escape. You have contracted obligations you know not how to annul, nor yet how to meet. What a helpless feeling creeps over you, possesses you. Bound, *bound*, BOUND! Oh! to break the chain and be free again. You are a wreck, a heap of ruins. You can never get back to where you were. Poor remnant of a broken life! What can you do with it? An old man is seen looking at the children as they play. What is he thinking about? How great advantage he has over them in being farther on with life's work, nearer the goal, nearer the great reward? Oh, no; far from it. He is thinking of his own misspent life; wishing he might once more stand at life's door of hope; thinking he would enter in, go on, and do well. But he is a ruin now, and has lost his time. It is sad! The picture stands for many.

Hosea, run to that man, and tell him the Lord can make the valley of his sorrow hopeful yet. Tell him God invites. Tell him the valley of Achor God can make a door of hope, though to his dim vision there is no such bright prospect yet revealed. In that valley songs of gladness, as in the olden days, may wake the silence, or change the sad refrain of hopeless grief to a note of sweet delight and purest joy.

Is there a troubled soul now here? Is there here a wrecked life? Come to the door of hope. Bring your ruins. Bring the fragments of your life, no matter how small. Bring the relics of your love, no matter how impaired. Bring your dishonored bodies, no matter how abused. Bring your polluted hearts, no matter how soiled. God wishes you. God has provided for you. God calls you. He wishes you to cast yourself down at his feet as a poor wreck, to be renewed, restored by him. Oh! what can there be made of this sinful life? Much, very much. God says he will blot out the wretchedness you have wrought. He will take you back, back to the first camping-place, a reminiscence still to you of earliest peace and sweetest joy. Come to the valley of Achor. He will make it to you a door of hope. You shall sing happy songs again, as happy as ever waked from its silence the lovely vale.

RELIGION NOT A VAIN THING.

BY REV. SAMUEL A. KING, D. D.,

Pastor of the First Presbyterian Church, Waco, Texas.

"It is not a vain thing for you; because it is your life."—
DEUT. xxxii. 47.

THIS testimony was given thirty-three hundred years
ago concerning personal and family religion. The
witness is Moses. Aside from his right to be
heard as a divinely-appointed messenger, as we believe
he was, the great Hebrew law-giver is entitled to an
audience, and the generations of men have given heed to
his words, because he was one of the world's foremost
men. Any one tall enough to cast such a shadow as
has been thrown by his conspicuous form across the
space of three and thirty centuries will be recognized as
one of the world's most colossal figures.

In considering his testimony, as it is conveyed to us
in the text, I remark—

1. That he was an *intelligent witness*.

No man is brazen enough to dispute the intellectual
greatness or the extraordinary culture of Moses; and
he was thoroughly informed in the matter about which
he speaks. He had not simply taken his belief on trust.
True, the faith he held was the faith of his father and
mother. There are some who cast slight on those who
hold to the religious beliefs in which they were brought
up. As for me, I think it no discredit to any man's intellect or intelligence to believe the Bible and walk in
the paths of piety because his father and mother cher-

ished the Christian's faith in life, and enjoyed the Christian's hope in death.   If the Bible was a sufficient lamp to the feet of my father and my mother along the path they trod; if it guided them in duty, sustained them in trial, was a solace in old age and a comfort in death, I blush not to avow myself a believer in that religion in whose faith they lived and in whose hopes they died.

But this witness had abundant and unusual opportunities to compare the religious faith in which he had been reared with those beliefs which were different and hostile.   He had been taught in all the learning of the Egyptians.   He knew what was the best that could be offered by the world's wisest men, who had no revelation from God.   He knew what fruits had been borne by the one form of faith and by the other.   And he gives, in the words before us, his deliberate and intelligent testimony on behalf of the religion which was made known by revelation from God.

2. He was a witness who had *tested* that of which he speaks.

Many persons show a disposition to discount the testimony of young and enthusiastic believers—a disposition which we cannot approve.   The faith and zeal of David and John and Paul was as real and as rational in the morning of their religious life as in the after-ripeness of their rich experience.   But when any are inclined to undervalue the testimony of a witness because he has not had his faith tested by time, they can offer no such objection to that of the man whose words we are considering to-day. He had embraced this faith when young, and held it through all the years till now he was old.   Through loyalty to God and to his people, he had turned his back, when a young man, on the most dazzling prospect of earthly greatness that could fire the ambition of any

youthful mind. And from that day forth, in banish-
ment, in poverty, in conflict with Egypt's king and
court, in trials from an unbelieving and fickle people
whom he was leading from bondage to liberty, in all
these weary years and through all these varied trials, his
religion had been put to the severest test, and he had
been able to make proof of its reality and its value.
With this long experience behind him he utters with
his aged lips the testimony in our text.

3. He was a *disinterested witness*.

He had nothing now to gain by speaking aught except the truth. He was now uttering his last words.
In our courts of justice the declarations of a dying man
are accepted as valid testimony. It is believed that the
hour of death is ''life's honest hour''; that when one is
on the border-line between the life that is and the life to
come the lips will speak the truth. Moses had been
told that he must die. Before ascending the mountain
to view the promised land and then to die, he spoke these
words, which were his ''dying declarations'' as to the
truth and the preciousness of that religion in the light
of which he had walked ''till travelling days were
done.''

I. The testimony of this witness.

(1), It is *not a vain thing*.

Our religion is not a vain thing in the sense of *lacking
sufficient proof*.

We who believe the Bible to be the word of God have
solid ground on which to rest our faith, and can give
to every one that asks us ''a reason of the hope that is
in us.'' We invite those who would know the grounds
of our confidence to ''walk about Zion and go round
about her, to mark her bulwarks and consider her
palaces.''

It is not a vain thing because it is not a *speculation* or an *unpractical belief*.

Religion is practical or nothing. It prescribes a rule of life. It sets a watch at the door of our lips, and demands that our words shall be loving and truthful and chaste.

It goes where no human law can enter and asserts authority where no human ruler can exercise dominion, in the secret chambers of the soul. It demands that the thoughts and affections shall be subordinated to its control. That which prescribes a law for the outward life, which brings us into judgment for even idle words, and claims to regulate the thoughts and intents of the heart, is far removed from being a vain speculation, or the unfruitful belief of a doctrine or a creed, it is intensely and preëminently practical.

It may be added that a religion which has borne such fruits in personal godliness, in household piety, and in the moral renovation of communities and states, whose presence in any age or land can be as surely recognized by its effects as can the course of a running stream by the verdure that adorns its banks, is not a vain thing when tried by the supreme test of being judged by its fruits.

(2), It is *your life*.

This is true as to *nations*.

Israel furnishes a telling illustration. Immediately following the words of the text it is added: "And through this thing ye shall prolong your days in the land whither ye go over Jordan to possess it."

While the people of Israel obeyed the commands the promised blessings were enjoyed. They did not continue in possession of the fair land bestowed upon them because they did not continue to set their hearts to the words of God's law to keep them.

Dispersed among the nations of the earth; scattered and peeled and without a local habitation, they are a standing proof of the truth of Scripture prophecies, and their history bears witness that religion is not a vain thing for peoples, and commonwealths, and kingdoms, because it is their life.

This great truth is in as full force to-day as when it was uttered by the renowned Hebrew leader, and its fulfilment afterwards registered in the sad chronicles of the Hebrew people. Righteousness exalteth a nation. Sin is a reproach to any people, and will work their ruin. The mills of the Almighty Ruler ''grind slow, but they grind exceeding fine.'' The history of states and kingdoms that have risen, and prospered, and then gone to decay and ruin, is eloquent and emphatic in confirmation of the truth of our text.

There is a lesson and a warning here for us. Our country is on trial.

The perpetuity of our free institutions and the continuance of that prosperity which has hitherto been enjoyed, the *life* of our republic, cannot be assured except on condition of loyalty to God and obedience to his commands.

All our vast resources, our teeming population, our intelligence and energy, our Anglo-Saxon blood and prowess will not prevent the sure coming of decay and ruin, if we cease to be a people whose God is the Lord.

The Bible, the sanctuary, the Sabbath and the Christian home are chief among the defences which will secure to us and to our children our fair inheritance. The Bible has, in times past, been fiercely set upon, but like the anvil in the smithy, it is surrounded by the hammers that have been worn out upon its surface.

The chief attack to-day is upon the Sabbath; and if we

let the Lord's day be despoiled of its sacredness and given over to worldly pastime, or trodden in the mire of worldly traffic by those who are led astray by the maddening greed for gain, we will have reached "the beginning of the end."

If the Sabbath of the Puritan and the Hollander and the Scot, the holy Sabbath of our fathers and our mothers, shall be exchanged for the " Continental Sunday" of modern Europe, or the fête-day of Mexico ; if instead of the holy day we have the holiday, there will follow a sure and perhaps a swift decay, and the time will come when upon all the temples of our prosperity and greatness will be written " Ichabod," for the glory will have departed.

It is true of *families* that *religion is their life.*

It is the godly families that last.

In the early days here in Texas there were some large and noted families whose names were familiar as household words. They were ungodly and dissipated and reckless of human life. Their stalwart sons were the dread of the communities in which they lived. Though numerous then, they are now extinct. Their names are almost forgotten, and most of those who bore them went down to bloody graves "unwept, unhonored, and unsung."

In many communities in the older states can be seen the workings of this great law of life. There linger there the memories of prominent families, who were gay and godless. They were possessed of large estates, and held high social place by reason of birth and blood and wealth. They lived high and fast, without the fear of God or consideration of aught but the lighter or darker indulgences of a worldly life. They have disappeared. Other names are known where theirs were once most prominent. Other owners hold their great estates and occupy the stately homes where worldliness bore rule and godliness was eschewed.

But there were other homes—some elegant and some humble—in which the parents set their hearts to God's word, and commanded their children to observe to do all the words of his law. The family altar was the centre of household life; the family Bible was enthroned in the place of honor, and the "sweet hour of prayer" was the gateway through which they went forth in the morning to the labors of the day, and at evening time to the peaceful slumbers of the night. The sons and daughters trained by the precept and example of parents who "lured to brighter worlds and led the way" have perpetuated the honored names their fathers bore. In many cases they occupy the old ancestral homes. The rolls of members in the churches and of those who are now ministers, elders, deacons, and Sabbath-school teachers are largely filled with the names of those who were the fathers and mothers in Israel in the generation that went before. Godliness is not a vain thing for families; it is their life, and through it they prolong their days.

For *individuals* religion is not a vain thing; *it is their life*.

It is not merely a preparation for death. It is not "life" in the sense of *being* or *existence*, though temperance and chastity and godliness tend to the strengthening and preservation of physical and mental health and life. Life is a larger word than mere existence. In common speech we recognize the distinction when we say that one has a great deal of or very little life, or when we say of one whose lot has been isolated, or his surroundings disagreeable, that he *stayed* in such a place for a given time, but that he did not *live*.

When one is possessed of the peace which comes from being justified by faith, and of a realized fellowship with God as our Father and with Jesus Christ as our Saviour and friend; when mind and heart are filled and fired with the high conception that man's chief end is to glorify God and to enjoy him forever; when "sustained and soothed by an unfaltering trust" that all things in life shall work together for good, and that dying will be but going home, then there is life in the full meaning of the large word, for then the whole man lives. All the faculties must be employed, and all the desires of man's nature must be met in order that life, in its fulness, be realized. Man's moral nature; his sense of accountability to God and his relation to the future and to immortality, these are as real as his possession of a body and a mind. His consciousness of sin and of his need to be reconciled to God in order to have peace of conscience and a hope of heaven cannot be denied or ignored. Only the gospel meets the requirements of man's religious nature, and makes provision for satisfying the desires of the soul.

A bird has a nature which prompts it to fly in the air, and its wings are fitted for free and graceful movement in the fields of space. You capture the little feathered songster and confine it within the bars of a cage. It may be a gilded cage, and its place may be amid the fair surroundings of one of earth's most luxurious homes. The little captive may be caressed and petted, and its dainty food may be served by a fair and jeweled hand. But that caged existence is not *life* to the little bird. If you would minister to its real life you must open the prison doors and permit it to go forth on eager wing to fly in the upper air and warble in cheerful notes its glad song of freedom.

The prodigal son existed in the far-off land; but was it *life?* He had the memory of his early home, of a father's care and a mother's love. He had, moreover, the consciousness of sin, and the remorse the sinner must sooner or later feel. He was far away from the well-remembered home, without friends or friendship; forced to occupy himself with uncongenial toil; fain to satisfy his hunger with the food of the swine he herded, and was far more miserable than the unclean beasts which it was his daily task to feed.

That existence was not life to him. But when "he came to himself," and his returning feet bore him back to the home he had left; when the deep penitence of his softened heart found expression in the words of confession that leaped from his lips, and he was embraced in the father's arms and welcomed back to sonship in the father's house, oh! then the lost was found, and he who had been dead was alive again.

Man does not live by bread alone. When creature-good is enjoyed in fullest measure it does not satisfy. The ox that feeds upon our plains can satisfy his hunger with the tempting grass, quench his thirst at the running brook, and then lie down in the nearest shade and be at perfect rest. Every want his nature knows has been fully met. He has no bitter memories of the past, no forebodings of the future, and no consciousness of wrong to make him ill at ease. But it is not thus with man. He cannot feed the hunger of his soul with the things of earth, nor satisfy its thirst with worldly pleasure, wealth, or fame. Only the bread of heaven and the water of life can feed and satisfy the soul. The gospel offers these. The Saviour came into the world that we "might have life, and that we might have it more abundantly." "In him is life, and the life is the light of men.'' Coming to him we obtain pardon, and with it peace. The soul that was dead in sin is quickened into life. Spiritual life breathes in prayer, rejoices in fellowship with God and all the good, and finds ennobling use for all the faculties and employment for all the days in consecrated service. The affections have an object suited to their heavenly birth in a divine Saviour, who is ''chief among ten thousand and altogether lovely.'' And this spiritual life, beginning in grace, will be perfected in glory. ''He that believeth on the Son hath everlasting life.''   .   .   .   .   .   .

How do you, my hearer, esteem this religion of which our text bears witness? You may say that you set high value on it, and that you believe the Scriptures and all they teach concerning Christ and the great salvation. This may be the utterance of your lips, but what is the language of your life? There is a familiar adage that ''actions speak louder than words.'' Do you act as though this were a vain thing, or to you the ''one thing needful''? To profess to believe the Bible and to acknowledge the importance of personal religion, and yet neglect the great salvation, is a fearfully inconsistent course.

The man whose heart has led him to be an atheist is consistent with his cheerless creed when he lives without God and without hope in the world. He who can walk amid the foot-prints of the Deity, which are impressed on all the acres of the globe; who can lift his eyes to yon heavens, where the Maker's name is written in syllables of stars; who can shut his eyes to all the proofs of God's being and wisdom and power that are above and about and within him, and say, ''there is no God,'' he is consistent with his cold and dreadful belief when he lives as though it were ''all of life to live, and all of death to die.''

The skeptic, who does not accept these Scriptures as the word of God; who is so credulous as to believe that this wonderful book was written by unaided men; who can believe that the character, and the life, and the words of Jesus of Nazareth were the product of the thought of the fishermen of Galilee, and that they died for bearing witness to the resurrection of a Saviour who did not rise from the dead; the man who can believe all this is consistent in refusing to yield to this Saviour the love of his heart and the loyalty of his life.

But not so with you, if you profess to believe the Scriptures to be the word of God, and to accept their teachings about sin and salvation, about heaven and hell, and yet treat as a vain thing ''the hope set before you in the gospel'' by neglecting to lay hold upon it. How have you been treating him who has been standing and knocking at the door of your heart through all your years? What of your attitude to the church, in which he asks you to take your place and confess him before men?

What does your action say when the communion board is spread, and that Saviour whom you honor with your lips says to you, '' Do this in remembrance of me,'' and you refuse to take a place among those who remember his love?

Were I to ask you on what terms you would barter away your faith in the Bible and your hope that some day you may be able to ''read a title clear to a mansion in the skies,'' I doubt not you would shrink with shuddering from the proposal, and declare that you would not make that fearful bargain for a price that worlds would rate for. But, dear dying friend, what is the language of your life?

My Christian friends, do we manifest such earnest

devotion to the Master we profess to serve, and give such diligence to make our calling and election sure, as to give proof that with us religion is not a vain thing but that it is our life?   May God help us to walk worthy of our high vocation, and to show, by the choices we make and the lives we live, that we "count all things but loss for the excellency of the knowledge of Christ Jesus our Lord."

This religion, to which the testimony of Moses was borne so long ago, is an *old religion*.   Some things are the better for being old.   Were we to seek a shelter beneath which to pitch our tent we would not choose the blooming and graceful vine that had sprung into being and beauty since the last frost and would perish with the next.   Rather would we select an oak, like that beneath which Abram dwelt at Mamre, and which, gnarled and knotted though it might be, has anchored its great roots amid the rocks beneath the sod, and with giant arms has waged victorious struggle with the winds and storms of centuries.   When we seek a place on which to build a home we do not go to the tide-washed beach whose sands may have been cast into forms of beauty by the movement of the waves, and strewn with shells and coral that have been lavished on its surface by the sea.   We would go rather to some firm ground beyond the reach of tides, and digging deep till we find the rock, we would there build our habitation, and then feel sure that though "the rains may descend, and the floods come, and the winds blow and beat upon our house, it will not fall because founded on a rock."

Were we about to cross the sea we would not choose the new and gaily-painted vessel that, fresh from the builder's yard, was just weighing anchor for her trial trip.   We would prefer the veteran ship whose timbers

23

had been tested by the waves, and whose sails had been tried and mayhap torn by the storms through which the staunch vessel had often borne her living freight to the desired haven.

In religion " what is new is not true, and what is true is not new."

We will only build wisely when we build on the Rock of Ages.

In choosing the bark on which to venture the precious interests of our souls and our hopes of heaven, let us take up with no speculation of "modern thought"; no faith that claims to be better, because newer, than that in which our fathers and mothers lived and died. But let us make our voyage, as did they, in "the old ship of Zion, which has landed many thousands and can land as many more."

Jesus' Supreme Authority.

BY REV. C. R. HEMPHILL, D. D.,
Pastor of the Second Presbyterian Church, Louisville, Ky.

"Ye call me Master and Lord: and ye say well; for so I am."—JOHN xiii. 13.

JESUS and the twelve were assembled in the upper room of some unknown host in Jerusalem to celebrate the passover. It was the same night in which he was betrayed, and while they were gathered about the table Jesus arose and laid aside his garments; took a towel and girded himself; poured water into a basin, and washed his disciples' feet. He takes his garments and sits down again, and says to his disciples, "Know ye what I have done to you? Ye call me Master and Lord: and ye say well; for so I am." Is he mistaken who finds here an acted parable of the incarnation? The Son of God had abandoned his throne in heaven; had laid aside the glory of his divinity; had girded himself with the nature of man, and set himself to the lowly service of cleansing and saving men. In a little while he is to return to the heaven whence he came, and to robe himself with the glory which he had with the Father before the world was. The Son of man is the Son of God. He that is among men as he that serveth is also over men as he that ruleth. "Ye call me Master and Lord: and ye say well; for so I am." These titles by which you address me, says Jesus, are no mere conventionalities of speech; in their broadest import they are true.

355

Master means teacher, Lord means owner or ruler;
fusing these ideas together, the authority of teacher over
pupil, of master over servant, of ruler over subject, we
arrive at the conception of supreme and absolute authority. The humble figure that a few moments ago
was discharging so menial an office now assumes to
himself a dignity and an authority none other of the
sons of men have ever ventured to claim. To vindicate
the right of Jesus to the supremacy he claims does not
fall within my purpose. I set before me the humbler
task of defining his authority in its nature and extent.

Many of his most familiar sayings carry with them the
strongest assertion of his authority, and serve to display
its nature. Here are some of them: ''Ye believe in
God, believe also in me''; ''I am the Bread of Life'';
''If any man thirst, let him come unto me and drink'';
''I am the Light of the world''; ''Thy sins are forgiven
thee''; ''The Son of man shall come in the glory of his
Father with his angels''; ''The dead shall hear the
voice of the Son of God''; ''The Father hath given him
authority to execute judgment.'' When one speaks in
this fashion it is natural for him to add, ''For one is
your Master, even Christ.'' To reach a more adequate
notion of the authority with which Jesus invests himself, let us dwell on some of his utterances. ''I am
the Way,'' he declares. Many are the roads, made
smooth by the tread of many feet, over which men have
travelled to find God. These paths end in darkness.
Jesus is clothed with the authority to lead men into the
knowledge of God, and to bring them into his presence;
he is himself the way. ''No man cometh unto the
Father, but by me.''

''I am the good Shepherd.'' The mark of the shepherd is authority, wielded, it is true, with sympathy and

tenderness, but authority still. The flock must follow
the steps of the shepherd, and yield to his guidance and
control. Jesus is the good Shepherd, the only true
Shepherd of the sheep; all others are thieves and robbers. At the head of the flock walks Jesus, and only
those who hear his voice and follow him will reach the
shelter of the heavenly fold.

"I am the Truth," Jesus affirms. Amid the babel of
human tongues, crying, "lo! here, lo! there," is heard
this saying of Jesus, so quietly spoken that we may fail
to hear it or to compass its meaning. The old fable is
that truth once existed in the beauty and unity of complete proportions, but was torn into fragments and
the fragments scattered to the winds. Men have been
haunted by the vision of truth's pristine unity, and,
cherishing the dream of its restoration, have been patiently seeking the severed parts. Jesus declares man's
dream fulfilled. The sovereignty of truth is imperial,
her voice is imperative to the minds of men, the voice,
indeed, of God. This sovereign authority of truth Jesus
takes to himself. The august functions of the Judge of
all the earth are among the prerogatives of Jesus. He
pictures the solemn scenes of final judgment, and
paints himself the central figure. Before his throne are
gathered all nations; in his hands is lodged the destiny
of every man; and from his presence march the long
files of the generations of men to their everlasting
abodes.

Observe how the acts of Jesus illustrate and lend force
to his words. The winds and the waves are untamed
by man, and are the very symbols of immeasurable
power. See Jesus amid the storm. He rises in the
little ship tossing on the billows, rebukes the wind and it
hushes to silence; says to the waves, "Peace, be still,"

and there is a great calm. "What manner of man is this, that even the wind and the sea obey him?"

Death is the last and mightiest enemy of man. In his fear man pictures death with crown and sceptre. See Jesus confronting those whose lips are now sealed and whose beating hearts are stilled. "Little girl, I say unto thee, arise." "Lazarus, come forth." The dead hear this voice of authority and power. Jesus smites the sceptre from death and flings his crown into the dust.

See Jesus face to face with the alien powers of hell which have invaded the inner life of man. He meets a man whose home was the tombs, whom no man could bind, no, not with chains; who was possessed of a legion of demons. At his word the demons tremble and flee; peace falls on the troubled spirit of the fierce demoniac, and he sits at the feet of Jesus, clothed, and in his right mind. The regnant spirit of Jesus betrays itself in his whole tone and attitude. It compasses him as an atmosphere. Compare him with the religious teachers of his time. They were men of learning and of prestige among the people. Venerable precedent and hoary tradition were the sanction of their teachings. The method of Jesus was altogether different. He uttered himself; he was a voice and not an echo. People were quick to detect the contrast, and to catch the tone of this new teacher. "The multitudes were astonished at his teaching: for he taught them as one having authority, and not as the scribes." This accent of authority is felt in passing from the prophets to Jesus. "Thus saith the Lord," is the formula of the prophet: "Verily, verily, I say unto you," is the formula of Jesus. Prophecy itself confesses his superiority. In John the Baptist Old Testament prophecy comes to its flower and consummation, and in him does homage to Jesus and veils its face before his brighter glory.

The bearing and tone of Jesus unite with his words and deeds to impress on us the authority, altogether singular and supreme, to which he lays claim. We no longer wonder that Jesus fails to rebuke Nathaniel, who calls him the Son of God; commends Peter, who confesses him to be the Christ, the Son of the living God; and shrinks not from the worship of Thomas, who hails him, my Lord and my God! "Ye call me Master and Lord; and ye say well; for so I am."

Authority may be absolute in nature, yet may be limited in range. Has Jesus traced limits within which he is to be supreme, and beyond which he is to be as other men? We discover none. His authority is coëxtensive with the faculties and acts and relations of man. The Lord Jesus is not a sovereign who commands obedience in certain spheres only; he is supreme over the whole man. He is the Lord of the reason. He comes within the realm of the intelligence, and requires subjection to himself. He is to be "the master-light of all our seeing." The truths he utters are fixed points from which thought is to travel, and to which it is to return. The findings of the reason are to be construed in relation to his teachings, and corrected by them. He does not argue, he declares. "Verily, verily, I say unto you," is reason enough for our reason.

Jesus is Lord of the affections. Our love we regard as peculiarly our own, and a stranger may not intermeddle with our affections; we will give or withhold, as we may choose. But Jesus prefers the highest claim upon our love. Even as his brothers' sheaves bowed before the sheaf of Joseph, so the affections that we cherish for father, mother, wife, children, must yield to the affection we give to him. The very centre is to be shifted, and the movement of life must revolve about him.

Jesus is the Lord of the conscience. It is a commonplace of our thinking that freedom of conscience is the inalienable right and the proper heritage of man; yet with a great sum of tears and blood have we obtained it. This holy of holies of man's nature, within which king nor priest may come, Jesus claims the right to enter. The voice of conscience is to be the echo of his voice, its decisions to be guided by his judgments, and to be registered for final appeal at his bar.

Jesus is Lord of the will. Through this executive power man translates thought and motive and purpose into action, and expresses himself. Here, too, Jesus asserts supremacy. This mysterious and masterful faculty of man must guide its movement by Christ's will.

> "Strong Son of God, immortal Love,
>   Our wills are ours, we know not how,
> Our wills are ours, to make them thine."

With claims so lofty, and covering the amplitude of man's nature, the marvel is that Jesus is not pelted from the world. We remember that for his pretensions the Jews more than once took up stones to stone him. A Socrates, or a Confucius, or a Paul, who would arrogate to himself claims like these, would be despised for his folly. There is something in man that restrains him from hastily resenting the claims of Jesus—an instinctive recognition, it may be, of the right of Jesus to be Master and Lord.

Not that the authority of Jesus passes without challenge. In unfolding the nature and extent of the claims Jesus makes upon the allegiance of men, I have had in mind some contrary teachings of our time. This comes not only from the avowed opponents of Christ. Some of those who count themselves his loyal disciples deny him knowledge, and, therefore, authority, in some regions where modern scholarship is most busy. It is said, for instance, that in regard to the history of Israel and the origin of Israel's sacred books Jesus had no knowledge, or, at any rate, delivered no authoritative teaching. Expressions of his which seem to indicate definite opinions and instruction must be interpreted by the doctrine of his self-emptying, or by the principle of accommodation to the beliefs or the modes of expression common to his day. Great caution must be observed in ascertaining what Jesus believed and taught, but he is on perilous ground who adjourns his faith in any teaching of Jesus, however incidental, to the results of even the highest scholarship. The disciples of Pythagoras confided in him so implicitly that to quote a saying of his was to them an end of all controversy. "*Ipse dixit*—he says it," was their very badge of discipleship. "Verily, I say unto you," falling from the lips of Jesus, should be to the Christian a bar to all further discussion.

Whatever posture Jesus assumed towards the Holy Scriptures, loyalty to him requires should be ours. Whatever he believed and taught regarding the providential movement of the history of Israel, and the origin and character and veracity and inspiration of the then sacred books, this we should not hesitate to accept, though all the critics and scholars of the world should be arrayed against us. *Ipse dixit*—he said it.

We do well to read again words long ago written of Jesus:

"Why do the heathen rage,
And the people imagine a vain thing?
The kings of the earth set themselves,
And the rulers take counsel together,
Against the Lord, and against his Anointed, saying,

> Let us break their bands asunder,
> And cast away their cords from us.
> He that sitteth in the heavens shall laugh.
> Yet have I set my King
> Upon my holy hill of Zion.''

Let me hasten to add, that subjection to Jesus is the truest freedom. Some may be tempted to think, ''Well, this must be a hard Master, the claims he makes are so strenuous and extravagant; it must be a bitter experience to be in his service.'' Far from it. His yoke is easy and his burden is light; and the liberty wherewith Christ makes free is the broadest and happiest. See what subjection to him does for men. He takes a few fishermen and publicans, slaves to ignorance and prejudice, and by their obedience to him he lifts them to a place among the leaders of human thought for all ages, and sets them as shining examples for all time. Saul, the narrow-minded and bigoted Pharisee, becomes the ''bond-servant of Jesus Christ,'' and is thereby transformed into the most illustrious exponent and champion of freedom of thought the world has seen. His unfettered intellect expands under the great ideas of Jesus, and his mind gives birth to ''thoughts sublime that pierce the night like stars.'' It is the thought of Paul that has brought freedom to the world. He is the universal thinker; for depth and reach and influence on men and institutions no philosopher or statesman compares with him.

But what is the effect upon character? Is not submission to the will of another deadly to aspiration and growth and true virtue? To be subject to the Lord Jesus is to win the beauty of holiness. Fishermen and publicans, under this influence, become the saintliest spirits of mankind. A Saul becomes a Paul. It was Paul's delight to think the thoughts of Jesus Christ after him; to guide his conscience by the judgments of Jesus; to pour upon him his great heart's wealth of affection; and to bow his imperial will to the will of the Lord Jesus. The traces of suffering upon his body he counted as brands by which Jesus Christ had marked him as his own. Yet where shall we look upon a character so splendid? Under the benign influence of the lordship of Christ every Christian grace ripened to a surpassing beauty. For perfection of character, only one name do we write above the name of Paul—the name that is above every name.

Loyalty to Jesus Christ is the need of the hour. For intellectual rest, for peace of heart, for guidance in duty, for enrichment of character, for motive and inspiration in the service of man, for bringing in the kingdom of God, the Christian must, with emphasis and deep devotion, salute Jesus as his Master and Lord.

Before the toiling, sinning, suffering men of our day stands Jesus, as of old, and in the tenderness of love he invites them to the rest and peace of bearing his yoke.

> "Oh! may our willing hearts confess
>   Thy sweet, thy gentle sway;
>   Glad captives of thy matchless grace,
>   Thy righteous rule obey!"

Trust in the Lord.

BY REV. JOSEPH R. WILSON, D. D.

"It is better to trust in the Lord than to put confidence in man. It is better to trust in the Lord than to put confidence in princes."
—Psalm cxviii. 8, 9.

IT is not meant that no man at all is to be at all trusted, that everybody is unworthy of confidence on the part of anybody, for such is not the truth. Men do, and ought to, have confidence in one another, not only, but *must* have, or society itself would fall to pieces, and each person (if he could think life to be worth having on such terms) would be compelled to live fenced around by walls of gloom resembling those of a grave. This earth would be an absolutely intolerable abode were there no play of mutual confidence. No doubt there are persons here and there who know little or nothing of the experience of a confiding disposition—who go through their ice-clad lives, from one frozen day to another, without finding, or caring to find, a single human being on whom to lean, self-poised and self-sufficing, who long for no friendship and yearn for no love. Why, even the wild animals must have their co-helpers and their alliances of mutual trust. The lion seldom hunts alone; the tiger is most defiant of danger when he has a companion near. It would seem that where there is intelligence, to *any* degree, whether in man or beast, there also is a feeling of dependence, and in this feeling is imbedded the principle of confidence. It is only the *insane* who wish to be always by themselves.

Far from God, therefore, we must conclude, is the purpose to forbid the trust which one person places in another, and which he cannot but place so long as he retains his sanity, or so long as he remains true to the very make-up of his being. This natural interchanging of trust is in obedience to one of his own laws, a law impressed as deeply upon our individual and social manhood as is the law of gravitation upon the material universe. The great Lord simply tells us that it is "*better*" to trust in him than in men, or in the princes of men; not that it is a bad and a wrong thing—our mutual confidence—no, it is a good and a right thing; but there is that which, in the comparison, is "*better*." He would not have us to cease trusting whatsoever creature *deserves* to be trusted, but would have us not to stop in this, as if thus we had reached the highest point to which we are capable of climbing in the same direction, and which we all are bound to reach if we would trust in a manner worthy of the nature God has given us, and unto the finest and noblest results.

The truth is, that, in yielding to the promptings of our implanted principle of trust, we are apt to go *too far*. We are apt to trust each other, not too little, but too much; *i. e.*, we are prone to expect *too great a benefit* from the trust that terminates upon the mere creature. That benefit is, indeed, considerable—often a very large source out of which a heartfelt gratitude should songfully spring; it may, however, be easily overestimated; for, always—yes, *always*—there is an element of disappointment in the most rewardful confidence that one human being ever placed in another—something being still lacking to render the satisfaction complete. In other words, no person can ever do for another person *all* that is wanted. Take even that instance of trust which is, perhaps, the purest, and the fullest of heart-ease, the instinctive trust of a little child in its mother. However trustful the trusting child, and however deserving of it the trusted parent, there is many an ache of this child's affections which lies beyond the most soothing touch of the most sympathizing mother; achings which it is compelled to sob out upon its lonely pillow in tears which can give no account of themselves to the very fondest of maternal coaxing—tears which thereby declare their need of a hand to dry them up which the whole world does not extend any one, the hand that tells of his presence whose love is beyond a mother's, and "*better*" than hers.

And it is just the same around the entire circle of human trust where it touches alone upon a human object. It is a trust that is always a more or less *defeated* trust; is thrown back upon itself, having, at this point or at that, missed its mark.

There are, indeed, many matters in which men do not vainly trust each other, the trusters getting all they expected from the trusted. You may trust a neighbor with portions of your property and find him true to your confidence. You may safely trust him not to lie when you are in want of his testimony. In a hundred supposable cases you can securely trust; can even sometimes go so far as to trust another to play with your very heart-strings, as is done every day where love exchanges itself for corresponding love, or for the promise of it; and yet you may, in all this, not have to regret what you have done. But your trust will be disappointed if you expect to get from man—be he ever so faithful, be he ever so honorable, be he ever so eminent for trustworthiness, be he ever so large in resources—*all* that your soul desires. You, perhaps, get the whole which that man is able to give; but there are some things which he cannot give, however loudly, however honestly even, he may promise them. He is not competent, for example, to give you happiness—not even that amount of happiness you have thought that he was in a condition to bestow, and which he himself believed that he was. Wives and husbands, to take an extreme instance, trust each other for happiness, as they ought to do, thinking that they have only to draw upon the rich treasures of their mutual affection for as much as they can want. Well, do they always get it? Is there not a drawback, sometimes nameless, yet real and felt? Is there not often an ache like that of the child, which no quantity or quality of human love, even the most assiduous and most self-sacrificing, can soothe—an ache which belongs to the soul's own independent and unapproachable individuality, and which, accordingly, it must just learn to endure, unless, indeed, it is at liberty to resort to a far higher and far choicer fountain of good than any that is filled from an earthly source?

Or take the instance of one who trusts another in a partnership whose object is to acquire wealth, and at the same time cement a friendship which has already stood the test of years. This chosen partner is all right; he discharges his whole duty; his undivided talent is devoted to the business; there is nothing about him which is not completely satisfying. The result is, ever-increasing riches. And yet, somehow, you are now and again forced to feel that he has not done all that you had expected of him. You have his utmost help, and still his help has not conferred happiness, even though it has brought wealth. You do not blame him; you are even sure that he is not at fault; nay, you are certain that the greater share of your success is what he has achieved. *So far* you have not trusted in vain; but, then, you trusted him for something *more*, which it was not in his power to bestow with all his other bestowments; you trusted that in his many helpings towards accumulations of property he would also add to it more and more peace of mind, or that both of you together would do this, for in this respect you trusted not only his capability, but also your own; and he has not disappointed you any more than you have disappointed yourself or disappointed him. The gold is there, but not the good you had thought was in it. There is still a void unfilled. The partnership has proved a failure on the highest ground of all—the ground where contentment ought to be awaiting your summons. No neighbor is richer than you in merchandise and money, but many a neighbor may not be so poor in the matter of that true treasure, heart-sunshine, the one only thing that was worth your partner's trouble and your own to gain and to lay up.

So the ambitious man trusts to the people to lift him into eminence of position. They raise him as high as he wished, higher even than once he had dreamed. They lavish upon him their honors and their stations. They place him at the very top. He is grateful; but, as he quaffs the bowl of their laudations, he by-and-by becomes conscious of a want that he had fondly hoped would also be met in the wine-taste of his gratified desires. Elevation has not made him happy; it has only made him cold and lonely, and envied—maybe hated—by some. The people had not that to give which comes exclusively from a satisfied mind, a mind restful, as on a rock of security; and, this being absent, all the rest resembles ashes. He evidently needs to go to a source of power higher still. People and princes can confer many favors upon those whom they greatly regard, and who know how to trust or to court them; but they cannot confer that smile which lights up the living-room of the soul, where the man is at home with his own thoughts, and where he holds converse with his immortality; and if that room remains dark, no lamps burning in any or in all of the other rooms can suffice to illumine the great house.

In what has thus been suggested, I have referred you alone to the fact that, for many of the things which are considered desirable, you have good reason to trust your fellow-man. Shall I now, however, turn the picture, and refer you to another and quite opposite fact, the fact that your fellow-man often deceives you, even when you trust him for such common assistances and even for such mere courtesies as every one needs from those with whom he mingles? In how many of your acquaintances, in how many of your so called friends, may you confidently trust when you are in actual want either of their sympathy or of their helping hand? How long would it take you to count the number of such as *seem* trustworthy when all is prospering with you, but the shallowness of whose assurances of good-will is discovered when a "friend in need would be a friend indeed"? Let the broken and scattered hopes of a too-confiding inexperience, the world over, answer the mournful question. I am not disposed to view with a gloomy eye the world about me, nor should any of you be so disposed. It becomes us all, on the contrary, to look with as cheerful an aspect as possible upon the characters and conduct of the members of the common family to which we all belong, to the very meanest member of which we are all related by a blood which is as old as the creation, and multitudes of whom are far better than ourselves. But, it cannot be denied, even by one who gives the utmost possible credit to the fair intentions and the fine words of his brother-sinners, that their promises are often larger than their

24

performances, and that the man who acts upon a contrary belief must at some critical hours of his life pay the penalty of his faith in not a few grievous disappointments. In truth, is not the whole earth a scene, throughout, of the war which men are waging with men because of the ill-starred trusts they mistakenly place in each other? How largely, how variously, how distressfully could this be illustrated, were the unpleasant task a necessary one! Your courts of justice are full of the evidences of the fact. Every person knows it in many a bitter experience, or may too easily learn the sad lesson from what others are able to tell him of their experience. On every account, therefore, is it not "better" to trust in the Lord than to trust in any man? and for the reasons I have given: no such earthly trust brings a steadfast happiness, and such happiness is what we all are pursuing—rightly pursuing, too. Only, let us learn what true happiness is, in what it consists, and we are at full liberty to secure it if we can, God himself being the approving witness of our efforts. But now the question arises, even on the part of those who think they *do* know what happiness is, does *God* make happy those who trust in him? I confess that it does not always *look* as if he did. It must be acknowledged that he leaves many of his trusters poor and forlorn, tossed and torn ; and that there is not one of them, however favored in a worldly point of view, who does not have reason, daily, to shed tears of more or less racking grief, or utter groans of more or less remorseful sorrow. You cannot listen to their public prayers or their private petitionings without feeling convinced that they have that to cause them unhappiness of which even the trusters in man know nothing, and at which they sometimes are constrained to wonder. How, then, can it be said that it is "better" to trust in the Lord? Well, were there no other answer to such a question, might we not wisely rest the whole matter on this: *He has said so*, and does he not *know?* Is not the entire history of our race open to his view as it cannot be to our own? and has he not seen the long result of such trusting as man places in his fellow-man when there was also no higher person in which he confided? Does God need to be told of that weakness in man which causes him, even in his best estate, to be as a broken reed to whomsoever, with his whole weight, leans upon him; does he need to be told of one man's treachery to another, of the selfishness which everywhere reveals itself in the intercourse of life, of the meanness which gets all it can whilst giving only as little as it may, of the inhumanity, even, which pushes dependence to the wall when it would trust to the stronger but dare not? And is not God so far acquainted with what he himself is as to know that he at least is a fit object of man's trust, being so full of mercy, so full of might, so full of truth, so full of wisdom, so full of tenderness? We may well, therefore, take his word for it that we had better repose our trust in him than even in the princes of men, who, to say the most, are as frail as others, and who, to say the least, are as false.

But, then, where is the *happiness* of trusting in him? is a question still to be asked. Why, it is found in the very act of our trust itself. For what *is* happiness? It is not a thing which you can see, or handle, or get into your embrace. It is not what you may *have*, it is what you ARE. You do not need to go one step out of yourself for it. Gold does not contain it. Pleasures do not conduct to it. Fortune-building does not construct it. Industry does not collect it. It is a possession of the soul, or, rather, is the soul possessing itself. It is a principle

and a power *within*, where no outward circumstances
can intrude to place a destructive hand upon it; a lighted
candle at the centre of us, which no wind can blow out.
It is *being what we ought to be*, right with ourselves and
right with our God; a rightness that shall last, therefore,
so long as the soul shall last, that is, so long as God
shall last. Out of such rightness, planted as it is in our
very immortality, springs happiness, in the just sense of
that much-used and much-abused word. And it is to
bring about this supreme rightness that we are exhorted
to put our trust in the Lord, which is altogether the
same as exhorting us to love him; for, otherwise, to trust
him were impossible, love being, indeed, only another
word for confidence. It may, then, be said, with an assurance which nothing can gainsay, that they who thus
love God are they who are right, in the very deepest
meaning of the term; right at the core of their being;
right as the saints and as the angels are. But, whilst
this is true, it is also true that his children's trustful
love is not yet complete; and it is because of their strug-
gles and of their Father's discipline to make it complete
that they experience most of the sorrows to which I have
referred; sorrows which are themselves more to be desired than the raptures of the world. They trust, but do
not trust perfectly, and will not until they see him as he
is, in the home towards which they climb. In thus climbing, however, they needs must suffer, for the hill is high,
and it is both steep and rugged, where progress is assured only at the expense of toil and trouble. Nevertheless, with all that it costs, it is "better to trust in the
Lord than to put confidence in man"; for so great a
trust must have a correspondingly great issue; so supreme a trust must have a correspondingly supreme reward. It is trusting in a *word* that never was broken,

and which nothing can ever break; in a *wisdom* that never was baffled, and which nothing can ever baffle; in a *watchfulness* that never has been thrown off its guard, and which nothing can ever throw off its guard; in a *will* whose decrees of good have ever been, and must always be, sovereign; and in a *welfare* that is as certain as eternity.   It is trusting in him who has proved himself the one Friend of the friendless, the one Father of the fatherless, the one who is faithful when all others are faithless. It is trusting the only Being who can destroy for us our sins, and dry up for us our sorrows, and bestow upon us a salvation compared with which the utmost blessedness of earth is as a dying lamp to the living sun.   It is trusting for peace of heart whilst living, for strength of heart when expiring, and for wealth of heart when the treasures of heaven burst upon the view.   It is trusting unto *holiness*, the fountain of *happiness*.   It is trusting GOD, as God is in CHRIST, which says all in one exhaustless word.

NOT ONE FORGOTTEN.

BY REV. T. D. WITHERSPOON, D. D.,
Professor of Homiletics and Pastoral Theology, Louisville Theological Seminary.

"Are not five sparrows sold for two farthings, and not one of them is forgotten before God?"—LUKE xii. 6.

THE thought of a particular providence, minute as to its details and special as to its ends, embracing all the creatures of God, however lowly, and all their actions, however insignificant, linking all in a single chain of divine prevision and control, is one of which men have never been able altogether to divest themselves, but to which they have been strangely reluctant to give full and hearty assent.

Of the causes that have operated to produce a latent and lingering skepticism in reference to a doctrine so consonant to reason and so comforting to the servant of God, there seem to be two particularly deserving of attention.

The first is the apparent insignificance of this world of ours when considered as a part of the measureless universe of God, and the consequent improbability that, amidst these vast myriads of worlds with their teeming millions of inhabitants, the Almighty Ruler should condescend to busy himself with the minute relations and infinitesimal concerns of all the creatures upon the earth.

The second is the apparent irregularity in the operation and enforcement of the moral law in the economy of nature, as contrasted with the invariable sequence of those laws that are purely mechanical and physical; a state of things which we would by no means expect if the hand of the great moral Ruler is in all the events of time.

These two causes have operated in all ages to produce skepticism in reference to the overruling providence of God. Thus it was in the days of the patriarch Job. "Behold," says Eliphaz the Temanite (Job xxii. 12), "is not God in the height of heaven? and behold the height of the stars, how high they are! And thou sayest, How doth God know? Can he judge through the dark cloud? Thick clouds are a covering to him, that he seeth not; and he walketh in the circuit of heaven." And so, as to the second cause, Job says (chapter xxi. 7, etc.), "Wherefore do the wicked live, become old, yea, are mighty in power? Their seed is established in their sight with them, and their offspring before their eyes. Their houses are safe from fear, neither is the rod of God upon them. . . . . One dieth in his full strength, being wholly at ease and quiet. . . . And another dieth in the bitterness of his soul, and never eateth with pleasure. They shall lie down alike in the dust, and the worms shall cover them."

And so, to make one further quotation, we have the same protest in the days of Solomon against the doctrine of a particular providence, the ground of protest being the chequered nature of human life, and the apparent inequality in the distribution of punishments and rewards. "All things" (Eccl. ix. 2) "come alike to all: there is one event to the righteous and to the wicked; to the good and to the clean and to the unclean; to him that sacrificeth and to him that sacrificeth not; as is the good, so is the sinner; and he that sweareth as he that feareth an oath."

Nor have these difficulties in the way of a firm faith in God's overruling providence at all diminished since the days of Job and of Solomon. On the contrary, as science has pressed her investigations and has extended her domain, we have gained conceptions of the magnitude of the universe and the comparative insignificance of our globe to which the men of Solomon's time were utter strangers. So, too, as the ages have advanced, the evil principles of the world have more and more developed in antagonism to the good. They have aggregated to themselves more and more power. Their votaries have become more and more skillful in the oppression of the right. In this day of vast moneyed corporations and consolidations of capital and labor, it is even more true than in former times, that "these are the ungodly that prosper in the world," and that "no man knoweth either love or hatred by all that is before him."

But, amidst all the confusion and disorder incident to a state of things like this, it is the great joy of the Christian heart to rest in the doctrine of the overruling providence of God, which is so clearly taught in his holy word; to think of the little sparrows, five of which brought less than a cent in the markets of the world in our Lord's day, and to remember that "not one of them is forgotten before God."

Let us, then, as we look out upon the unknown future—many of us with thoughtful solicitude; some of us, it may be, with anxious forebodings—bathe our spirits for a little while in the sweet thought of the text, "not one of them is forgotten before God."

I. And first let me say that this is the view of the providence of God presented all through the Scriptures; not simply that of a general superintendence under vague and indefinite laws of nature, but a minute and detailed personal supervision, a particular and definite personal control, extending to the least as well as to the greatest works of his hand. Many persons are willing to admit that the hand of God is in the great events of nature and of human history. When the pestilence is on the air and thousands are falling victims, when some great earthquake has engulphed cities, or some furious tempest at sea has carried down strong ships with their hardy seamen and their terror-stricken passengers, there are few who believe in a God at all who do not recognize his hand, and say, ''Surely God is here.'' But that the God who kindled the blaze of the sun supplies also the glow-worm's lamp; that he who ''rides upon the stormy wind'' fans also the cheek of the invalid with the gentle zephyr's breath; that he who upholds the stars in their courses guides also the sparrow in its flight; these are the things reckoned incapable of belief. And yet the Scriptures do not more clearly teach the one than the other. Its language on this point cannot be mistaken. Turn to whatever part you will, and you will find this truth everywhere expressed, believed, acted upon, that the hand of God is as truly in the least as in the greatest; nothing so obscure as to escape his notice, nothing so trivial as to lie outside the schemes of his providence, and the purposes of his will.

Let us hear the testimony of Elihu (Job xxxvi. 27, etc.): ''He maketh small the drops of water: which the clouds do drop upon man abundantly.'' ''With clouds he covereth the light; and commandeth it not to shine.'' ''God thundereth marvelously with his voice.'' ''He saith to the snow, Be thou on the earth; likewise to the small rain, and to the great rain of his strength.'' ''By the breath of God frost is given; and the breadth of the waters is straitened.'' ''He scattereth his bright cloud, and it is turned round about by his counsels, that they may do whatsoever he commandeth.'' He causeth ''it to rain on the earth where no man is, to satisfy the desolate and waste ground; and to cause the bud of the tender herb to spring forth.'' He '' sendeth lightnings, that they may go and say unto him, Here we are.'' He ''stayeth the bottles of the heaven when the dust groweth into hardness and the clods cleave fast together.'' He ''hunteth the prey for the lion, and provideth for the raven his food.''

Let us hear what the Psalmist says (Psalm lxv. 9, etc.): ''Thou visitest the earth, and waterest it: thou greatly enrichest it,'' etc. Psalm civ. 14, etc.: ''He causeth the grass to grow for the cattle, and herb for the service of man.'' ''Thou makest darkness, and it is night: wherein all the beasts of the forest do creep forth. The young lions roar after their prey, and seek their meat from God.'' ''These wait all upon thee.'' ''That thou givest them they gather: thou openest thine hand, they are filled with good.'' But why multiply passages. The Old Testament is filled with these statements of the universality and the minuteness of the providence of God.

Let us turn for a moment to the declarations of our Lord: ''Behold'' (Matt. vi. 26, etc.) ''the fowls of the air: for they sow not, neither do they reap, nor gather into barns, yet your heavenly Father feedeth them.'' ''Consider the lilies of the field, how they grow; they toil not, neither do they spin: and yet I say unto you, That even Solomon in all his glory was not arrayed like one of these. Wherefore, if God so clothe the grass of the field, which to-day is, and to-morrow is cast into the oven, shall he not much more clothe you, O ye of little faith?'' And so in the passage before us: ''Are not five sparrows sold for two farthings, and not one of them is forgotten before God." Or, as Matthew has it, "One of them shall not fall on the ground without your Father; for even the very hairs of your head are all numbered."

It is evident, then, that if the plain meaning of these passages be taken, we must believe that the providence of God is in the little things as well as in the great. And when we consider how precious and comforting such a doctrine is, does it not seem strange that men should endeavor to persuade themselves to believe that when our Saviour says, " not one of them is forgotten before God," he really does not mean it? and that when he says, "the hairs of your head are all numbered," he is speaking in hyperbole?

II. But this skepticism in reference to the minuteness of God's providence rests upon two assumptions, each of which is altogether untenable. The first is, that objects and events sustain to each other in the mind of God the same relative dignity and importance that they do in ours; so that what are great and important in our eyes are so in his, and what are puny and insignificant in our view are so in the view of God. We are prone to forget that nothing finite can in itself appear great or important in the sight of God. There is such an infinite disproportion in the scale on which his being is projected and that which appertains to all created things, that the distinctions of great and small do not apply. As one who climbs some lofty mountain and looks down on the plain beneath sees not the inequalities of the surface, but looks upon it as upon a map with even face lying before him, so from the height of God's infinite perfection he looks down and there is nothing in itself great in his sight. All things take their relative magnitude and importance from their relations to him, to the fulfilment of his purposes, and the manifestation of his glory. The things, therefore, which seem least to us may seem greatest to him. There is an element of power that enters into our conception of the sublime, so that things are grand and impressive in our view as they reveal a power that overawes us by its superiority to our own. The roar of Niagara, the thunder of the ocean in a storm, the wild sweep of the tornado, and the sullen moan of the earthquake, seem great to us by comparison with our own impotency, but they are not so to God. The overthrow of a kingdom, the crumbling of a throne, the conflagration of a world, are, in his view and in comparison with his power, but as the falling of a leaf or the withering of the grass under the summer's sun.

The second false assumption is, that there may be such dissociation of the great things and the small things that the former may be directed and controlled without attention to the latter. No great event has ever yet occurred to which a number of minute and apparently insignificant events have not stood in such relation of cause and condition that the great event could only be brought about by close attention to these apparently trivial ones. The little things are the pivots upon which the great ones turn. As the whole machinery of a watch will come to a standstill if one of the almost-invisible jewels be dislodged, or if a grain of dust adhere to one of the thousand tiny cogs in its various attachments, so, if one of these minute events should go awry, the whole order and course of providence would be arrested or disturbed. I stood, not a great while ago, looking at a splendid locomotive about to be put upon its trial-trip. The engineer, proud of his beautiful engine, at a signal from the conductor, placed his hand upon the lever and applied the steam. But, though there was a quiver, as if every nerve of the iron horse were strung to its utmost tension, there was no motion of the great wheels. A second time the lever was applied, but with the same result. Then the quick eye of the engineer detected the cause. A single thumb-screw had been insufficiently turned. There was but the light touch of the fingers upon it, and again the steam was applied, and the train moved gracefully away. These little things which men think beneath our heavenly Father's notice, what are they but the valve-screws of the great engine? What but the cogs and jewels of that secret mechanism which causes the hands of all human destiny to move upon the dial-plate of time?

But it is time to assume that of which I am happily persuaded, namely, that whatever others may think of the doctrine of a particular providence, you, to whom I am now speaking, find delight in its belief, and will not have it wrested from you by all the specious arguments and haughty cavils which its enemies may employ. Let me, then, as we look forward to-day to the life that lies before us, as we seek to gird ourselves for its duties and responsibilities, as we take each his staff in his hand and go forth to its unknown vicissitudes and trials, draw for you some practical lessons of instruction and comfort from the words of the text, "not one of them is forgotten before God."

And, *first*, let me remind you what a sanctity it gives to the little things of life that God's eye is upon them, and that we can have fellowship with him in them. So much of our life is taken up with little things—things that do not seem to tell upon the great issues and interests of Christ's kingdom in the world—that we are likely to feel as if the time spent in them is lost from the service of God. The mother with her little brood about her, the housewife with her busy cares, the merchant with all the inventory of his active brain, the teacher with the tedious routine of the class-room—one and all with the daily throng of little duties, little vexations, little cares— let us remember that not one of all these is forgotten before God. There is a sanctity and a blessedness given to life when we can see God's hand in everything—in leaf and flower, in pebble and stone—and the dull monotony of the most humdrum life may be relieved by this thought of the ever-presence and sympathy of our heavenly Father.

Again, let me remind you that if not one of the least of these dumb creatures is forgotten before God, they should not fail of all due consideration and kindness from us. How much wanton cruelty, how much thoughtless neglect would be avoided, did we always keep before us the consideration that "not one of them is forgotten before God." How this thought of our heavenly Father's watchful oversight and tender care binds us, as with a band of gold, not only to the humblest and poorest of our kind, but to all that vaster family whom his loving arms enfold, and who rest upon the bosom of his care.

Thirdly, and lastly, while we know not what the changes or trials of coming life may be, there is one thing we do know, and that is, that not one of us in any of them shall be forgotten. However dark the pathway, God's eye will be upon us as we walk it; his infinite arm will be about us to protect us; his wing of love will overshadow us, and he will make good to us his precious promise, that "as our days so shall our strength be." And if at this hour there be in the sanctuary some child of adversity or bereavement, whose cup seems to be full to overflowing with sorrow, let me say there is comfort for you here. Thou, O child of affliction, art not forgotten. Forgotten before man thou mayest be, forsaken of kindred, deserted of friends, but not forgotten before God. His eye of love is upon thee. His pitying arms enfold thee. He will be with thee in all the way thou goest. "Fear not," is his message, "I will help thee." Say, O timid one, "I will trust and not be afraid"; for "the eternal God is thy refuge, and underneath are the everlasting arms."

THE SABBATH-DAY.*

BY REV. W. F. V. BARTLETT, D. D.,

Pastor of the First Presbyterian Church, Lexington, Ky.

"And it shall come to pass, that from one new moon to another, and from one Sabbath to another, shall all flesh come to worship before me, saith the Lord."—ISAIAH lxvi. 23.

IS the Sabbath a divine institution of permanent and universal obligation? Is it of God, and did God intend it for all mankind? This is the question that lies at the root of the present-day Sabbath controversy. Many are losing a sense of the sacred quality of the day. Many are turning it from a holy day to a holiday. Corporations are turning it from a rest-day to a work-day. Many who teach that it should be set apart for a rest-day and a day for religious purposes affirm this upon grounds of expediency, and not as a matter of divine requirement. In the midst of so much diversity of opinion, the question is a pertinent and an important one, Is the setting apart of one day in seven a divine ordinance, and did God intend it to be permanent and universal? If it be, we should know it, and we should want to know it. If it be, then to speak otherwise of it, as though the Sabbath were a mere human arrangement, which men may treat as they please, is to profane it. It is to dishonor God and to trample his will under our feet. It is a sin. Let us see what Scripture teaches on this subject. Certainly what Scripture requires we are bound to accept,

---

*A sermon delivered before the Synod of Kentucky.

I call your attention to three separate declarations of the word of God, which ought to settle this matter. One is the account given in Genesis of the origin of the Sabbath; the second is the fourth command of the decalogue, and the third is the utterance of our Lord.

These three passages, like a threefold cord that cannot be easily broken, contain the scriptural argument.

In the first place, we may argue for the permanent and universal obligation of the Sabbath from the nature and date of its origin.

In the second chapter of Genesis the first three verses read as follows: "Thus the heavens and the earth were finished, and all the host of them; and on the seventh day God ended his work which he had made; . . . and God blessed the seventh day, and sanctified it, because that in it he had rested from all his work which God created and made."

These words follow upon the description given in the first chapter of the six days of creation. They tell us that God's six days' work was followed by God's resting on the seventh day; and, therefore, he appointed the seventh day, or, what is the same thing, one day in seven, as a day for rest and a sanctified day.

It seems to me that our whole contention is contained in that declaration. How any one who accepts the Bible as the inspired and infallible word of God can escape it, I do not see. What does it teach? Certainly that the Sabbath is a divine ordinance; that it is not a human invention. It is God's arrangement; that is clear. God, says the record, blessed the seventh day and sanctified it. This setting apart, then, of one day in seven, was ordained by God. You must bear that in mind. You must remember that in dealing with the Sabbath you are not dealing with a mere human device. It is

25

not like a tariff bill or a lodge bill that men may quarrel over. It is not an enactment of the state. It is God's institution; the creation of God's will and armed with God's sanction. As, then, God made it, no man has a right to unmake it. Only God can do that. But has God done that? Can you point to a single passage in his word where he has done it? In this passage God distinctly says that one day in seven shall be set apart as a blessed and a sanctified day. Where, in all the pages of inspiration, from Genesis to Revelation, will you find any utterance of God to the contrary—that one day in seven shall not thus be set apart?

But this passage not only teaches that the Sabbath is an ordinance of God; it just as plainly teaches that God intended it to be permanent. That appears in the reason assigned. When a law has a temporary ground or reason for its enactment, its obligation will be temporary. The obligation to observe it will cease with the reason for enacting it. But where the reason of the law is permanent, the law itself will be permanent, too. Is not that sound logic? Apply it here. What was the divine reason assigned for instituting the Sabbath? Because God rested after his six days' work. Is not that reason as good to-day as it was then? Will it not be as valid in the last generation of mankind as it was in the first? Because God, having worked six days, rested the seventh. Can time change the force of that consideration? Who shall dare to say, until God bid him to, that that reason is not as good now as it ever was?

And then, too, not only the permanency, but also the universality, of the Sabbath obligation appears in these words. Of what time do these words in Genesis speak? Is it not the time immediately following upon the creation? Hear them again: "Thus the heavens and the

earth were finished, and all the host of them; and on
the seventh day God ended his work which he had
made; . . . and God blessed the seventh day and
sanctified it, because that in it he had rested from all his
work which God created and made." Is it not plain
that the time referred to here is the time that followed
directly upon completing the heavens and the earth, and
all the host of them? Is not that the natural sense?
Anti-Sabbatarians try to get away from that sense, but
is not that the plain meaning? After the heavens and
the earth, and all the host of them were finished, then it
was that God rested on the seventh day and blessed and
sanctified it. If that be so, the Sabbath is coeval with
the creation. It was instituted at the beginning. It did
not first appear in later ages. God established it at the
outset. It was, therefore, given to all mankind; intended for the whole human family. If the Sabbath had
first appeared among the Hebrews, in God's legislation
for them, it might have been supposed to be intended
only for the Jews. But here we see that it appears at
the beginning of human history, with the very commencement of mankind; therefore it must have been intended for mankind. Even Dr. Paley admits that. He
says that if the divine command was actually delivered
at the creation, it was addressed, no doubt, to the whole
human species alike, and continues, unless repealed by
some subsequent revelation, binding upon all who come
to the knowledge of it. That is exactly the fact, and
yet that admission comes from one of the strongest of
the anti-Sabbatarians. It is an admission that contains
the whole argument.

The fact is that, as I read these words in Genesis, I
cannot but feel that in them God intends to tell us that
the principle of the Sabbath, viz., that of one day in

seven for cessation from labor and for rest, is wrought into our nature and implanted in the constitution and laws of the universe. Men are so made, and animals too, that they need to have that interval to recuperate their wasted energies. So physiologists tell us. So experience demonstrates. The daily nocturnal rest is not sufficient. The human system is like a seven-day clock. That is the law of our being. That is the way our nature has been created and things around us have been fixed. That being the case, I take these words in Genesis as God's announcement of that fact. They may be paraphrased after some such fashion as this. It is as if God had said to mankind, just as they were starting out on their world-wide career: "I have just got through the work of creation; you are now about to commence your course. There are some things you must at once understand. One is, that in creating your nature and things around you, I have fixed it that one day in seven must be set apart as a rest day. I have also constituted it to be a blessed day and a sanctified day. It is so woven into the constitution of your being. It is the law of your nature. Be sure to keep it in mind and observe it. For if you do not, the economy of your well-being will be disturbed. Your body will suffer; your mind, your heart, every part of your nature, will suffer. It is absolutely necessary, if you want to rise to your best and noblest development." That is the way I would read these words in Genesis. When read that way, it is apparent that the Sabbath was intended to be permanent and universal; for if it be a law implanted in our nature, then that law can never be abrogated until our nature has been re-created.

These statements may be confirmed and illustrated by the case of marriage. In the same chapter of Genesis we read: ''God said, It is not good that the man should be alone. I will make him a help meet for him. . . . . And they shall be one flesh.'' That is the law of marriage, one man and one woman, man's helpmeet, and both together a unity. That law is woven into our nature. It is not an arbitrary enactment in such a sense that any other arrangement would answer just as well. We are made and constituted that way. When, then, God said, It is not good for man to be alone, he needs a woman for helpmeet, and the two shall be one flesh, he was not enacting a law, he was simply enunciating the law of our nature, telling us how we were made, what must be the order of our life in the sexual relation for our best development. Exactly the same is true of the Sabbath. The fact is, that marriage and the Sabbath are twin institutions. They are both coeval with creation. They both stand at the commencement of the world's history. They both indicate the order and constitution of our nature. They are not like paper laws, not like the enactments on our statute-books, but they are set in our very being, like as gravitation is set in the orbs of the sky. They are written all over our bodies and our minds. They are the lines in which our nature is appointed to act—just as there are certain lines in which the rose bush matures into the flower, or the fig tree or the orange into the luscious fruit. They are so wrought into our being that marriage lies at the root of our earthly welfare, and the Sabbath at the root of our spiritual and eternal welfare. This is so true, that if marriage, which the enemies of mankind want to destroy, and the Sabbath, which the enemies of God want to destroy, were got rid of, all order would be upset and the world be turned into a pandemonium. So true is this, that always wherever the law of marriage and the law of Sabbath have been most faithfully observed the nations have been most mighty and prosperous. You see, then, that in the nature of the case, the Sabbath was designed to be a permanent and universal institution. If, like marriage, it is fixed in man's nature, and woven into the constitution and order of things, even God himself could not do away with it without making our nature all over again.

Our second argument is based upon the fourth commandment. The presence of this command among those delivered on the top of Sinai, when properly understood, is proof of the universal and permanent obligation of the Sabbath.

What was the first thing God did after the creation was finished, and before the human race had started upon its historical career? It was to announce the law of the Sabbath. What was the first thing God did when he took a people from out the world which had wickedly departed from him, and before he started them on their national career? It was to revive and reinforce the law of the Sabbath. Does that look as if God intended the institution of the Sabbath to pass out of existence?

It is sometimes said that because the fourth commandment was addressed to the Jews, it was designed only for the Jews. But why is not that said of the first, or the second, or the third, or any of the others? Why should that be said only of the fourth? Why fasten objection on that one alone, and not make the same assertion as to the other nine?

There are three things that ought to correct such a notion. One is the word "Remember." "Remember the Sabbath-day to keep it holy." Did it ever occur to you that that is a very remarkable word to put at the beginning of a law? No other law in the decalogue be-

gins with such a word. No other law in the Bible begins with such a word. I do not know that any law on
our statute-books begins with such a word. Why, then,
does the fourth commandment begin with that word?
Because God having established the Sabbath in the beginning, and the world having forgotten it, God is charg-
ing the people whom he had taken out of the world to
be his peculiar people to remember it. His people must
not do with the old Sabbath ordinance, which had come
down from the beginning, what the world had done with
it—forget it; they must remember it. It is as if God
had said: "I am now giving you a code of laws lying at
the foundation of all individual and national prosperity.
They are laws that are set in the nature of things. No
nation can attain to real and lasting greatness without
them. In selecting you to be my peculiar people, I announce them to you. The other nations, who will have
nothing to do with me, I leave to themselves. They
have got to learn, by rough experience, that in departing from my statutes they have deserted the way of happiness and power. The ten commandments are the way.
There is, there can be, no other way. Among them is
the law of the Sabbath. Be sure to remember that. The
other nations have forgotten it, and so must suffer the
consequence. Do not be like them. Remember it. Not
only your greatest power and prosperity, but even your
existence, is interwoven with its remembrance." I take
that to be the meaning of that remarkable word. A proper understanding, then, of that word shows how false
is the idea that the Sabbath was intended only for the
Jews.

A second thing is, because it is not found among the
ceremonial regulations of the Hebrew commonwealth.
Had it been put there, the opinion that it was intended

only for the Jews might have had some force. When those ceremonial rules passed away, it would have passed away, too. But, instead of being among the ceremonial regulations, it is in the decalogue, and one of its principal precepts. It belongs to the ten commandments, which the ceremonial arrangement did not. It is one of the longest of the ten commandments, one of the most conspicuous of them, one of the most strongly emphasized of them. Like the other nine, it was spoken by the mouth of Jehovah, amid the awful solemnities of Sinai. Like the other nine, it was engraven on stone, as a symbol of perpetuity. Like the other nine, it was laid in the ark of the covenant. It occupies so important a place in the series as to come before the commands against filial disobedience, against theft, murder, adultery, covetousness, and the like. Is it possible that God could have associated it so closely with the other nine, confessedly intended to be permanent and universal, and have given it such a conspicuous and prominent place amongst them, if he had not intended it to be permanent and universal too? Is he a God of confusion? Is he not a God of order?

The third thing is, because the fourth commandment is the keystone of the arch. Take that away, and all the others will soon fall to the ground. How long would men remember the first command, to have no other gods before Jehovah; or the second, not to worship idol images; or the third, not to profane the holy name, if one day in seven were not set apart for them to learn of God and to worship him? Even as it is, how ignorant and careless men become in relation to their duties towards God! Or how long would it be before men would cease to honor and obey their parents, and fall into crime, if this day were abolished? Take away the fourth command, and you will break down all the others. Do you doubt this? See, then, the atheism, the vice, the crime, the lack of filial honor, the weakening of family ties, the robberies, the murders, the rapes, multiplying on every side of us at the very time men are being taught that the Sabbath is no longer of divine obligation. In the history of our country there has never been the amount of criminality of every sort that exists now; in the history of our country there has never been a time when the Sabbath has been so neglected and ignored. Do you not see how the two things go together? This is according to the observation of the great men who sit on the watch-towers of the world. Blackstone says: "A corruption of morals usually follows a profanation of the Sabbath."

Prideaux says: "It is not to be doubted that, if the Sabbath were dropped from amongst us, the generality of the people, whatever else might be done to obviate it, would, in a few years, relapse into as bad a state of barbarism as was ever in practice among the worst of our Danish or Saxon ancestors."

Does that seem too strong? Then you know but little about the history of criminology, and of communities and nations. Let the Sabbath be devoutly observed, and the other commands will be observed too. Let the Sabbath be habitually profaned, the other commands will be disobeyed too. Break down that one command, and all the others will soon follow. Suppose the Sabbath were observed all over our State; among our mountains, in our valleys, and in every part of the State; do you imagine that we should have the lawlessness and disorder that now darken and blacken the civilization of this commonwealth? Therefore it is that God put it in the middle of the decalogue; and its presence there ought to convince every right-minded person what the significance is that God attaches to it, and what his purpose was in framing it.

But we may go further, and, in the last place, argue for the universal and perpetual obligation of the Sabbath from the direct utterances of our Lord. Strange that persons who will have nothing to do with the Old Testament suppose that in giving that up the Sabbath goes with it. Hear what our Lord says: "The Sabbath was made for man, and not man for the Sabbath: therefore the Son of man is Lord also of the Sabbath." Could there be a clearer recognition of the Sabbath than that, or a stronger authentication of it? Do you not see that in these words our Lord is doing just what was done at the creation and upon the organization of the Hebrew commonwealth? At the creation, as the human race was starting out on its historical career, God ordained the Sabbath. At the organization of the Hebrew commonwealth, when God is starting his peculiar people out on their national career, he re-ordains the Sabbath. At the inception of Christ's kingdom, when our Lord is starting it out on its world-wide mission, he takes up the Sabbath again, and makes it one of his institutions. He does not annul it. He does not ignore it. What he does is to remove the errors and corruptions grown around it, and exhibit it in its true nature. He claims it as his institution, invests it with his authority, and constitutes it a vital part of his kingdom. Mark his words: "The Sabbath was made for man, and not man for the Sabbath: therefore the Son of man is Lord also of the Sabbath." What do these words mean? I think the key to them is found in that little word "also." The idea is this, that the Son of man was made Lord of the Sabbath because the Sabbath was made for man. Let us expand this statement. You will observe that we have a syllogism here, with the major premise omitted. The full syllogism might be expressed as follows: The Son of man is Lord of everything intended for man and for man's good; but the Sabbath was intended for man and man's good; therefore the Son of man is made Lord also of the Sabbath.

Now, with that syllogism before your eyes, you can arrive at our Lord's exact meaning in these words. He is talking to the Pharisees. He is telling them that they have perverted the real meaning of the Sabbath. You have supposed he would say to them that God originally gave that day to you as a peculiarly Jewish institution. As such, you have supposed that it should be observed in a peculiarly Jewish way. But you are mistaken. It is not a peculiarly Jewish institution at all. God originally made it for man—for all men; not for you alone, but for man universally, and made it for man's good. "But you have perverted it from this purpose; you have made it a Jewish day; you have made it a hard day; you have turned it into a day that, instead of doing good, brings harm and evil. Well, now, as everything that pertains to man and man's welfare has been put into my hands, so I have been given charge of the Sabbath; and I have been given charge of it that I might recover it from your perversion of it, and see to it that its original purpose of being made a blessing to mankind is carried out."

That, I understand to be the meaning of these words, a meaning so plain that I wonder anybody could have missed it. Do you not see, then, that in these words there is no intention on the part of our Lord to weaken, by a hair's breadth, the obligation of the Sabbath; that, on the contrary, his purpose is to confirm and strengthen it; nay, more than that, to liberate it from its Jewish limitations and restore it to its original universality? Do not his words plainly teach that, instead of its being less true under the gospel that the Sabbath is an institution of universal and permanent obligation, it is more true now than ever before? And is not this exactly what the ancient prophet predicted in our text, when, in speaking of Christian times, he said that "From one Sabbath to another shall all flesh come to worship before me, saith the LORD"?

With two brief remarks your patience shall be relieved.

One is, that while Scripture teaches that the Sabbath is a divine ordinance of perpetual and universal obligation, it does not identify it with any particular day of the week. It does not command its observance on Saturday or Sunday or any other day of the week. What the ordinance exactly says is, that God blessed the seventh day and sanctified it, but what day is to be regarded as the seventh day is nowhere indicated in the command. The reason is plain. It is because it is a matter of indifference which day of the week is taken, if so be that one-seventh of our time is given to that purpose. Under the old Hebrew dispensation, Saturday was the day observed, although it may be doubted whether that was the day appointed at the beginning. Since our Lord ascended, Sunday is the day that is taken. It is easy to understand why the change should have been made.

Why was Saturday preferred as the day for the Sabbath under the Jewish dispensation? Because that day was the day which commemorated the deliverance of the chosen people from Egypt (their deliverance, it is thought by scholars, being accomplished on Saturday), and it was so great an event that it was incorporated into the meaning of their Sabbath. But under the Christian dispensation we have an event to take the place of that, and far greater than that; that is, the resurrection of Christ, by which our eternal deliverance has been effected. His resurrection took place on Sunday, therefore Sunday is the day preferred for the Christian Sabbath. That is one reason for the change.

The other is, because the design of the Sabbath is that it should be a day of delights, of rejoicing, a festal day, not a sad day; a day of joy, not of gloom and fasting.

Do you not know that in the early church men were forbidden to pray on their knees on the Sabbath? They were to stand erect, exulting in the accomplishment of the work of God's redeeming love. That being the design of the Sabbath, you can at once see that Saturday would not be the proper day for it, because on that day our Lord was in the grave under the power of death, and our redemption had not been accomplished; whereas on Sunday he arose, bringing full redemption with him.

Hence it was on Sunday, the day of his resurrection, that our Lord met his disciples assembled together. Hence it was on Sunday of the week following that he met them again assembled together. Hence it was on Sunday, called Pentecost, that the Spirit descended in a miraculous and glorious manner upon the apostles. Hence it was on Sunday the disciples were wont to assemble to break bread and make charitable contributions to the suffering brethren. Hence it was that the Apostle John, in the Book of Revelation, styles this day "the Lord's day," and hence it is, too, that God has perpetually and gloriously annexed his blessing to the Christian Sabbath. Wherever throughout the Christian world Sunday has been observed as the Sabbath-day, it has been followed by all the blessings God has pronounced upon a proper observance of his day; and it would be hard to find a more invincible proof of the actual resurrection of our Lord than that the church from the beginning selected Sunday, the day commemorating it, for its Sabbath-day.

Our last remark has respect to the observance of the Sabbath. On this point I have said nothing, because the great need of our time is to have a sense of the sacredness of the day revived in the hearts of Christian people. It is useless to talk about the manner in which the Sabbath should be observed, unless the people are convinced of its sacred character; and if they are convinced of its sacred character it will be easy for them to understand how it should be observed. The point demanded to be emphasized at the present time is that the Sabbath is a sanctified day, set apart by God to a sacred and holy use. That is what is being lost out of the consciousness of Christian people. That is what we must labor to restore. Impress the people with the divinity of the day—that it is a divinely appointed season, and that in dishonoring it they are dishonoring a distinct ordinance of God. Make them to feel that it is not a mere institution of expediency; not a mere matter of civil or ecclesiastical decree, but a day enjoined by God himself. Unless they feel that way, the current of worldly business and pleasure will sweep it from the church. The only alternative is either a Sabbath set apart by divine authority, or no Sabbath at all. We must labor to inculcate the sacredness of the day upon the minds of our people alike, old and young. Otherwise they will do pretty much as they please on the Sabbath; will travel on the Sabbath; entertain socially on the Sabbath; read novels, and newspapers, and magazines; be careless about the requirements of the sanctuary, aud let their conversation run upon business, crops, politics, fashions, and other worldly things.

THE GOSPEL AS FIRST REVEALED.

BY REV. W. T. HALL, D. D.,

*Professor of Didactic and Polemic Theology, Theological
Seminary, Columbia, S. C.*

"And I will put enmity between thee and the woman, and
between thy seed and her seed: it shall bruise thy head, and
thou shalt bruise his heel."—GENESIS iii. 15.

THIS verse, though often quoted, is seldom made
the subject of public discourse. Yet, in itself and
in its relation to other Scripture, it is eminently
worthy of such consideration. It is the first form in
which the gospel was revealed, and the germ of all subsequent revelations concerning Christ and his kingdom.
We read it with the interest of an explorer who gazes
into the fountain-head of some mighty river. There is,
too, an advantage gained for the study of the nature of
the gospel, by taking our stand at this first revelation.
The plan of the Bible is not logical, as of a treatise, but
historical. If we wish to study the political institutions
of this country in which we live, we go back to the co-
lonial period, and begin with the seeds and tendencies
contained in the early deliverances of our fathers.

I. This first gospel was not addressed directly to Adam
and Eve. That they heard it, and were saved through
faith in what it announced, is not questioned. The
words themselves teach that the heart of the woman was
renewed. And Adam proclaimed his faith by calling his
wife Eve, a name identifying her as the mother of the

seed that should bruise the serpent's head. All this is true, and yet the words of the text are a part of the address to the serpent. This is a significant fact, and calls for our consideration. It intimates the radical character and wide scope of the gospel. Adam and Eve had sinned in eating the forbidden fruit, and the divine displeasure against them for their sin was signally manifested. But the real author of the ruin wrought in the garden of Eden was the devil, who is a liar and a murderer from the beginning. (John viii. 44.) So he is first addressed, and the curse is laid upon him. The effect of the gospel is not confined to the release of the captives of the serpent, but extends to the tempter as well. The serpent's head is to be bruised. The gospel goes to the root of the matter, and makes an end of sins. "Forasmuch then as the children are partakers of flesh and blood, he also himself likewise took part of the same, that through death he might destroy him that had the power of death, that is, the devil." (Hebrews ii. 14.)

II. Another circumstance that claims attention is that this first gospel is found in the bosom of a curse. The first curse and the first promise come to us in the same sentence; and the form of the utterance is the curse upon the serpent. There is more in this association than the general fact that the salvation of God's people is always attended with judgment upon their enemies. This interview in the garden follows closely upon the sin of our first parents. No one can read it and not recognize the intrinsic demerit of sin and the awful character of the retributive justice of God. God made man holy, and gave him dominion over this beautiful world. He made a covenant with man upon the easiest of terms, and gave to man the opportunity, under that covenant, of securing eternal blessedness by a brief period of obedience. The tempter entered, and man fell. At once he felt in his soul both nakedness and guilt. God is just as well as merciful. Sin is death to the soul. This is the plain import of the shame and dread of Adam and Eve after they had sinned. They were now under the curse of the violated covenant of works. It is in this situation the first promise is made to them. To provide relief for their guilt and shame was the object of the first promise, so far as they were concerned. It was a promise of salvation to them through the coming seed of the woman. He was to bruise the head of the serpent, and to put enmity between him and the family of man. In accomplishing this the serpent was to bruise his heel. The deliverance was to be effected by suffering, by vicarious suffering. This much is plain from the promise itself; and that the suffering was to be expiatory in its nature was signified by the institution of sacrifice in the family of Adam. The great doctrine that without the shedding of blood there is no remission was imbedded in the gospel from the first. There was no hint to the heads of the fallen race that a great teacher, or one who should seal his testimony by his death, could save them. They were not treated as unfortunate dupes of Satan, who needed only a spectacular exhibition of self-sacrificing love to win back their hearts to the love of God. No intimation was thrown out that God, as the moral Governor of the world, must make an example of some sufferer, in order that he might not be misconstrued when he forgave sin. Nothing of all this. In fact, it is wonderful how all the false gospels that men have devised were anticipated by the first promise, and condemned in advance. The language of the New Testament reads like a commentary on the first promise: "For as many as are of the works of the law are under the curse: for

26

it is written, Cursed is every one that continueth not in all things which are written in the book of the law to do them. . . . Christ hath redeemed us from the curse of the law, being made a curse for us; for it is written, Cursed is every one that hangeth on a tree.'' (Galatians iii. 10, 12.) ''For as by one man's disobedience many were made sinners, so by the obedience of one shall many be made righteous.'' (Romans v. 19.)

III. Passing now from the form to the matter of this first gospel, we have an intimation of a conflict, ending in victory. The conflict is threefold. We take the features in the order of the record.

A personal conflict is first announced. ''I will put enmity between thee and the woman.'' Literally, I am putting enmity between thee and the woman. The conflict has already begun; and having begun, it is to know no end in this world. Such seems to be the import of the phrase, ''I am putting enmity.'' The unholy alliance between Eve and the serpent has been broken. Instead of concord there is enmity. Eve has new views, new feelings, and new purposes. A new heart has been given her. This great change is expressly said to be the work of God. In its beginning and in its progress he claims to be the author of it. It was a work of grace. And the work is done through a mediator. The context shows this. In fact, when Eve says, in Genesis iv. 1, ''I have gotten a man from the Lord,'' she speaks as if she already *possessed* the deliverer. The Scriptures teach everywhere that two great objects were accomplished by the work of Christ, the removal of the curse due to sin, and restoration to the image and fellowship of God. The first he accomplished by his obedience to the precept and penalty of the law; the second he secures by the renewing and sanctifying power of the Holy

Spirit, purchased for his people. It would seem that Eve was the first subject of saving grace, as she had been first in the transgression. And that the evidence to herself and to others of the reign of grace in her heart was a war against the serpent. In this she is the type of all her descendants, who, like her, are renewed by the Spirit of God. There is a personal conflict for every believer with the evil one. The seat of the war is in the heart. The dominion of sin is broken by the new birth, but the seeds are not all exterminated. Satan does not yield his prey without an effort. The Saviour sustains faith and all the graces; Satan injects doubts, weakens confidence, seeks to seduce by his guile. The conflict is inevitable. It is sometimes prolonged, and it is always distressing; but it is to end in victory. Christians sometimes complain that they have not the joys of salvation. They forget that this is not the period of reward. This is the day of battle. It is not to be expected that a battle-field will be particularly a place for comfort. The great question with all of us is, are we fighting the good fight of faith? Religion has its joys even here, but its real rewards come after we have fought a good fight and have finished our course. Let us give attention to what principally concerns us here. Are we born again? Have we undergone that great change represented in Eve? Do we hate evil? There are but two classes of men upon the earth, those who are the enemies of the evil one, and those who have in them the carnal mind, which is enmity against God. It may seem strange to some that enmity can be the fruit of the grace of God, or taken as evidence of a gracious state. The thought is, God is love, and to be like him we must be full of love. Paul says, "Now abideth faith, hope, charity; but the greatest of these is charity." But it

must be remembered that the Scriptures also say, "The
wrath of God is revealed from heaven against all ungodliness and unrighteousness of men." We have also
the command, "Ye that love the Lord, hate evil."
The fact is, that the moral quality of our affections is
determined by the objects to which they are directed.
It is right to love holiness, it is wrong to hate holiness.
It is right to hate evil, it is wrong to love evil. We can
never love God too ardently; we can never hate the evil
one excessively. A heart that does not love God is not
pure; a heart that does not hate evil is corrupt. Possibly
there is a suggestion in the text that the best evidence
of a renewed state is enmity to the devil and his works.
The enmity is certainly represented as progressing. The
statement, "I am putting enmity," sounds very much
like our Lord's language about the leaven. It was put
in the meal, where it worked till the whole was leavened.
Such a settled and growing enmity to sin harmonizes
well with the precept to avoid in the life the very appearance of evil. If such is the state of the heart, there
can be no yearning after worldly conformity, and self-
denial will be habitual. The thought of the heart will
be, how can we be delivered from the evils of our nature;
rather than, how near may we live to the world and yet
escape its doom!

A general conflict is next proclaimed. I am putting
enmity "between thy seed and her seed." That this is
a conflict distinct from the one mentioned in the last
clause of the verse is clear, because there the parties
are the serpent himself and the seed of the woman.
Who are the parties to this general conflict? To limit
the seed of the woman and the seed of the serpent so as
to make the conflict nothing more than the mutual
antipathy between all men and literal serpents is puerile.

The seed of the woman, in the strict sense, is Christ.
So Paul says expressly, in Galatians iii. 16. But in saying so he speaks of Christ as the head of the body of
believers. That the word "seed" is used in a secondary
sense is clear both from the Old Testament and the New
Testament. The two lines of descent from Adam, through
Cain and through Seth, indicate the import of the phrases
"seed of the woman" and "seed of the serpent." The
first is the ungodly line, in which is found polygamy and
murder. The second is the line of life, spiritual life. In
John viii. 44, Jesus said to the wicked Jews, "Ye are of
your father the devil." And in his interpretation of the
parable of the tares he said, "The good seed are the
children of the kingdom. But the tares are the children
of the wicked one." It is plain that the parties to this
general conflict are two sections of the descendants of
Eve. Satan set up a kingdom in this world when he
triumphed in Eden. He is called the god of this world,
and he is the head of an organized conspiracy of evil.
Christ's people are also an organized host, going forth
under his leadership to conquer this world. For six
thousand years this mighty conflict has been waged.
The battle has been fierce, as well as long. Beginning
with righteous Abel under the Old Testament, and again
with holy Stephen under this dispensation, the church
has her roll of martyrs to the truth. And yet victory is
certain. In these last days we see the promise of approaching triumph. The church of God confronts the
kingdom of darkness in every quarter of the earth. It
was my privilege once to witness a review of a great
army. Stretching across a broad plain in double lines,
composed of strong men with brave hearts, the burnished arms flashing in the sunlight, while the waving
banners mark the various organizations—the sight

was inspiring to the heart of a patriot.   In a moment,
however, my mind reverted to the church, and I felt the
force of the exclamation, '' Who is she that looketh forth
as the morning, fair as the moon, clear as the sun, and
terrible as an army with banners ! ''   Brethren, are we
good soldiers of Christ ?   Do we sympathize with the
purposes of our great teacher ?   Are we obedient to
orders, patient under discipline and present for duty ?
Are we sustaining the church at home and abroad ?

Last of all, we have the announcement of a special conflict.   '' He shall bruise thy head, and thou shalt bruise
his heel.''   The parties here are Christ and the devil.
That Christ is intended has always been the faith of the
church ; and for it there is good reason.   He is identi-
fied, as we have seen, by the Apostle Paul as the ''seed''
of the woman.   The term did not begin with Abraham
and the covenant with him, to which the apostle refers.
It had its introduction in the Eden gospel.   From the
mother of the race it descended, narrowing as it went, to
Abraham and then to David's line, and was fulfilled in
Christ.   Besides this, why is he the seed of Eve and not
of Adam ?   In the covenant of works Adam was the party
made prominent.   And so it was in the case of Noah,
of Abraham, and of David.   There must have been some
peculiar sense in which the word ''seed'' was used in
this first promise—a sense like that realized in the son of
Mary.   And still further, it is only at this feature of the
conflict that victory is proclaimed.   The result of the
personal and the general conflict is not stated.   The
victor comes in at the special conflict, not only triumph-
ing gloriously over the great enemy of God and man, but
reflecting triumph back upon the Christian conflict, both
in its individual and general aspect.   He is represented
as a person, as the son of the woman, and as the con-

queror of the devil; a true man, and yet more than a man. The voice of prophecy continued to hold up the coming seed of the woman to the faith of the ancient church as a mighty conqueror. The apostles proclaimed that the risen Saviour had assailed principalites and powers. The authors of the life of our Lord represent him as specially engaged in conflict with the devil at the opening and the close of his public ministry. All the guile of the tempter was brought into play in the assault in the wilderness, and all his malice and power in Gethsemane and on Calvary. This world has no other battle-field like these. The serpent had power to bruise his heel. This does not denote the slight injury supposed by some. A gallant officer, a friend of mine, received a Minie ball in the heel, by a flanking column, in one of the great battles of the late war between the States. Hearing of it, I inquired about it of the surgeons. They said, "Not necessarily fatal, but serious." The heel, they said, had so many bones that a wound there was serious. And so it was. He suffered much and long, but lives to-day to be elected for the third time to the Senate of the United States. What the Saviour of sinners endured in the garden and on the cross no heart can conceive. But the victory was never for a moment doubtful; and it was thorough and complete. He bruised the serpent's *head*. Through death he destroyed him that had the power of death. And now, my hearer, is not this enough? May I not ask you to look to this victorious sufferer and live! He had no battle of his own to fight, he entered the lists as our friend. He met our enemy and overcame him for us. He has the right in view of his triumph to say, "Come unto me, all ye that labor and are heavy laden, and I will give you rest." He said in anticipation of his death, "And I, if I be lifted up, will draw all men unto me." Shall it not be true of you?

Printed in the USA
CPSIA information can be obtained
at www.ICGtesting.com
JSHW021742091023
49829JS00006B/17

9 781599 252001